FROM WHERE WE CAME

The story of four families
the Stubbs, the Worleys, the Watkins and the Bakers

BY JEANE WEISBROD

IBSN: 9781955342841

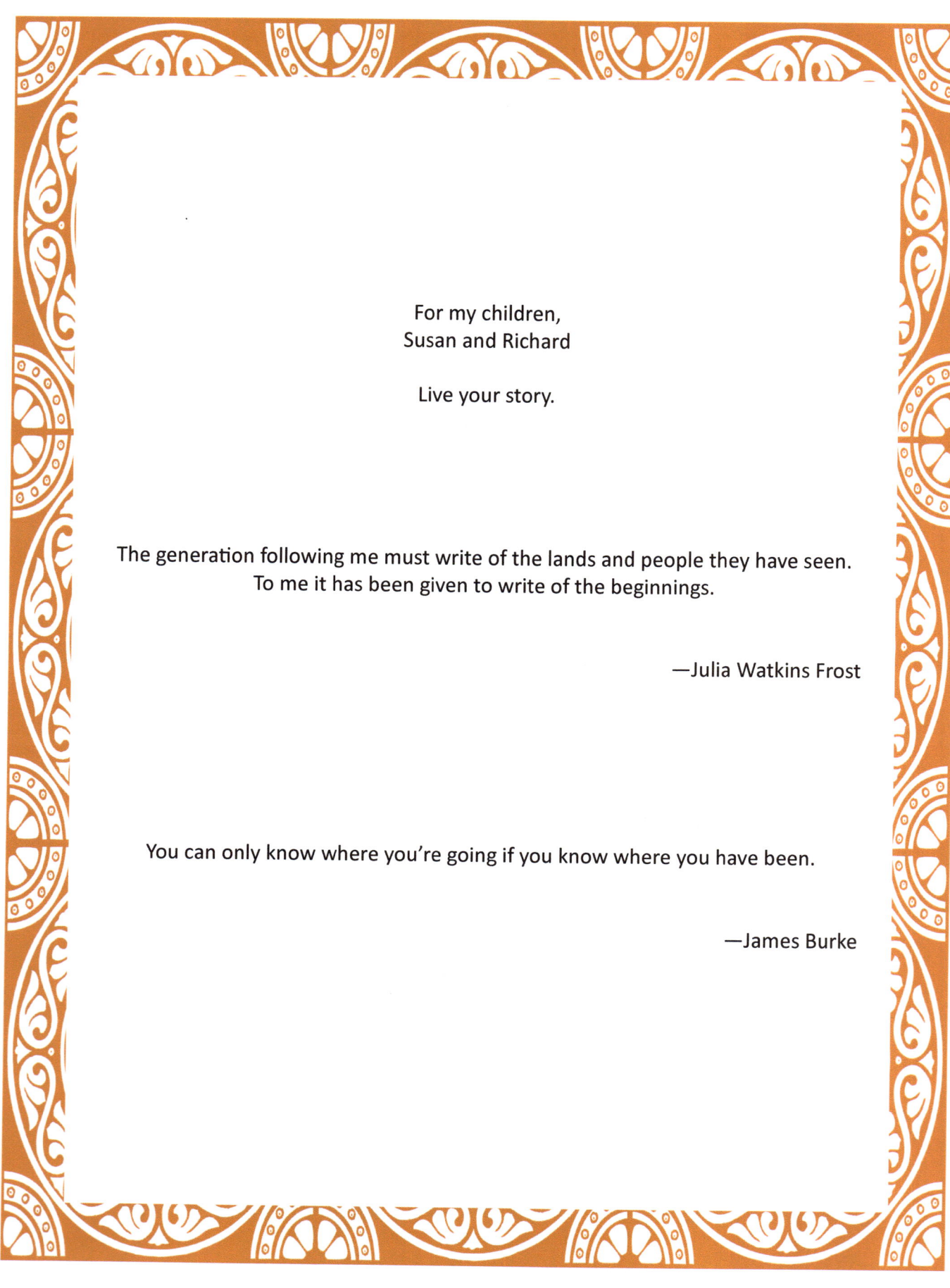

For my children,
Susan and Richard

Live your story.

The generation following me must write of the lands and people they have seen.
To me it has been given to write of the beginnings.

—Julia Watkins Frost

You can only know where you're going if you know where you have been.

—James Burke

TABLE OF CONTENTS

INTRODUCTION

There came a time as the years rolled on in my childhood that I out grew my toys. I doubt if my mother reflected sadly on this time for I was the last of three children born in a fifteen year period. On the first floor of our farm house, the toy room was conveniently off the living room. In place of my dolls, books, puzzles and a record player, my mother gradually moved in antiques and treasures from my father's side of the family. Only the old player piano remained in the room. Soon there hung a charcoal painting of Grandma Toms over a Jenny Lynn day bed. A framed flyer advertising the mills which operated right down the road

also hung on the wall. A shaker chair was at the foot of the daybed. The teacher's desk from the one room school house at one time up the road held a thick ledger showing the transactions of the mills more than a hundred years ago. A phonograph that one cranked and a case of thick cylinder records sat on the hearth of the fireplace along with a foot warmer that was used in a buggy. There was also a Jenny Lynn cradle that my father slept in as a baby which many babies in the family have slept in since.

When friends and family came to visit, my mother was delighted to lead them into what was once the toy room and tell the old stories that went with the old family pieces. I would tag along listening to the stories time and time again. I heard of my pioneer ancestors and their courageous ambitions as they settled right here in the wilderness long ago. There were tales of those who became teachers, millers, farmers, salesmen and musicians. There were also Indians which are now referred to as Native Americans. For many just survival alone was an accomplishment. Our ancestors suffered through hardships and excelled through success. Most of them married and had many children. Many had high morals and deep a faith in God.

As an adult I realized that the fascinating stories that I had heard were no longer known throughout the family. These stories should not be lost, but should be passed on. My children knew very little of the rich history of their ancestors in this area. They did not grow up as I did with the treasures of our ancestors on the land where they once farmed.

So this is what I have written about with the hopes of keeping the family history alive. In Warren County, Ohio along the Little Miami River, I am related to four families that settled in the early 1800's – the Stubbs, the Worleys, the Watkins and the Bakers. Though we may not know them personally, we can grasp what they were like by their commitments and actions.

We all have a story to tell. It's the story of our life. Here are some of the stories of many lives to which I am connected. For our family now and those to be born in the future to know, this is from where we came.

I

PART 1 – THE STUBBS FAMILY

OLD STUBBS HOMESTEAD BUILT 1822

JOHN STUBBS
1732—1803

John Stubbs left Pennsylvania to be part of a march against the forces of the combined French and the American Indians. The group encountered General Braddock (of the British forces) in their march. Braddock fought in Maryland, Pennsylvania and Ohio.

Later, John and his wife, Esther (Maddox), left Pennsylvania and moved to North Carolina where they had their first six children of fourteen. In 1768 Quaker friends and relatives of John and Esther moved to a newly opened area in Georgia. This group established Wrightsboro, Georgia. After the death of their father, John, their children with the exception of one, moved to southwest Ohio.

John Stubbs was one of many, many people who came to settle in the British Colonies, what we know today as the USA. John and others like him, left all that they knew to be home and all that they owned except for a few items. They came with the faith and hope of finding a new life, a better life. After travelling across a vast ocean, they would settle in the New England area. Some would never leave the area, but others would venture on and, in some cases, be a part of establishing a new settlement or town, just as John and Esther did.

MILLS AND MORE MILLS

The Little Miami River meanders for 111 miles through fields and valleys in southwest Ohio eventually emptying into the Ohio River. Its headwaters are located in Clark County, and it flows through four more counties – Clinton, Warren, Clermont, and Hamilton County. It empties into the Ohio River just east of Cincinnati. It is a beautiful, scenic river named for the Miami Indians who lived in the area. The area was also home to other Indian tribes. Near its headwaters the river is noisy as it gushes and races through a forty foot deep but narrow gorge that cuts through natural limestone walls. This spot is named Clifton Gorge in John Bryan State Park. The gorge is the location of Darnell's Leap. In this area after Daniel Boone's scouting party was captured by the Shawnee Indians, one member of the scouting party, Cornelius Darnell, escaped captivity. His escape did not go unnoticed, and soon the Indians were in hot pursuit. As Darnell frantically ran, he soon realized that he was approaching the gorge. He quickly decided to jump from rim to rim across the gorge. He was not totally successful but caught the branches of shrubs on the opposite side and made his getaway while the Indians watched him disappear through the thick trees to safety on the other side.

As the river flows into Warren County near Oregonia, it opens into a wide valley with steep sides. As a part of Interstate 71, the Jeramiah Morrow Bridge spans more than two thousand feet across the valley. It is Ohio's tallest bridge, 230 feet above the river. It is named after Jeramiah Morrow who was the governor in Ohio from 1822 to 1824. He was also a member of the railroad board along with Isaac Stubbs which not only proposed that the railroad be built along the river but monitored its operation. Above the river on the hill top near the bridge is Fort Ancient, which did not really serve as a fort but as an old Hopewell Indian ceremonial and burial ground. The ceremonial area is surrounded by large earth mounds as barriers. This "fort" was established around the year of 1000 by descendants of the Hopewell tribe which died out over time. In the 1700's and 1800's it was occupied by the Shawnee tribe as a settlement. The range of vision from the crest of the hill gave the Indians a spectacular view of the surrounding river valley. Fort Ancient is now a state park. Downstream from the bridge is the village of Morrow which was also named after the Warren County statesman.

The Treaty of Greenville was signed in 1795 by Anthony Wayne and Chief Turtle of the Shawnee tribe after a long battle between the colonists and the Native Americans. After the colonists won The Battle of the Fallen Timbers, a peace agreement was made. Basically, the northwest portion of Ohio would remain in the possession of the Indians while the rest of the state would be open for the colonists to settle. In exchange for the land, the Indians received clothing, utensils and animals. Unfortunately not all of the Indians were aware of the treaty, and attempts were made at various times by the Indians to regain the land. This caused frequent skirmishes between the settlers and the local Native Americans.

Historically, the Little Miami River formed the boundary between the Symmes Purchase to the west and the Virginia Military District to the east. Those serving in the Revolutionary War were given land in The Virginia Military District. The first settlement in Warren County was Beedle Station north of Lebanon in the summer of 1795. Right after Beedle Station a settlement called Mounts Station was formed in the autumn of 1795. William Mounts had served in the war and was given the land near the Little Miami River between Morrow and South Lebanon. William and Catherine Mounts founded a small settlement which was called Mounts Station where a few other families built log cabins in a circle around a natural spring. A station or settlement usually had a building of some type of fortification such as a blockhouse. No such building was located in Mounts Station.

Isaac Stubbs would later buy a mill near Mounts Station. Before roads or railways were built, the river was the thoroughfare for travel. The river also was a source of natural energy to run mills. Pioneers gravitated to its banks to settle in a time when mills were important to the life of early settlers. The pioneers would find the means to survive by farming or by establishing a trade. One of those settlers was Isaac Stubbs. Generally, the name Stubbs is of English descent and was given to those who were woodcutters. When cutting down trees, they would leave stumps or "stubbs". Earlier generations of the Stubbs were most likely wood cutters.

Isaac Stubbs I and his wife, Margaret (Carter), moved from Georgia to Warren County, Ohio with their son, Isaac II who was ten years old. They found the area to be new and wild with great opportunities. His brother, Nathan Stubbs, also moved six miles north of Waynesville to operate a mill on Elk Creek. They were Quakers and raised their children with strong morals. The Stubbs family was quite the pillars of the Quaker church in Waynesville, Ohio. As the church grew, Isaac II and his brother, John Stubbs, were on the committee to finish the upper part of the Meeting House in Waynesville on the corner of Third Street and Miami Street. Providing food and clothing for a family was not easy. Isaac was quite unassuming and worked hard to meet his family's needs.

RESIDENCE AND MILL OF A. AND I. STUBBS
OREGON POST OFFICE, WARREN CO. O

When Isaac first moved to Waynesville, he worked in a mill on the Little Miami River. This is where he acquired the skills and learned the trade of milling. As one might say, he literally "put his nose to the grindstone". It was necessary for a mill hand to watch the flow of the water into the grinding stone. If the water was too fast, it would turn the stone too quickly causing great friction with the grain being crushed. The grain would begin to burn causing the flour to be burnt. The mill hand would keep his nose close to the grindstone in order to smell any burning and regulate the flow of water.

In 1804 Isaac built a mill in Millgrove just downstream from Waynesville. He also built a mill in Oregonia that had a flour mill, a paper mill and a general store. Close by he also built a house for his family that was later occupied by his grandson, Zimri O. Worley. This was the first mill that Isaac owned. In an old Warren County Atlas, dated 1875, there is a sketch of the residence and the mill with I. and A. Stubbs as the operators. The location is Oregon Post Office which was renamed Oregonia in 1882. One might guess that the I. was Isaac Stubbs III, and A. was his brother, Albert Stubbs.

East Branch was a stream that emptied into the Little Miami River in Morrow. The stream is only ninety-nine miles long which is one mile short of being identified as a river. Simon Kenton renamed the stream Todds Fork after John Todd. John Todd was an officer in the military who died in the last battle of the Revolutionary War in Blue Lick, Kentucky. Unfortunately, the battle occurred ten months after the war had ended with the surrender by Lord Cornwallis in Yorktown. John Todd's life might have been saved if they would have known the war was over. Word was slow to reach the soldiers in Kentucky, and they fought not knowing the war was over.

Jabish Philips owned a mill farther downstream, two and a half miles from Todds Fork in Morrow that Jabish had built in 1801. It had a flour mill, saw mill and a woolen mill. This was very close to Mounts Station. Isaac bought the mills in 1819, and he built the homestead for his family close to the mills in 1822. When one spoke of Stubbs Mills, these were the mills they were talking about rather than the others. Isaac I operated the mills until he sold them to William Nixon in 1860. In 1867 Isaac I's son, Zimri, bought the mills once again, and later they were operated by his sons, Samuel and Quincy

 OREGONIA MERCHANT MILLS.

Stubbs. They were each married, and Quincy's wife was Martha Washington Young. They had one child, Clara. The mills required several people to keep them running. There were as many as thirty employees at the mills at Stubbtown. Zimri sold his flour to various bakeries in Cincinnati. He would hire wagons to haul the flour into the city. Most of the time, the recipients could not sign their name. With two others to witness, they would simply write an "X" on the receipt. The woolen mill ceased to operate in 1860. There was a great flood in 1897 which destroyed the flour and saw mills.

Zimri Stubbs married Mary Irons, and they lived in the Stubbs homestead. They had fifteen children. Zimri's grandson, the son of Noah, died in the Little Miami River when he was nine. He was bathing in the river near his home, one half of a mile above Stubbs Mills. This was reported in *The Western Star* newspaper on July 26th, 1884. Another son of Zimri and Mary, Samuel, married Letitia Bush, and they had seven children. Samuel served in the Union army for a brief period from May to September in 1864. He reenlisted and served again from 1865 to 1866. Before he died at the age of 93 in 1937 in his son's home in Morrow, he was considered the last Civil War soldier in Warren County.

The Woods Mills were built in 1799 by William Wood. They were located at Gainesboro which is now known as Kings Mills. Later the mills were bought by Hunt and Lowe. They were sold again to Isaac Stubbs I. Isaac I sold the mills to the King family in 1877. They operated the mills for many years. During World War I and again during World War II, the Kings built a gun powder plant along the river known as "Kings Great Western Powder Works". They produced ammunition during the war and long after. Several buildings still stand. My father would tell of hearing explosions occasionally from that area eight miles away from our home. The next day the news would be of someone dying in the explosion at the plant. The plant had many small buildings so that if there was an explosion, few workers would suffer from the blast.

The Nebo Gauntt Mill was built in 1804 in Freeport which is now known as Oregonia. This flour mill was destroyed by a fire on Christmas Day in 1852 due to careless firecrackers. It is believed that Isaac I built this mill. After the fire he transported machinery from Whitehall Mill to replace the machinery that was destroyed in the fire. Whitehall Mill was on the Warren County Canal three miles west of Lebanon. This mill was named Stubbs and Sherwood Mill until 1873. Isaac II was married to Elizabeth Sherwood, and it is assumed that Elizabeth's family had a part in the operation of the mill. After 1873 their sons, Albert and Isaac Stubbs III operated the mill. The mill sold in 1903 and was then called the Spencer and Monroe Mill.

Isaac Stubbs I and Margaret had six children. Not all of their children worked in the mills. Their third child was Samuel Stubbs who was born in 1844. Samuel married Rachel Whitacre, and he bought 1200 acres along the Little Miami River between Morrow and Stubbs Mill Road. He farmed the land until he sold it to Levi Baker who much later sold 129 acres of that parcel to Samuel and Rachel's son, Jonas Stubbs, in 1882. Levi Baker was no relation to the Bakers who later married into the family in the 1900's. This farm was on the opposite side of the river from where the Isaac Stubbs homestead stood where his brother, Zimri, lived.

Little Miami Scenic River

Warren County, Ohio. Location of mills along the Little Miami River in the 1800's.

Mill owned by Issac Stubbs at Kings Mill. He later sold this mill to the King Family. They operated the mill for many years.

Jonas, son of Samuel and Rachel Stubbs, married Elizabeth Pierson. The land that his father owned included a serpent mound built by the Indians near the Stubbs homestead but on the opposite side of the river. The mound attracted people occasionally, and it was commonly called the 'Stubbs Earthworks". There were 129 maple trees on and around the mound. Jonah's son, Stephen, was given the task beginning when he was eight years old to drive a horse and sled in the winter over and around the mound to collect the sap from the trees to make maple syrup. There was a sugar camp near the tail of the serpent where the sap was boiled down into syrup. It was common for most people to tap their maple trees because the sap could be boiled into homemade sweeteners. In 1889 Jonas was approached by Warren K. Moorehead to buy the property where the serpent existed. Moorehead had married a daughter of the wealthy King family in Kings Mills and therefore was not confined to earning a living. Jonas refused Moorehead's offer, but allowed him to excavate part of the mound. A tent was set up with tables to display his findings. A few men came to the dig under the supervision of Moorehead. Several flat rocks were found within the mound standing on end which Moorehead took with him at the completion of the dig. Stephen Stubbs remembered this happening but could look at the rocks on the tables only from a distance since he was a child. The men shoveled the dirt back onto the original area leaving the mound as they had found it. Stubbs Earthworks no longer exists as the land was sold. It is currently used as a gravel pit.

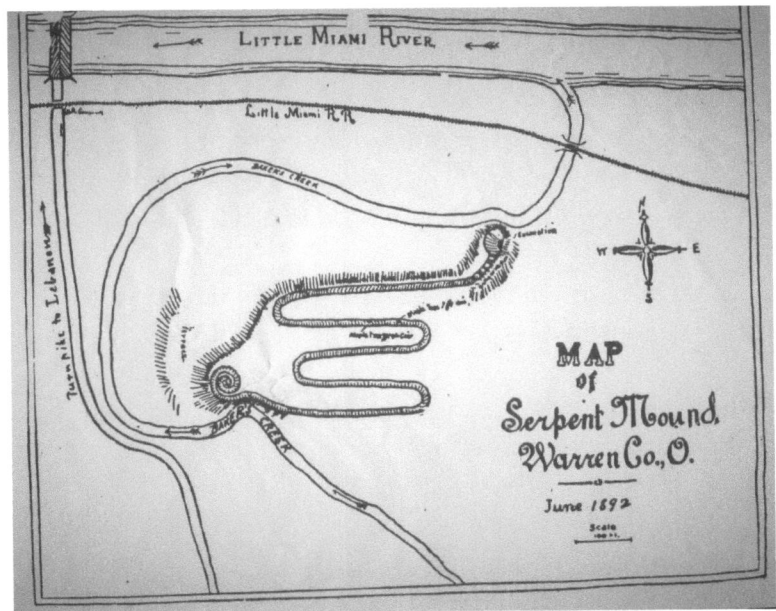

There were two Indian mounds north of the Stubbs Mill at the top of the hill on each side of the road. They were round shaped mounds. On the west side, many pieces of flint, arrow heads and tool-like pieces were once found. One can only speculate that the area had some special purpose to the Indians. One reason is that flint is not found in the southern part of the state. The Indians were known to trade items for flint in Newark, Ohio more than a hundred miles away where flint was naturally found. When a pond was built in the field, the dirt from the pond was spread across the field covering the flint pieces. In the mid 1900's a hired hand, Carl Roberts, once found a flint drill, spiral in shape while hoeing the field. The mounds were gradually leveled as they were cultivated.

Shawnee Indians coexisted with the settlers in this area at the time. There were thousands of Shawnee Indians in the Midwest. Their headquarters was in Chillicothe, Ohio which is now known as Old Town. Later the name Chillicothe was used to name a different settlement which was once the capitol of Ohio

At one time, there were twenty-two mills along the Little Miami River. Milling was big business. To say the least, Isaac Stubbs I was quite renowned in the area as being a mill owner. Collectively he owned mills in Oregonia, Millgrove, Stubbtown and Kings Mill. Isaac Stubbs was ambitious and worked hard. One might say figuratively that he "put his nose to the grind stone" which now means to work hard for a very long time. In another document it was said that Stubbs "left a unique impression on a rural neighborhood". One certainly cannot argue with that fact.

Below you will find an article that was extracted from the *1865 Warren County Atlas*. I include it here for those who are not familiar with the history of Mr. Issac Stubbs.

Isaac Stubbs (II)

This gentleman was born in Georgia March 4, 1794. When he was ten years of age his father's family came North and settled at Millgrove, Warren County, Ohio. His boyhood was partly upon a farm and partly in a mill, where he learned the miller's trade which latter business he followed for nearly half a century.

His wife was Elizabeth Sherwood, by whom he had five children, three sons and two daughters. One son and daughter died quite young. The surviving children are Margaret, now Mrs. H. W. Irons, of Warren County Albert and Isaac who are engaged in business in Freeport. They carry on a saw mill and grist mill, and also a store.

Coming here in 1805, Mr. Stubbs had but few and meager opportunities for learning. The country was new and wild, and the toiling pioneers had all they could do to provide food and clothing for their families. Hard work was the order of the day with both parents and children.

Mr. Stubbs spent the greater part of his life in Union Township, but subsequently changed his residence to Turtle Creek. He was a sober, industrious, hard-working man, very exact, careful, and conscientious in his dealings. He possessed an inflexible integrity that commanded a power where ever he was known. He observed a marked economy in the expenditure of money, and by close application and frugality accumulated a large property. His religious connection was with The Society of Friends, in which faith, he reared his family, and he was particularly strict in the moral training of his children.

For some three years previous to his death his mind began to fail him, and to such an extent indeed at times he was not himself. He passed away on the 15th of April at the advanced age of eighty-one.

Mr. Stubbs was a very quiet, unassuming man, took no part in public affairs, but gave his whole attention to his business and pushed it with an indomitable energy and resoluteness of purpose that insured success. His wife died before him on May 3rd, 1878.

Departed Glory
Stubbtown, August 21, 1886

The Little Miami is no classic, but that is not its fault. Amid all the prose of a restless age, and, despite the hourly scream of the locomotive, it keeps its beauty from year to year. "The axe of the White Man" has not desolated its banks and made it like Yarrow, "a river bare that flows from the dark hills under." As in earlier days, its banks are set with tall sycamores, through whose green tops the clean white of the branches shows, or with huge elms, some near six feet through, or in almost every place with smaller grain, over which the wild vines run gadding. At intervals along the bank, little saw mills are seen in the shade of overhanging trees, and piles of new boards show that they are still busy. Grist mills too, still run and grinds in days of yore, save that in some cases the new process has displaced the old mill stones. Deserted mills are not so common as in the big Miami, and yet there is here and there one with its sad story of departed prosperity.

Stubbtown, though upon this quiet and beautiful river, in sight of the wonderful basky dells, so charming to city eyes tired of the hot glare of stony streets, and overshadowed by fine sycamores, and horse weeds so large that the falling of them in Aug. is reckoned dangerous, with all these advantages, is not thronged with visitors. Nor has anyone in our hearing expressed his faith that when its merits became known the wealth and fashion of the city will pour in. Stubbtown has no hope or aspirations. Its glory is in the past.

Here stands the big framed mills which Grandfather Stubbs that capable old Quaker, built in early days. The timbers are still sound and the roof good, but the weather-boards have begun to fall one by one. Two large mill stones form the steps. If you look through the cracks you can see a pile of wheat on the floor, and note that it is now used only as a granary. The old fashioned sawmill nereby still does a little work, but beside it the race rushes past the broken forebay of the grist mill, and its wheels are silent forever.

Just below it, where the horse weeds stand so rank and stand so scythe-defying, stood the carding mill. To this laborious housewives sent their wool to be made into long, loose rolls, which could be spunon the great wheel at home into stocking yarn of thread to be woven into broad cloth at home or in the weaving house opposite the mill. Several old frame houses stand about in different stages of decay, most of them having lost some weather-boards and showing that they are filled in with brick after the fashion of our grandparents period. On the other side of the river, through the long covered bridge, are some empty shops, where once trade might have flourished. If the Stubbtowners ever get a postoffice, it should be called Ichabod. Amid a smiling landscape the glory has departed, and all the works of man show decay. But the glorious soil of the valley still remains renewed in fertility from time to time by floods, and the corn stands thick and tall like bodies of troops standing under arms.

This was Grandfather Stubbs farm of many hundred acres, now divided among its descendants; that is his house of old-fashioned red brick, and that wonderful barn was large enough to hold the great crops and shelter scores not to say hundreds, of cattle. Under on of these sheds, safe in the dry, lie the ox yokes, under which a forgotten generation of steers toiled and groaned. In the barn, now full of hay, with its spacious floor covered deep with this year's threshed barley, are some planks of curley oak, which will one day find their way to the city to serve as parts of costly cabinet work. Our old house is finished throughout with walnut. But Joe and Clint are bent on fishing, and I must away. The fishing of the Little Miami is excellent, but you must wait till my next to learn about the catching.

Signed W.W.

Author's note –

This note was found typed which I doubt is the original. Errors in the writing were copied as they were found. One can guess that W.W. is possibly William Watkins (1836 – 1889) who would have been a cousin to Clinton Watkins and a brother to Joe or later known as J.R. Watkins. William Watkins lived on Green Tree Road in Lebanon.

AN ANNUAL SPRING JOURNEY

Isaac Stubbs moved to Warren County from Georgia sometime in 1804 leaving some of his relatives behind. Those relatives later served in the Civil War on the Confederate side. Letters to and from a soldier and his wife have been preserved. So Morns the Dove: Letters of a Confederate Infantry and His Family by Alto Loftin Jackson was a novel based on the letters. The wife who wrote the letters was Martha Stubbs Jackson. Those letters were revealed in a television documentary series, The Civil War by Ken Burns on The Public Broadcasting Service in 1990.

Isaac I was married to Mary Carter and together they had six boys John, Samuel, Zimri, Ephraim, Hezekial and Isaac II. Of their sons, Hezekial, served in the Revolutionary War. Isaac I would own and operate the mill first, and much later the mill would be owned and operated by his sons, Isaac II and Zimri until 1860. This is the mill Isaac I bought on the Little Miami River near Morrow from Jabish Phillips. The mill was placed where the river could be easily forded. This would allow

WOOL CARDING AND
Cloth Dressing.

THE subscriber is now ready to card Wool, or full and dye Cloth, which he is prepared to do on the shortest notice and in the best manner. Having three double Carding Machines clothed with new cards, and his fulling mill rebuilt, and all his machinery in the best order, and experienced workmen employed, he will warrant all work entrusted to him to be done in the above manner. He has a large stock of woolen goods of his manufacturing on hand, which he offers for sale, for which he will take Wheat, Rye, Corn, Barley, Buckwheat or Flaxseed, Wool, Flax, Linen, Feathers or Rags, Bacon, Lard, Tallow, Beeswax, or any other approved country produce at the highest market price, (delivered to him at his mills on the Little Miami, five miles south of Lebanon, Warren county, Ohio.) And lastly, though not least needed, he will not refuse cash, or the currency of the country, in payment for work, goods, or debts due him, and he does hope that those in arrears with him will pay him shortly in some way or other, as he is much in need of all that is due him, and cannot get along with out it.   ZIMRI STUBBS.
May 10, 1844.

customers from both sides of the river to reach the mill. Mills were big business at the time. The Stubbs profited well from their mill business. There were three mills – a grist mill, a woolen or carding mill, and a saw mill. Each mill had a different peak season in the year which kept the Stubbs family busy continuously throughout the year. Farmers would come from miles around to have their grain made into flour in the fall, their wool made into yarn in the spring when sheep are sheared or their timber cut into boards any time of the year. Soon the Stubbs built a hotel to accommodate farmers who had come a great distance. The hotel was on the opposite side of the river from two of the mills and homestead. The river bank was much steeper there which would prevent the hotel from being flooded. The spot was first called Millsbourough then later Stubbtown. A very old, large, metal commercial-size cooler chest exists in our family. It was made in Cincinnati and although no proof can be made of it, many believe it came from the hotel. This was very close to Mounts Station.

Since no cash system was established, the Stubbs would barter as payment for the hotel and/or services of the mill. There exists in our family a large old ledger which shows many of the transactions of the mills. There is also an old hand-drawn map of the river that was found in the attic floor of Charlie Baker's house. This map is drawn on a piece of leather approximately ten inches by twelve inches mounted on a board. It's interesting to see that the course of the Little Miami River and the mill run have noticeably changed in the last two hundred plus years. (See photo above.)

The Stubbs also had a large farm of more than three hundred acres along the river that provided more than enough for the family. The exact size of the farm is hard to tell on maps because the maps show measurement in poles rather than acres. Having a large farm and bartering gave them an excess of supplies, flour and lumber. Each spring the Stubbs would take their extra flour and whatever else they might want to sell to market in Cincinnati, St. Louis or wherever the market prices were good.

At times they would float downstream as far as New Orleans for it was a big market, and they could get top dollar for their goods. They would build a large, flat, wooden raft to travel on the river and then wait for the spring rains to arrive. It was a long arduous trip – down the Little Miami River, onto the Ohio River, and then finally onto the Mississippi River. If they went to New Orleans, they floated down the rivers for more than 1,400 miles which took more than a month. They waited until after spring rains making the water rise on the river which in turn would make the river swift and quick so their journey would be easy. A few mill hands would go on the trip including a local Indian. We're not sure, but we believe the Indian's name was Yellow Horse. He was a friend of the family and very important to the success of the trip. Because Yellow Horse was along, it would ward off attacks from other Indians along the way. It was dangerous as the river wound among densely wooded areas with few residents. Other Indians could easily attack, steal their goods and might even kill the Stubbs and the men in their group. At night it was even more treacherous for they would have to dock the raft among the banks and sleep. The Indians in this area were Shawnee Indians.

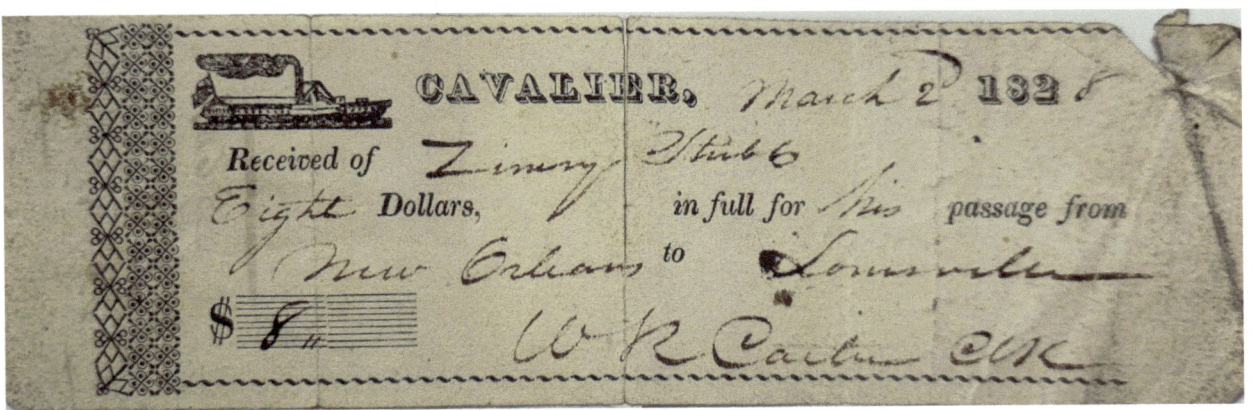

Once they reached New Orleans, the men would sell their goods, break up the raft and sell the boards. They would buy a ticket for a steam ship that took them only as far as St. Louis or Louisville. In Louisville there were some rather large falls on the Ohio River that prevented the ship from going farther north. A ticket receipt shows the price of the steamboat trip as $8.00 to travel. Each man would buy a horse in Louisville, and off they would go on horseback to return home. Now their journey had a different venue, by land instead of water. Again, Yellow Horse played an important role by providing protection for the small group.

While the men were on their journey down stream, the women and children were on their own, caring and fending for themselves at the Stubbs homestead. It was early spring, and the weather especially at night would still be rather cold causing the women to have a fire in the fireplaces. The nearby Indians would soon detect that the women were alone with no men to protect them. At night they would climb the outside walls of the house and onto the roof. They took blankets and covered the top of each chimney. This would prevent the smoke from escaping the house. It was the hope of the Indians to smoke the women and children out of the house or suffocate them in their sleep so they could steal from their home. The house would soon fill with smoke, but the strong-willed women would not leave. The women and children would lie on their tummies near the outside doors of the house with their noses close to the bottom crack of the doors to breathe fresh air. This would continue through the night until dawn when the Indians would give up. It made for some long nights in the house, and weary days without adequate sleep.

The homestead was located near the northeast corner of Stubbs Mill Road and Morrow-Mason-Millgrove Road at Stubbtown. It was built at a safe distance from the river on a small rise of land to avoid being flooded in the spring. However, one spring the floods reached the house. The Stubbs lifted their piano onto chairs as the river water began to rise. The flood covered the chairs reaching the bottom of the piano sparing it from damage. Most likely the house was small when it was first built, a single room with a fireplace. We know it was built before 1811. There was an earthquake late in 1811 with aftershocks in 1812. The earthquake put a large crack in a wall of the house. The house became larger as time went on. As they could afford it, additions were added one by one. Eventually it was a brick two-story house with four large rooms on the first floor and four large rooms on the second floor.

On the north side there was a large covered porch made of the same brick that probably served as an outdoor kitchen which had a hand pump to the water in the well. On the south side and the north side there was a rectangular gable marker which read "I.S. 1822 Z.S. 1868". The house had two chimneys giving each room in the house a source of heat in the winter. The house stood for a very long time, but was finally razed in the early 1970's when it was sold to a local gravel company which dug up gravel from where the house once stood. Before it came down, I walked through the dilapidated house that had stood empty for several years. Efforts were made to preserve the gable markers, but they crumbled when the house was razed.

The men had to deal with the threat of being attacked by Indians on their journey, and the women had to manage with the threat of Indians at home. One Indian was a friend. This was the Indian who accompanied the men down the river. Perhaps he disowned his own tribe to be a friend of the Stubbs. At the top of the hill on the east side of the road, there is an old cemetery with several graves of the mill hands. These workers from the mill were too poor to be buried in a cemetery and had no relatives in the vicinity. It's small and hard to find, for one must look for a small area heavily covered with fox vine. The vine was purposely planted because it has a nasty odor which deters dogs from digging at the graves. There is only one gravestone with the name James G. Stewart. This gravestone shows the date of his death in 1856. The rest of the nineteen graves are marked with a flat rock having no names and no dates. Among the graves are also the remains of the Indian. This is where Yellow Horse, a friend of the Stubbs family, was also buried when he died.

Letter written to one of the Stubbs family members in regard to a trip to New Orleans in 1835.

Cincinnati, Ohio Sept 2nd, 1835

Friend Stubbs

I have not yet received any funds from New Orleans. I have received from C Dorsey a letter of the 25 he says he has 5 16 lbs of Bacon sides on hand and that may every article of produce is null except fresh flour which is very scarce and advancing. We have met with many disappointments in respect to our flat boat the pilot we expected to go disappointed us as we have no prospect of getting a pilot soon that we can put confidence in and without we can get the boat off in a few days. I think there will great uncertainty in the adventure the river continues to fall and is now lower than it has been this season within these last few days flour has advanced 12 ½ cents in consequence of large quantities being bought up by speculations for flat boats. I have seen nothing yet to cause a rise and cannot expect these prices to sustain if I & S Stubbs should now think it not to their interest to ship by flat boat. I have it now in my power to withdraw. You will please show them this letter. Fresh flour made of new wheat could be sold by the quantity at 5,25.

Yours sincerely,
P Andrew

Samuel Stubbs

Author's note –

I have copied this letter as it was written without correcting errors or adding punctuation.

CUT OFF THAT BRANCH OF THE FAMILY TREE

The Golden Lamb is Ohio's oldest inn located on the corner of Main Street and Broadway in Lebanon. It was establish in 1803. The location was ideal for stagecoach travel. Lebanon is thirty-five miles from Cincinnati and thirty-five miles from Dayton. Thirty-five miles is a good day's trip even when the team of horses is replaced every ten miles. When traveling from Cincinnati to Dayton or back, the coach would stop in Lebanon for the night. Passengers would eat their dinner and rent a room. The next day they would continue their journey on to their destination. The Golden Lamb has continued to operate as a hotel throughout the years. Additions were made as the number of visitors increased. The structure was enlarged in 1815 and again later.

The building is rich with history. Twelve presidents have lodged there dating back as far as John Quincy Adams and as recent as George W. Bush. Other well known people have stayed at the inn including Charles Dickens and Mark Twain. The inn and the restaurant are still in operation. One can walk through the entire building, and if any of the rooms aren't occupied with overnight guests, the doors are open for viewing. The rooms are all different in décor and beautifully furnished as they were in the 1800's with fine antique furniture. A sign board still hangs outside the hotel with a picture of a golden lamb. Such pictured sign boards were common so that the illiterate could identify and find the place. The hotel faces Broadway which is a four-lane street with parking on each side. The street was purposely built wider than the

other streets so that horses with carriages could easily turn around. This also allowed ample room for the passengers on the stagecoaches to board off and on.

In the early 1800's Robert H. Jones was the owner of the Golden Lamb. His ancestors lived in Georgia on an adjoining farm to the ancestors of Isaac Stubbs II. Isaac bought the hotel from Jones in February, 1841 for $3,150. He sold it in March, the following month, to Calvin Bradley for $6,700. Bradley operated the hotel for a few years but was not successful. Isaac Stubbs bought the hotel again in 1846, and the family owned it until 1914. At this time the name was changed to the Stubbs House. A sketch of the building from 1878, shows the name painted in large letters above the second story windows. At different times in history, it was also named the Lebanon House.

On March 7, 1845 Isaac Stubbs advertised in the local paper, *The Western Star*, that the hotel was for sale or rent. No one showed interested in purchasing or renting the business, so he remained as the owner. Isaac added a three story wing on the north side in April, 1854. Later in 1878 the family added the fourth floor to the hotel with a windmill on the roof. The windmill would pump water throughout the building which was an added convenience to the guests. The fourth floor was built to accommodate the railroad workers. Other risqué accommodations were known to exist during this time. The railroad workers had a reputation of requesting the services of women. The Stubbs House became a house of prostitution while the railroad workers were there. The hotel served liquor, and it was not much more than a saloon. It was a rather rough place. My family was never proud of the Stubbs allowing the hotel to become this way surprisingly since their ancestors were strong and moral Quakers. My great uncle, A. John Watkins, would reluctantly tell this story. He was a stout, dignified man whose penmanship was beautiful, and his command of the language was one of a distinguished man. When Uncle John told the story of the Stubbs owning the Golden Lamb, he would shake his head with shame and say, "This is a branch of the family tree that should be cut off."

In 1860 the boarding cost was anywhere from $2.50 to $5 a week according to the amount of meals requested. In 1870 the cost rose from $4 to $6 a week.

When the Civil War began, a group of men from Warren County with their captain assembled for breakfast on April 23, 1861 at the Golden Lamb before leaving to serve in the war.

In 1865 an ad appeared in *The Western Star* claiming a new proprietor of The Lebanon House. It read, "We intend to make The Lebanon House a first-class hotel. No pain will be spared to promote the comfort and convenience of guests." Perhaps The Lebanon House turned the corner from its days of despair and ill repute.

In 1874 Isaac Stubbs II died. It is not known if his son Isaac III was already involved in operating the hotel along with his father. Isaac III assumed the responsibility of the hotel at this father's death.

From 1878 to 1898 the Lebanon House was a local place of culture offering plays, concerts, and lectures, readings, and minstrel performances. Naturally the performers who roamed from town to town lodged at the hotel. Many of the lectures were given by the teachers from The National Normal School which had almost as many students as there were residents in Lebanon. The National Normal School once occupied several buildings in town. The only remaining building is beside the post office on East Street in Lebanon.

The first train to travel through Lebanon was in 1882. This was a day of celebration with over two thousand residents at the station to greet the train.

In that same year, Isaac Stubbs III died, and his brother, Albert, assumed the responsibility of the hotel. Albert was a leader in the community and became the mayor of Lebanon in 1914. Isaac left behind a wife, Eunice, and two young daughters, Sarah and Elizabeth. The family called Sarah "Sallie" and Elizabeth was known as "Bessie". When Issac died, Sarah was five years old and Bessie was only five months old. While it is not documented as to why, Eunice

Albert Stubbs, outside the Lebanon House, with several employees.

and her daughters moved to the Golden Lamb and resided in what is now the President Room on the second floor and their sleeping quarters were on the fourth floor. Sarah worked in the stables to earn money, by attending to the stagecoach horses. Sarah's room is open for viewing in the hotel showing many of her belongings. Many believe that the ghost of Sarah is still there. Some have even claimed sightings of her ghost in and around the room.

Directly across Broadway from the Golden Lamb was the Town Hall. For several years on the second floor of the Town Hall, was Mechanics' Institute reading room. This served as a library for those who paid to be a member. In 1903 Andrew Carnegie offered ten thousand dollars to build a library in Lebanon. Carnegie, who was the president of U.S. Steel, was known to build libraries in small towns across the country. The city of Lebanon would need to provide the land and agree to the maintenance costs which would be one thousand dollars a year. The proposed site for construction was voted on by the community and was decided to be on the corner directly across from the Golden Lamb on Main Street. By a two-thirds vote of city council it was passed that a one mill tax on all property would be collected to pay for the maintenance of the library. The Stubbs were against the tax and filed a lawsuit against the construction. Another suit from other citizens was also filed. They were opposed to any building on the vacant lots that the town owned. Some citizens believed that money from Carnegie for a public library should not be accepted. The Stubbs were very conservative and thought the tax was too high. The law suits were debated in several courts before going to the Ohio Supreme Court. At that point a decision was reached allowing the library to be built. By this time it was three years later in 1906 when the library was approved. The library opened in 1908.

The Stubbs family owned The Golden Lamb for sixty-eight years. Its name changed from The Golden Lamb to The Lebanon House and Stubbs House to Lebanon House and back to The Golden Lamb. The hotel endured through periods of change and diverse events. Its guests ranged from stagecoach passengers and presidents, to railroad workers, to entertainers and lecturers, and later train passengers. As much as it was an embarrassment to my great uncle, there were many proud moments. One might say there are enough good events that perhaps this branch should remain on the family tree after all.

The Golden Lamb is now owed by Robert Portman who is known to enjoy history and served as a U.S. Senator.

Lebanon House

LEBANON, OHIO.

Headquarters For Traveling Men.

RATES $2.00 PER DAY.

ALBERT STUBBS, Proprietor.

PART 2 – THE WORLEY FAMILY

The Worley homestead, Bluechin, Salem Township, Ohio late 1800's

THE WORLEY FAMILY'S HISTORY FROM ENGLAND TO AMERICA

Going back in history with the Worleys, there are a few interesting tales. The family lineage can be traced as far back as the birth of Stephen Worley in 1516 in Tonge, England. Tonge, named for nearby River Tonge, is near Manchester in England. His son, Henry Worley (1538 – 1583) moved to Hackney, England which is now considered a borough of London. It is the life of Henry's great-great grandson, Henry Worley II, which is fascinating.

Henry Worley II's parents were Henry Worley I and Lady Anna Young of London. He became a wealthy merchant in London and married Ann Stone. He was considered a religious martyr and was imprisoned at one time for refusing to attend The Church of England. He died of a fever in 1674 just seven years after his marriage leaving a widow and two boys, Francis and Henry.

Ann remarried Caleb Pusey (pronounced Poozey) in 1681. Caleb was a lastmaker by profession in London. A lastmaker is one who carves from wood the forms which are used by a peddler to make leather shoes. Caleb and several of his four brothers were approached by William Penn to be the first to buy property from Penn in an area which would become Pennsylvania. Caleb and his brother, John, agreed to invest with Penn. Caleb might have drawn the attention of William Penn after publishing, "A Serious and Seasonable Warning unto All People" in 1675. They were probably of like minds. Penn would become influential in the writing of The Constitution and would have the state of Pennsylvania named after him.

Caleb agreed to travel with his family along with William Penn to America where Penn planned to establish several mills over time. The structure of a mill was ready-framed in England and loaded upon a ship before coming to the wilderness of America.

In July of 1682, Caleb, Anna and their daughter and Anna's two sons boarded the ship "Welcome" for the ten week journey across the Atlantic Ocean. The ship was said to be of 182 tons with many Quakers aboard. Not all of the people made it to their destination, for smallpox claimed the lives of many.

"Welcome" was one of two or three ships in a fleet. One of the other ships was "Freedom".

The ships arrived in October of the same year (1682) and docked at New Castle County, Delaware which is now known as Port Penn. Along with William Penn, the small group traveled to Upland, outside of Philadelphia, Pennsylvania to build a saw and grist mill. They were considered the first settlers in Pennsylvania. Caleb and Anna (Worley) Pusey built a house in 1683 on their one hundred acre farm which they called Landingford Plantation. Their home was near the mill race of Chester Creek, where a mill was built. The mill was named Chester Mill. Caleb first operated the mill and then Anna's son, Henry, later joined him in managing the mill. Their home at 15 Race Street in Upland is standing as the second oldest English house in Pennsylvania. It has been restored and tours are offered to visitors. While living in Upland, Caleb was considered a peacemaker between the colonists and Indians in Chester County. In 1688 Caleb calmed a potential Indian scare at the frontier of Chester County.

While Henry worked with his step-father at the mill, Anna's other son, Francis (1667 – 1728), became a surveyor. Francis married Mary Brassey in 1693. He became a justice of the peace and was a member of the city council of Philadelphia in 1718. He was sent by the governor along with two others to survey beyond the west side of the Susquehanna River in the area of Springettsbury Manor in central southern Pennsylvania in 1722. Springettsbury was named after the grandson of William Penn, Springett Penn. Francis was a member of the Episcopal Church unlike his ancestors who were Quakers. In 1782 he bought 750 acres in Lancaster County and moved.

Francis and Mary had six children. One son was named Brassey (1696 – 1783) who was nicknamed Brice. Brice served in the Revolutionary War in Virginia and Pennsylvania. He moved with one of his brothers in 1766 to Blacksville, West Virginia. He received a land grant in 1792 of 330 acres in West Virginia just outside of the Pennsylvania state line. He married Lurena Christopher and had five children.

One of the family stories is that once there was a young gentleman in the Worley family that was traveling a long distance in the New England area. After travelling for a day, he stopped at a home and asked to spend the night which was not an uncommon request for the times. It was the Brice family that offered him accommodations and introduced him to their lovely daughter. The young man continued his trip the next day, but returned later to see the daughter he met at the Brice home. They eventually married. The first name, Brice, became a common name in the Worley family.

Brice, the son of Francis and Mary Worley, had a son named William. William Worley (1760 – 1828) married Nancy Walling, the daughter of Colonel James Walling. Col. Walling took part in the siege of Yorktown which caused the surrender of Lord Cornwallis and England. William was a sickle smith and did very well in this trade. William and Nancy Worley moved to Deerfield, Ohio along the Little Miami River in 1815. This is how the Worleys came to be a part of my family. William and Nancy Worley are my great-great-great grandparents. They had nine children.

Brice had a brother named Caleb Worley. Caleb had a son named Caleb Jr. who was a lieutenant in the Revolutionary army. After his first wife died, Caleb Jr. married Rebecca Allen. They moved to Augusta, Virginia where Rebecca was from. Rebecca's father, Malcolm Allen, was a Presbyterian minister. He moved with his wife and fifteen children to Lexington, Kentucky. Malcolm and his brother, who was also a Presbyterian minister, participated in the "Great Kentucky Revival" in 1800. Caleb Jr. became a surveyor, road keeper, was often on jury duty, and he grew hemp. He also grew wheat for the Revolutionary War soldiers from 1780 to 1784. He did not follow the Quaker ideal of nonviolence. Caleb and Rebecca followed her parents and moved to Lexington.

Caleb Jr. had a son named Malcolm Worley (1762 – 1844). He was a great-grandson of Francis Worley. Malcolm Worley married Miriam "Peggy" Monfort who was from Beedles Station near Lebanon, Ohio in 1804. They made their home in a nearby area called Turtlecreek which was four miles west of Lebanon. In 1805 a few representatives of a religious group known as United Believers of Christ's Second Appearance or Shakers traveled to Lebanon. The Shakers were known to have "shakes" during loud and rousing sermons. The Shakers had hopes of establishing a community of Shakers in Lebanon, but they were turned away by the people of Lebanon. Malcolm was deeply influenced by the "Great Kentucky Revival" in which the Shakers had participated. Malcomb was an active member of the Turtle Creek Presbyterian Church, but broke away to attended a local independent church where Richard McNemar preached. Malcolm and McNemar were interested in this new religion and way of life that the Shakers proposed. There was a meeting arranged between Malcomb and his wife, McNemar and the Shaker missionaries that went late into the night. The next morning Malcolm's wife, who was pregnant, was overtaken with a jerking fit or "shakes" which she had experienced during revivals. With that Malcomb converted to be a Shaker. He was the first Shaker convert west of the Appalachian Mountains. A month later McNemar was converted to being a Shaker. Malcomb offered his farm to the Shakers. Malcolm's house would become their office, and they would build a Family Center. The Shakers believed in a dual God, male and female, and the separation of sexes. They also strongly believed in the confession of sins and being separated from the world. Shaker historians said that Malcolm was "a deep thinker on great themes, intensely and actively interested in religious matters". In 1839 Malcolm was ordered by McNemar to leave the group. Some of the Shakers thought Malcolm was blameless. It was probably difficult for Malcolm and his family to adjust to being separated by gender since they were married and had children. After Malcolm died, his children sued the Shakers for the farm, but lost the case. The suit cost the children $1200. The Shakers remained in Union Village, their settlement in Warren County, until 1913.

The Worleys are a family with a long traceable history. Its history stretches for more than four hundred years containing a legacy rich with courage and adventure. What a decision it must have been for Caleb Pussey and his wife to leave everything behind – their homeland, family and friends. They knew that most likely they would never return to England. Just as Caleb was influenced by William Penn, Malcolm was influenced by the Shaker missionaries. So many in this family were brave in their quest to change careers, travel to unknown places and seek out different beliefs. This was all within their pursuit of happiness.

Pictured to the right is the Irons Family Reunion which was held at the Worley homestead on August 28, 1931. Zimri Worley was born in this home and lived there for 67 years (at the time of the reunion). The home was formerly owned by Issac Stubbs, great-grandfather of Zimri Worley. The house was purchased from Issac Stubbs in 1864 by John Worley. Althe Worley Watkins is in the picture, seated beside her husband, Clinton in the second row. Zimri is seated in the middle of the second row, holding a child.

FAMILY CONNECTIONS TO MALCOMB WORLEY

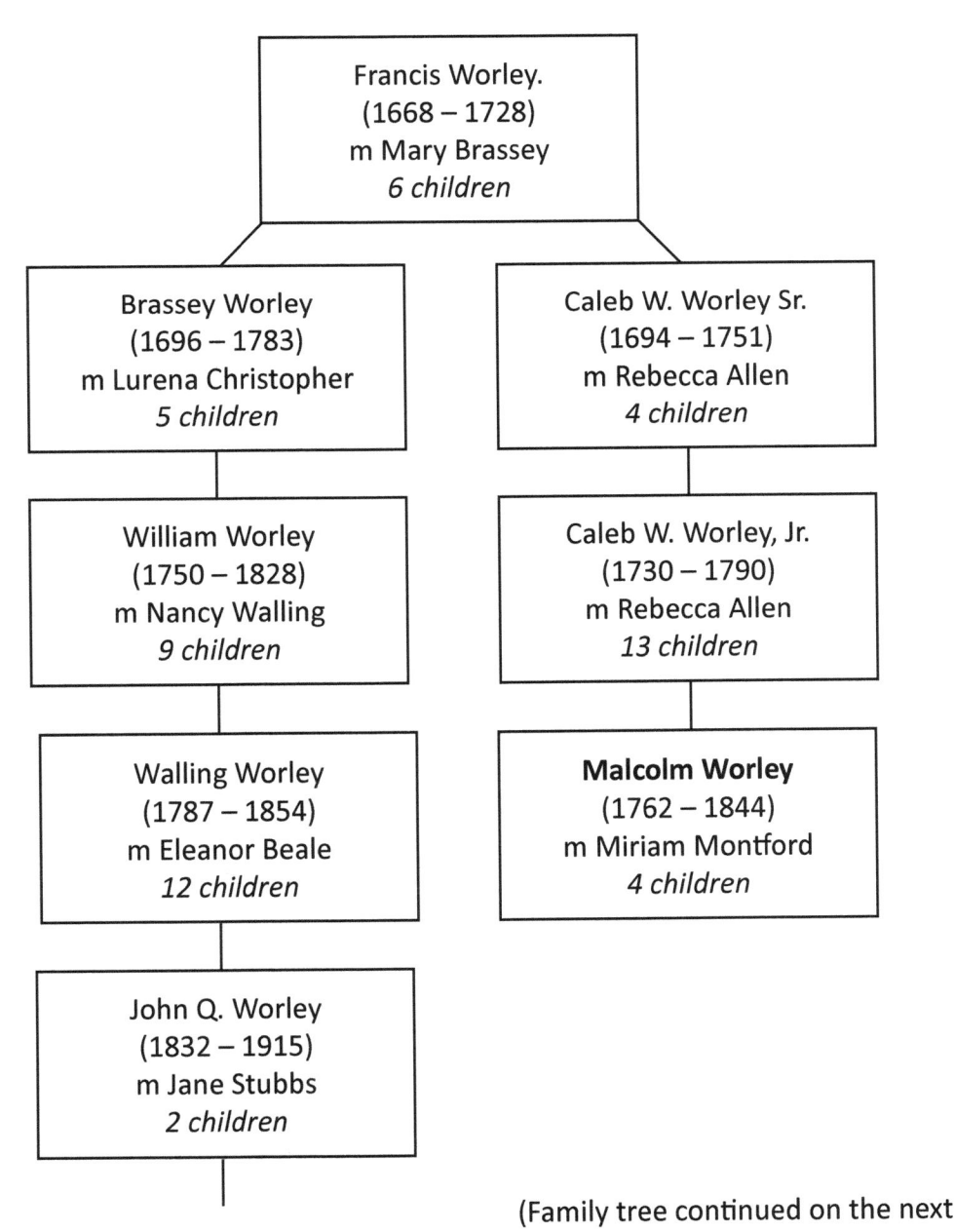

Francis Worley.
(1668 – 1728)
m Mary Brassey
6 children

Brassey Worley
(1696 – 1783)
m Lurena Christopher
5 children

Caleb W. Worley Sr.
(1694 – 1751)
m Rebecca Allen
4 children

William Worley
(1750 – 1828)
m Nancy Walling
9 children

Caleb W. Worley, Jr.
(1730 – 1790)
m Rebecca Allen
13 children

Walling Worley
(1787 – 1854)
m Eleanor Beale
12 children

Malcolm Worley
(1762 – 1844)
m Miriam Montford
4 children

John Q. Worley
(1832 – 1915)
m Jane Stubbs
2 children

(Family tree continued on the next page)

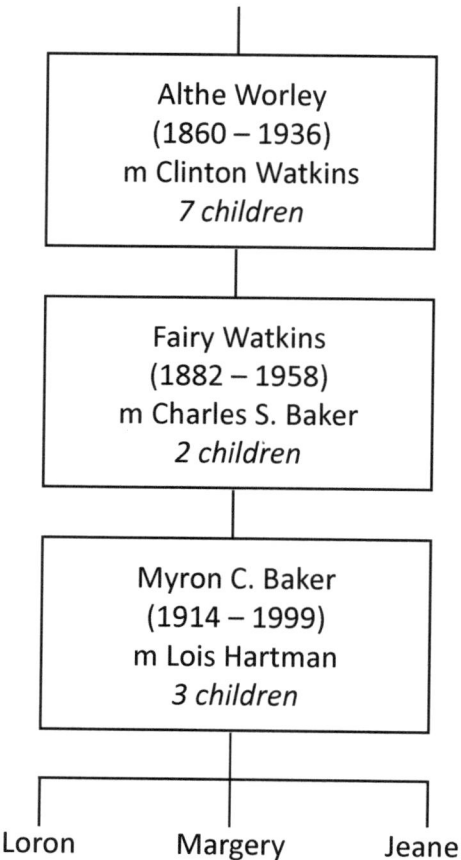

Althe Worley
(1860 – 1936)
m Clinton Watkins
7 children

Fairy Watkins
(1882 – 1958)
m Charles S. Baker
2 children

Myron C. Baker
(1914 – 1999)
m Lois Hartman
3 children

Loron   Margery   Jeane

See appendix for the full family tree.

THE WORLEYS OF WARREN COUNTY, OHIO

There were several settlements along the Little Miami River which are now gone. The river was a main thoroughfare for traveling in the 1800's. As other means of transportation increased, these settlements along the river disappeared. What is now known as South Lebanon was once Deerfield. Going upstream about three miles, one would come to Stubbstown. These two settlements were in Union Township. Going farther upstream about five miles, one would come to Morrow on the south side of the river, and across the river from Morrow would be Fredericktown. Continuing upstream as the river winds around, it takes a northern direction. In the five mile stretch between Morrow and Fort Ancient there was one settlement after another. The next settlement north of Morrow was Bluechin on the west side of the river. Just beyond Bluechin as one approaches the Washington Township line, Millgrove was on the west side, and Hammel was on the east side just north of the township line. Millgrove and Blueshin were in Salem Township. Another settlement was close by on the east side known as Senior which was named for the Senior Powder manufacturing plant. The next settlement north on the river is Fort Ancient in Washington Township. All of these towns have disappeared with the exception of South Lebanon and Morrow.

The connection of my family with the Stubbs is through John Q. Worley. John Q. Worley (1832 – 1915) was married to Jane Stubbs (1836 – 1913) in March of 1859. The Worley ancestors originally came to this country from London, England. John's parents were William Walling Worley and Jerimiah Eleanor Beall. William and Eleanor were born in Virginia and married in Virginia. Later, William and Eleanor, along with William's parents settled in Union Township, Ohio. They had twelve children.

JOHN WORLEY   MRS. JOHN WORLEY

John and Jane Worley settled on a farm in Bluechin near the banks of the Little Miami River and raised their children. This is where my great grandmother, Althe, and her brother, Zimri Oren, grew up. John Q. Worley, like most who settled in the late 1800's, was a farmer. He also had horses.

He produced and manufactured dried sugar corn. During this time corn was dried to preserve it through the winter months. Usually it was stored in a corn crib or in a drying house (barn) under cover. The corn could then be sold, and the buyer could take the corn to a mill and have it ground into cornmeal.

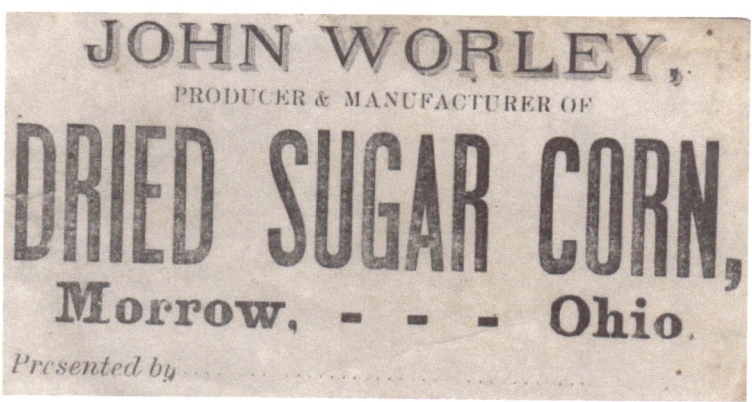

Jane was the daughter of and Zimri and Mary (Irons) Stubbs. Jane had at least twelve brothers and sisters. Jane probably grew up in the Stubbs homestead. Her grandparents were Isaac Stubbs I and Margaret Carter. Her uncle was Isaac Stubbs II.

When I was growing up, the house across the road from the Stubbs homestead was often referred to as the Worley house even though the Worleys no longer owned it.

Facing north on Stubbs Mill Road in Warren County, the Worley house is on the left and the Stubbs homestead is on the right. Both houses have since been torn down.

Some believed that Jane and John married because they grew up as neighbors. It isn't until 1903 that a map shows the Worleys owning the property. Jane and John married long before in 1859. This disproves the family legend. Most likely Jane and John simply met because the Stubbs lived about seven miles downstream from the Worleys. One must not forget that Jane's grandfather learned the milling business at the mill in Waynesville in 1805.

When Jane and John Worley lived in Bluechin just to the west, adjoining their farm, there lived a fine family. It was the family of Joseph Watkins. Joseph and Catherine (Pierson) were their neighbors and had nine children. In 1881 their son, Clinton, married the Worley's daughter, Althe. Clinton and Althe Watkins are my great grandparents. Later in their marriage, they would live in the Stubbs homestead. (See title page <u>From Where We Came</u>.)

Worley home across the road (Stubbs Mill Road) from the Stubbs homestead

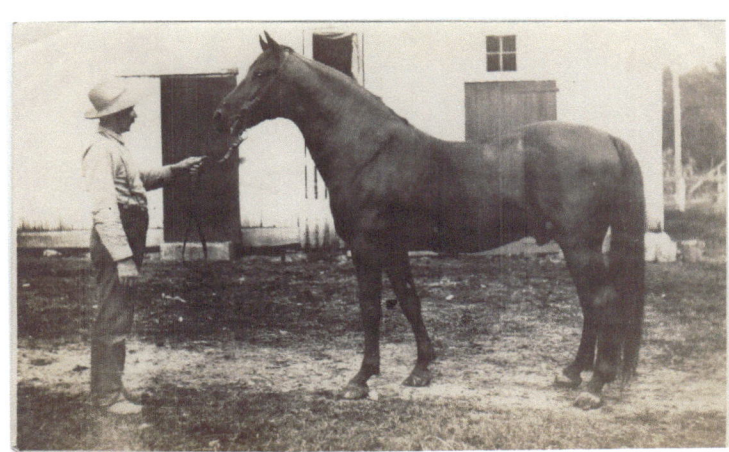

Zimri Worley, son of John and Jane Worley

Zimri Worley

PART 3 – THE WATKINS FAMILY

Walnut Tree Farm in Finneytown, Ohio. Watkins family
The Coffee nut tree on The Watkins Homestead with Nettie and Sam, next to the tree with Althe and
Clint underneath.

WALNUT TREE FARM

One can trace the Watkins family back to Joseph Watkins who lived in the early part of the 18th century and was of Welsh decent. This was also during the time of the Revolutionary War. Joseph lived in Elizabeth, New Jersey and was contracted to supply beef to the Revolutionary army. At the end of the war, he had earned a large sum of money through the sale of beef. Joseph described the money as being "as large as is it high". He might have once felt quite rich, but only for a period of time. He later burned the money because it was continental money which had no backing and was

Watkins Homestead in Finneytown, Ohio

deemed worthless. Joseph was married to Elizabeth Spinning and they had six children. Of their four sons, Jonathan, Hezekiah and Joseph, served in the Revolutionary War. They also had two daughters, Elizabeth, and Sarah. Joseph was "a fine man of mind and great energy", according to Julia Watkins Frost. He was described as being five foot in size, very hearty and strong.

Joseph's fourth son, James, lived from 1764 until 1848. James lost his hearing at the age of eight after swimming with an ear infection. James married Rachel Balgley Utter. Rachel's parents were Robert and Rachel (Vreeland) Badgley. Robert and his sons served in the Revolutionary War. Rachel was of Dutch descent and was born at sea as her parents traveled to America to settle. Rachel could not read because her father would not send her to an English school. Anthony Badgley, a brother of Robert, was born around 1650. In 1668 Anthony had a plantation in Flushing with his wife and their children, Anthony, George, and Phoebe plus one Negro. In 1701 he purchased a plantation of 17,000 acres from the Indians in New Britain, Pennsylvania. He paid the Indians two hundred pounds in money and goods. Anthony was also a sergeant in Captain Jonathan Wright's company in 1715.

James lived in Elizabeth, or as it was sometimes called Elizabethtown, until July, 1800. James Watkins began his work as an apprentice to a hard Master who provided a wretched shelter which was a log cabin with a leaky roof. Because it was hardly an ideal condition, he sought other employment. In Elizabeth James was later a mechanic and operated a business of sailboats plying between New Jersey and New York City. When the Revolutionary currency collapsed, he lost everything. James soon learned that there was plenty of good farming land in Ohio. Soldiers who had travel with Washington returned with such tales of "wine and corn". With that James left New Jersey with his family, a horse named Star, and oxen team, a wagon filled with his blacksmith tools and a crude, hand-powered nail cutting machine. He traveled through Pennsylvania and crossed the mountains of West Virginia into Ohio with his wife, Rachel (Utter), her son and her mother. While on their journey Rachel wrote the following poem:

> *Arise my true love and present me your hand,*
> *And we'll march in procession to a far distant land,*
> *Where the girls will card and pin*
> *And the boys will plow and sow,*
> *And will settle on the banks of the Ohio!*

It was not easy for Rachel to leave Elizabethtown. She was a widow when she married James and had two young boys, William and Robert Utter, from her first husband. It had been hard for her to provide for herself and the boys after her husband's death. Her husband's parents had taken the oldest, William, into their home to raise. Before Rachel left for Ohio, she went to gather William for travel, but her in-laws refused to release William. They promised that when he came of age, they would send him to Ohio with a horse and saddle, $50 and a suit of clothes. Rachel pleaded for them to let him go with her. They still refused. Rachel's heart ached as she left without William.

Once they reached the river, they boarded a flatboat and floated to Columbia, the first settlement in Cincinnati. Julia Watkins Frost wrote a book, <u>Annals of Our Ancestors</u>, that includes a description of their journey as well as the Watkin's history.

James was one of the first settlers in the Symmes Purchase, an area between the Miami River and Columbia. There was only one brick house in Cincinnati and several small framed houses. Because it was July, it was too late to plant crops for the season. Instead he set up a blacksmith shop and worked for Colonel Israel Ludlow. Ludlow was a surveyor. He laid out most of southwest Ohio including Cincinnati, Dayton, and Hamilton. In each city a street was named after him. When James Watkins brought the nail cutting machine, it was the first of its kind west of the mountains. James produced many nails that were used in the construction of the area. During the War of 1812, the nails sold for thirty-five cents a pound in Spanish silver. His family still owns the original anvil that he used in his blacksmith shop. It is engraved with his name and date.

Julia Watkins Frost

When Rachel's oldest son, William, was close to his twenty-first birthday, she watched every day for her son to ride up Winton Road (in Cincinnati, Ohio) toward her house. There was no mail service across the mountains, so she had not heard a word about him from her in-laws since she had left. She anxiously questioned a new family that had arrived in the area from New

Jersey about her son in hopes of hearing something, anything about him. They knew of him! However the news broke Rachel's heart. Unfortunately William had died the previous year.

Eventually James and Rachel bought a farm eight miles north of Cincinnati. The farm was eighty-six acres and was purchased from Mr. Finney. They named the farm Walnut Tree Farm because of a large walnut tree that stood in the front yard of the home. This suburb of Cincinnati is now named Finneytown. They cleared the timber and grew crops in the fields and fruit in orchards. They raised cows, sheep and other farm animals. The family would entertain friends and family beneath the sprawling branches in the shade of the large walnut tree for many years to come. Later, their son, Benjamin and his wife, Sophronia would raise a family on this farm.

THE FIRST MONEY BACK GUARANTEE

J. R. Watkins' heritage included men who were ministers, farmers, blacksmiths and those who traded goods during the Revolutionary War. These men were hard-working, industrious individuals who carved careers out of opportunities that they found or were presented to them at a given moment. He was born on Walnut Tree Farm, originally owned by his grandfather, James, and then his parents, Benjamin and Sophronia Watkins. JR's older brother, William, went to college for three years and earned a teaching certificate. William's first teaching job was near Green Tree Tavern north of Lebanon in Warren County, Ohio. This location was approximately a half day's journey by horse from the family home in Finneytown. William

Green Tree Tavern located at the corner of OH 741 and Greentree Road. This building is being restored by the Warren County Historical Society.

acquired this position through a friend, Isaac Morris. William's father, Benjamin, was a Christian minister and money was not too plentiful, therefore, the family was very grateful when William secured a teaching job from Morris. Morris was a very influential man in the area and lived in a luxurious house. William told his family that the house had a large hall down the center. It was built of brick, two stories tall in 1832 by a man named Ichabod Corwin. Corwin later sold the house to Nathan Sharp. This house was far nicer than the house on Walnut Tree Farm. In the next year (1858), William fell in love with Isaac Morris's daughter, Julia, and they were married. William invited his parents and siblings to visit him the following year (1859), and his siblings stayed for the winter. After months in Warren County, J.R. and his sisters returned home. As his father had taken a new pastoral position, the home was located in Harrison, Ohio.

For a short time J.R. worked as a salesman for Dr. Richard Ward who was an old friend of the family and owned a company called Wards. Dr. Ward also lived in Harrison and sold various items including extracts, spices and medical remedies. He was best known for his product, "Dr. Wards Vegetable Anodyne Liniment". It was concocted from evergreens and red peppers. This item would later become "Watkins Liniment". The Watkins family was familiar with the liniment, knew of its efficiency and popularity. After working for Wards, J.R. concocted some of his own remedies and went out on his own.

Original Watkins bottle with cork top

During the mid-eighteen hundreds, many people sold potions such as snake oil and liniment to cure all types of ailments. Some of those people were considered gypsies. They would travel about, sell their products, take your money and would never be seen again. Because very few remedies did as they were promised to do, it caused people to be very skeptical. J. R. wanted his products to be authentic, made with integrity and actually help people with their ailments. After his experience with Wards, he concocted several items to sell; he gathered them in a covered wagon and hit the road. He went door to door selling his extracts and remedies. To prove the authenticity of each product, he offered a money back guarantee. J. R. introduced what he called a "Trial-Mark Bottle". Every bottle was etched with a sample line on the top half of the bottle. The buyer was told at the time of the sale that if the product was not true to its promise or did not meet the expectations, they could return the bottle or simply leave it on their window sill in plain view and their money would be reimbursed. It was America's first money back guaranty! The only stipulation was that no more of the product should be used beyond the sample line. This was a huge marketing ploy, and, as a result, J. R. Watkins would some day have a thriving company on his hands. J.R.'s marketing tactic brought him great success.

J.R. Watkins

In the early part of 1860, news began to circulate regarding the possibility of a civil war. With this news, Benjamin decided to move to Minnesota in 1862 with the hopes of avoiding such a conflict. He sold the homestead in Finneytown, Ohio and booked a steamboat for the family on the Ohio River. He was first assigned to a church in St. Cloud, Minnesota, where they suffered raids by Indians but survived with little harm or destruction. Later Benjamin settled with his family in Plainview, Minnesota, where he became the minister at the Church of Christ. J.R. was twenty-two years old at the time, and he, along with his sisters, moved to Minnesota. J.R. began to make liniment in the kitchen sink of his parent's home in Plainview, Minnesota. For a while J.R. would travel back and forth from Minnesota to Ohio to visit his brother and relatives which he missed in Morrow, Ohio. On one of those journeys, he met Mary Ellen Heberling in Cadiz, Ohio.

In 1868 they were married, and in that same year, J.R. bought the rights to Wards products. They moved to Minnesota, and J.R. built what was to become a multi-million dollar business that would eventually become international.

Mary Ellen Heberling Watkins

J.R. fell in love with the Winona area in Minnesota. Because of the Mississippi River and the railroad along the river, it was an ideal place to transport raw materials in and transport products out. He moved his business to Winona, and it grew from there. He began to hire other salesmen and each would eventually be known as a "Watkins man". They were scrutinized carefully when applying for a job. The written application was long and J.R. would interview them personally

One of the "Watkins Men" circa 1900

to see that they were of fine, upstanding, moral character. Not just anyone could be a "Watkins man". To be a distributor of his product, J.R. would ask if they attended church, if they abstained from consuming alcohol and tobacco, and if their reputations were clear of any accusations of being a womanizer. Many of the employees would give their farm as collateral for the job of selling Watkins products. This gave the Watkins company credibility.

On the Watkins farm in Morrow, Ohio, where his cousins lived, J.R. shipped hundreds of cases of liniment and his other products. These products were stored in the "medicine house" on the farm for the relatives to sell. A common sight in the early 1900's would be a Watkins wagon driven by JR's younger cousins, James Watkins or Alfred Watkins. Alfred did so well in sales that he used his income to finance his musical education in Europe. Another cousin, Clinton, sold the products in Clermont County, Ohio, and another cousin, Samuel, went to Missouri and sold them there. Many years later the stones from the old medicine house were used to build a fireplace in a newer house on the Watkins farm by Alfred's son, William.

 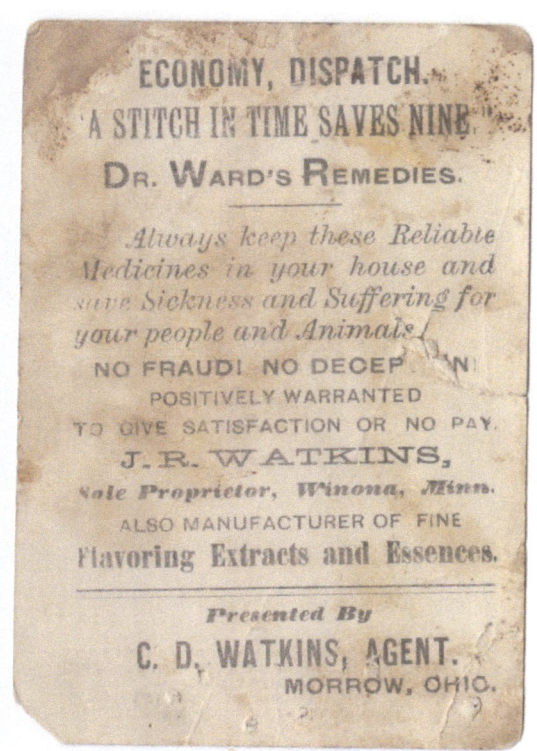

Clinton Watkins business card, front and back

One day my great-grandfather, Clinton, was crossing the Little Miami River in his wagon filled with his cousin's bottles of remedies and extracts. He was prepared to sell the products to others in the vicinity. As he crossed the river, the wagon tipped and all the bottles fell out of the wagon and into the water. The water washed off the labels! Even the bottles Clinton could retrieve had no identifying information. All was lost. This discouraged Clinton terribly, and he returned to farming.

J.R. felt the need for new ideas in the business and hired his nephew, Paul Watkins in 1892 to work for him. Paul, 27, was the son of William and Julia Watkins in Lebanon,

Paul and JR Watkins, about 1910

Ohio. Paul gained experience working in the grain business in Toledo, Ohio. After gaining that experience, he moved to Columbus, Ohio where he was a purchasing agent for an iron and coal company. Later he was secretary and treasurer of Central Ohio Natural Gas and Fuel Company. Paul accepted J.R.'s offer and shared the leadership of the Watkins Medical Company with his uncle in Winona, Minnesota. The company began to grow and expand to locations in Winnipeg, Canada, Memphis, Tennessee, Newark, New Jersey, as well as Europe and South America. Its products expanded into toiletries and cosmetics. One of his most famous products was his vanilla extract which he began selling in 1895. The vanilla extract was of top quality and widely known.

The historical marker outside the home reads, "The house that vanilla built". The house still stands as a residence for senior citizens. Many of the art pieces were donated to a college in town.

The Watkins families enjoyed a posh life. In 1924 Paul built a large Tudor-style house in town for his wife and four children which took three years to complete. He and his wife, Florence, traveled to Europe on art buying sprees. Paul transported and donated European marble pillars and statues to an elementary school that was being built in town. Paul's house had its own telephone booth and elevator. Paul and Florence each had their own private suites adjacent to private baths and bedrooms. In the huge drawing room there hung oil portraits of Paul and Florence. The great room even had a small elevator that lifted firewood from the outdoors for the large fireplace in the room with its vaulted ceiling and fine wood paneled walls. There was

once a large pipe organ with 5,975 pipes in the great room and a grand piano in the entrance hallway.

The Watkins Company was growing and thriving beyond anyone's expectations. In 1910 the Watkins Medical Company would become the world's largest direct sales company. However, in 1904, before reaching that great achievement, J.R. personally experienced both great sorrow and great joy. His wife, Mary Ellen, died in April. In November, Grace, his only surviving child, married Ernest Leroy King whom she had met in New York City. As a result of his marriage to Grace, King would assume the post of vice president of the Watkins Medical Company.

Grace built a huge home that was

Paul, Florence and their 4 children

designed by a protégé of Frank Lloyd Wright on the banks of the Mississippi River near Winona, Minnesota. She loved adventures and traveled on two different safaris in Africa with her husband and young son, E.L "Bud" King.

Picture of the first building of Watkins Medical Company. JR Watkins is the third from the right in the top hat.

As the company grew, a rivalry developed in the family between Paul Watkins and Grace's husband, E.L. King. They were known to never be in the office at the same time. Sometimes they would alternate six months at a time when Paul was traveling to other offices or plantations belonging to the Watkins Company. Paul had increased the Watkins products from ten to over one hundred items. The company expanded with offices around the world. The company also bought plantations in various parts of the world that grew the raw materials used in their products. Paul wanted the company to have complete control of the making of their products in every aspect. They printed their own labels. They owned their own bank. They grew their own raw materials. They had their own publishing company which printed cookbooks. They were dependent upon no one.

JR Watkins with chauffer

E.L. King was a shrewd businessman, but in this case there is a fine line between shrewd and corrupt. Some described him as greedy. In contrast to such claims, he was highly regarded by his previous employer, a company which manufactured typewriters. His employer said that E.L. was such a fine salesman that he would welcome him back at any time.

King invested heavily in real estate for the Watkins Company, and he was involved in banking. King bought real estate in Daytona Beach, Florida that was adjacent to property owned by the Rockefellers. King built a house in Daytona Beach as a family resort. That house has now been replaced with condos. Along with the Rockefellers, they built their own private golf course on their land.

King also bought four hundred acres in California along the coast. At one time E.L. owned more Ford auto dealerships than anyone in the country. During E.L.'s tenure at Watkins Medical Company, the relationship between J.R. and E.L. was weakened due to charges of tax evasion by the government.

J.R. remained a widower for seven years. In 1911 he married E.L.'s mother, Maud King. This made E.L. not only a son-in-law but also a step child! Soon after the marriage J.R. learned that Maud was still married to an alcoholic who lived in Chicago. The family sent money to Maud's husband in order to keep him quiet about his marriage to Maud. J.R. died four months after his marriage to Maud at the age of 71 while vacationing in Jamaica where he often spent time in the winter. The death certificate declared the cause of death as indigestion. J. R. was considered to be in good health at the time. The family became suspicious of foul play. Some thought J.R. was poisoned in order for the King family to inherit the company.

Paul Watkins continued to work with E.L. King despite their differences. In 1931 Paul Watkins died and E.L. King assumed the leadership of the company. It was a hard time in the U.S. with the onset of the Great Depression. Because of the prohibition of alcohol, J.R.'s famous liniment was found to contain too much alcohol at a whopping 47 per cent and could no longer be sold. King held onto the company and in fact, their products entered the international market in 1935.

E.L. King died in 1949. Before his death, he plead guilty to charges of falsifying information to the Winona ration board in seeking the approval for the purchase of six automobiles. He was fined $3,000.00 at a federal court in St. Paul, Minnesota. Such rationing laws were established during World War II to ensure that all needed resources were available for the war effort. These charges that were levied against E.L. King, including drug labeling violations and federal tax violations, caused E. L. King to step down from the presidency of the Watkins company.

King's son, "Bud", became the president in 1944 when his father stepped down. Bud had married a local Winona, Minnesota girl and had three sons. The Watkins's approach to sales and marketing door-to-door no longer fit the consumers' tastes. The company suffered, and many family members encouraged Bud to sell the company. He refused to sell.

Four years after E.L. died in 1949, the son of Paul Watkins, was shot and killed in a parking lot near Harvard University. The victim, Paul's son, was named James Ray Watkins after his great uncle. James was a graduate of Harvard Law School and had established a Manhattan brokerage firm, Brooks and Watkins, in New York City. There had been a huge financial dispute after James dismissed his partner when he learned that $75,000 had been stolen from the firm by Brooks. Later Brooks contacted James begging that they meet for dinner at Princeton Inn to discuss his employment situation. Before James had even left his car, he was shot by Brooks. Medics were called and found James dead slumped over the steering wheel of his car.

In 1964 Bud was maneuvered out of office at Watkins Medical Company by the company's board and replaced by James Doyle. This was the first time in history that the Watkins Medical Company was no longer controlled by a family member. The company continued to decline. By 1973 Bud regained control of the company and replaced Doyle with his son, David King.

In 1977, even after using personal money to keep the company afloat, the Watkins Company filed for Chapter 11 Bankruptcy. A local business man, Irwin Jacobs, gave two million dollars for the purchase of the Watkins Company. Jacobs revamped the marketing approach and improved the product line to get the company out of the red. Jacobs said, "The Watkins product was so strong that even thirty years of mismanagement couldn't kill it." His son, Mark Jacobs, is currently running the company.

The J.R. Watkins Company has over four hundred products now boasting its products to be crafted in the U.S.A. since 1868 with all natural ingredients. It's advertised as "the company that has been soothing coughs and colds for over 150 years." My mother always used Watkins's vanilla extract in her baking claiming it to be the absolute best vanilla. The products can be found on line at jrwatkins.com or in many stores across the country.

Oh, and the original concoction of camphor, oil of spruce, extract of capsicum and other ingredients known as Watkins Liniment is still available. It is item No. 02317.

Watkins Medical Company, Winona, Minnesota

The J.R. Watkins Medical Company complex located at 150 Liberty Street in Winona is on the National Register of Historic Places.

Stop by the J.R. Watkins Museum and Store to learn more about the company and the products that have earned a place in history.

Building Location:
150 Liberty St., Winona, MN 55987

Museum & Store Hours:
Monday – Friday: 10 a.m. - 4 p.m.
Saturday: 10 a.m. - 2 p.m.
Sunday: Closed

Learn more now at:
JRWatkins.com

TRAP SHOOTER

J. R. Watkins became quite a wealthy man as his company grew in Minnesota. He and his wife, Mary Ellen (Huberling), had one surviving child, a girl which they named Grace who was born in 1877. Grace grew to love hunting with her father in Minnesota. J. R. noticed great shooting skills in Grace as she became more and more proficient. At one time Grace received lessons from none other than Annie Oakley, and together they shot clays. Grace soon became competitive in trap shooting. She participated in tournaments and became internationally known. In 1922 and 1923 she won the Women's World Trapshooting Championship in Vandalia, Ohio. At one time she held the women's record of breaking 186 targets straight. She is a member of the Trapshooting Hall of Fame.

Grace Watkins

Grace lived an elaborate life as she was chauffeured about town in her very own horse and carriage which had her name written in gold on the door. Grace also enjoyed collecting Indian artifacts with her father in Minnesota. Most of their items came from the Plains Indians. Together Grace and her father wrote a booklet focusing on the Indians and the history of their area in Minnesota. One story told of an Indian chief's wife, Winona, which is where the Watkins lived.

Grace met Ernest L. King in New York City, and later they married. Grace and E. L. had two children, a daughter, Mary Eleanor and "Bud" E. L. King. E.L. King was a typewriter salesman, but soon after moving to Minnesota, he became vice president of the Watkins Company. Mr. King was also internationally known as a sportsman, big game hunter and trap shooter. Grace was a strong and intelligent woman, but in

those days it was not acceptable for a woman to be in business. Some elude that her husband may have had a title in the business, but it was Grace who was actively involved. As one author surmised, "Had Grace been male, she undoubtedly would have been groomed to assume control of the Watkins Company but in that day and age female executives were so rare as to be nearly unthinkable."

Grace had a love for adventure and was well acquainted with firearms. She purchased her first heavy rifle from Dr. Richard Sutton. In 1922 and 1927 she traveled to Africa with her son and husband. On the safaris they hunted buffalo, lions, elephants and large cats. A newspaper clipping from 1925 shows Grace and two men with a downed elephant. The caption boasts that it was the largest elephant ever killed by a woman. The tusks alone weighed 120 pounds. She donated many specimens to the American Museum of Natural History in New York City and to the University of Minnesota. At that time no one knew what an African animal truly looked like. She also wrote a book about her many adventures in Africa , Hunting Big Game in Africa. The proceeds of the book were donated to the trapshooting organization. Because she published the book herself, copies are difficult to find. In the book it tells how Grace and her husband established a camp in Tanzania on the N'Goro Nderi River. Along the Guaso Nyro in Kenya, they bagged an elephant and hippo. In the book she tells of a time when she and her young son were on the trail of an animal and had ventured quite far. She realized that it would be too long and strenuous to walk back to the camp. She sent a native to go back and retrieve her husband along with a tent and supplies. He came with the tent and supplies, and they slept off and on through the night in the African wilderness hearing hyenas and lions close by. The next morning they rose to find a buffalo that had been killed and half eaten near their tent. It was not much of a surprise to them after hearing noises all night. There is also a booklet available through antique dealers, African Game Trophies by Mr. and Mrs. E.L. King. The booklet is filled with pictures of their African adventures.

There are twenty exotic taxidermy animals on display from their African safaris in the Winona National Bank in Minnesota. It was built in 1916 and was originally known as Winona Savings Bank. The bank is known to the locals as "the lion bank" with a lion atop the exterior sign representing strength and power. The building presents a visual for stability and strength with its structure and bars. This is before the FDIC (Federal Deposit Insurance Corporation) was established, and therefore there was a great attempt to make

the building look secure. The building itself was designed by George Maher, an architect from Chicago who worked with Frank Lloyd Wright. The outside walls have several concrete busts of lions along with huge columns made of granite from North Carolina. The building style is Egyptian Revival with Prairie School influences. Inside the building the walls and floors are made of white marble from Italy and green marble from Greece. The finely carved railings of the spiral stairway going to the second floor are mahogany. There is also a gun collection on display in the board room upstairs that belonged to Grace. There are several beautiful windows, one quite large, all made of Tiffany glass. One large window is in the ceiling of the atrium in the center of the lobby. Quite innovative for its time, as one enters the bank, the floor mat in front of the doors cause the doors to open electronically. Very noticeably a huge vault is the first thing that one sees encased by large bars.

The vault was built first in the center with the rest of the bank built around it. Large taxidermy African animals are on display under glass cabinets throughout the lobby. It's not every bank that has a rhinoceros right outside the men's restroom. One person described the quiet, subdued atmosphere of the building as being more like a museum than a bank. Children from local schools tour the bank each year.

In 1911 this same architect, George Maher, designed a grand 10,000 square foot home for Grace and her husband. It was named Rockledge. The stunning house with terraces and porches was nestled between two large limestone cliffs along the Mississippi River. The Prairie School motif was used throughout the home. Many of the features were distinctly like those of Frank Lloyd Wright such as high backed chairs

Rockledge. Home of Grace and EL King.

around the dining table. Wright believed that tall chairs at the table gave a cozy, contained feeling to those gathered around. Much like Wright, Maher brought the outside of the surrounding area to create an earthy interior. Lilies that grew outside appeared throughout the house on various pieces. Maher also designed all of the furnishings including the silver service which bore lilies etched on each piece. In 1931 the house was redecorated in an Art Deco décor. The original furnishings were stored in a barn until much later when they were auctioned. Some items are at the Minneapolis Institute of Art while other pieces are privately owned. The home was redecorated in bright colors and even zebra covered couches. Grace and E.L. also had homes in Lake Tahoe, Nevada and Daytona Beach, Florida where they spent most of their time the last ten years of their life together.

One of the most festive and extravagant occasions at Rockledge was the marriage of Grace's daughter, Mary Eleanor King to Ralph Bolt in 1927. On the day of the six P.M. wedding in June, many guests arrived before noon and enjoyed the scenery.

Some swam in the $75,000 pool while others were out on the river in the new King launch.

Other guests arrived later in their Rolls Royce, Pierce Arrows and other expensive cars. The wedding took place in the Japanese gardens of the estate. No expense was spared. Chauffeurs, maids and butlers assisted the three hundred guests.

One of the ushers arrived by a private plane which landed on one of the links of the Winona Public Golf Course. The wedding was complete with a string quartet and soloist. The bride wore a quaint dress of duchess rose lace and satin made from her mother's wedding dress. After the receiving line guests mingled about the pool and were amused by the three lion cubs in cages that Mr. and Mrs. King brought back from their African safari. Dinner was served

Wedding of Mary Eleanor King to Ralph Bolt in June of 1927.

to the guests on terraces, porches and in the garden. The bridal party was served in the dining room of the house decorated with baby breath, ferns, lilies of the valley, white candles, crystal goblets and tulle. The wedding couple departed for their wedding trip to New York and the Atlantic coast. The wedding proved to be a beautiful event enjoyed by all.

Mary Eleanor or Mariel, as she was called, later became noted as a conchologist. She searched the South Pacific Ocean for unusual shells in cooperation with various groups, including the National Geographic Society. Mariel also had kennels for retriever and black Labradors on her estate, Kingwere. She was the owner of the first dual champion golden retriever in America. Mariel died in 1969.

E.L. King died in 1949 and Grace moved to Hawaii in 1950. Their daughter lived down the road from Rockledge on an estate named Kingwere, which was given to her as a wedding gift. Their son, E.L. Jr., lived in the Rockledge home only in the summer. He refused to have the building put on the national registrar of historic buildings. Large impromptu parties were known to be held there with no one to

cleanup. Rockledge began to deteriorate. One winter the heating fuel ran out causing the pipes to freeze and break. Water damage was extensive, for no one discovered the condition for weeks. Before it was razed in 1987, there were holes in the walls so large that one could walk through them. The estate is now remembered only by pictures.

The trap shooter, Grace Watkins King, built a house on Oahu in the secluded Kaaawa district on the site of an old Hawaiian temple. She surrounded the home with fruit trees and tropical flowers. Many of her garden plants were cultivated from seeds that she had brought from Minnesota. She died at the age of ninety-eight in 1975 in Hawaii. She was survived by her son, three grandsons, one granddaughter and seven great grandchildren.

SAMUEL HUNT WATKINS

James Watkins traveled from New Jersey to Cincinnati with his wife and mother-in-law in search of a better life. James began as a blacksmith and eventually acquired a farm and named it Walnut Tree Farm for it had a large walnut tree where they chose to build a house. They had two sons and a daughter – Joseph, Benjamin and Sarah. All three of them were afflicted by cataracts in their eyes at a young age which caused them to have great difficulty in seeing most of their life. Benjamin was more scholarly than this older brother Joseph, but they both attended school. Even though Benjamin became a Christian minister, as adults, Joseph decided to allow his brother to have the farm where they grew up, and Joseph brought a house and a lot in Cincinnati.

Some time later Joseph became restless. He purchased and operated a saw mill one and a half miles from Morrow on Todds Fork. Before leaving his home, he fell in love with Susan Bruin who lived close to Walnut Tree Farm. She was very ill and remained in her parent's home after they were married. Despite the distance from Morrow, he visited her often. A year after their marriage, she died. In time he traded his house in Cincinnati for one hundred sixty acres which was two miles from the mill. This land was solid timber. When he wasn't at the saw mill working, he alone cut the timber on his land, cut it into boards and then sold it. Gradually he farmed the land and built a house near the mill. He married Catherine Pierson in 1836, and they had one child in the house beside the mill before they moved to a newly built house on the farm. There they had eight more children

Joseph Watkins

which included Clinton and Samuel. Clinton later married Althe Worley, a playmate from childhood.

Times were hard during the 1800's after Joseph and Catherine were married. It wasn't always easy to feed and clothe their children. Catherine became deaf at one point, and many other ailments were about the countryside such as flux, consumption, small pox and typhoid fever. Money sharks roamed from farm to farm, and they found flaws in the farmers' land titles. In order to settle such a dispute, Joseph gave all the wood he had cut, thirty cords, and all of his furniture from his house. His son, Samuel, wrote a book which tells of such incidents. It's an autobiography, <u>The Tribe of Joseph</u>, which tells of his life growing up in a pioneer family. This book was published in Winona, Minnesota at the J.R. Watkins Medical Company which was owned by his cousin, J.R. Watkins.

Alexander McGuffey purchased a farm adjoining the Watkins farm on the south side. It was to be their summer residence, and it was on the bluffs overlooking the Little Miami River.

HE CINCINNATI TIMES-STAR—Wednesday, Aug. 16, 1933

BLISHED NEAR CINCINNATI

FORMER ALEXANDER McGUFFEY SUMMER HOME-MORROW,O

Summer home of Alexander McGuffey

Alexander was a rich, downtown Cincinnati lawyer and brother to William McGuffey who wrote the McGuffey readers. Alexander rode the train to and from Cincinnati to go to work. They entertained friends from the city continuously. They had six children and five servants. The parents had very little to do with the Watkins family, but the boys became friends. The oldest McGuffey boy was a fine young man. The younger McGuffey boys lacked morals which were not a good influence on the Watkins children. This concerned Joseph.

Joseph's children attended the school at Mill Grove upstream from Morrow in the early 1850's. When it closed, they went to school at Jack and then later at White Oak. The Watkins family was very devoted Christians and also strong abolitionists as most Republicans were. In fact, their daughter was named Harriet Beecher Stowe Watkins. She was born on January 31, 1858.

Generally the Democrats in the area were in favor of slavery. Since they objected to black children attending school, they were banned where the Watkins children went to school. Lee Edwards was a black man who owned a farm and had a family. Even though he paid taxes for the school, his children were not permitted to attend school. The school master showed no opinion as to whether the children should or should not be allowed in school. Being very angry and drunk, occasionally Mr. Edward would come to school in the middle of the day and threaten to kill the teacher. The teacher began to carry a gun to school in order to ward off Mr. Edwards. The students, being quite fearful, would witness such altercations. To clothe his children, Joseph would take raw wool to a nearby woolen factory and exchange it for bolts of gray cloth.

Catherine may have been deaf, but she could sew the fabric into clothing for the children. They all wore gray. Another source for clothing was a shop in Morrow with a sign that read, "Lewis Fairchild's Dry Goods Store". From time to time, boats would sink in the Ohio River near Cincinnati and the clothing on board would go up for auction. Lewis Fairchild would buy all the clothing, put it out to dry and then sell it. Many thought his sign was deceiving for it should have said, "Wet Goods"! During the Civil War, there would be blue uniforms for sell in his store. Many times they would have fancy brass buttons on the shirts or pants, and the jackets would be finely tailored. These items were snatched up quickly for every boy wanted to be a soldier or at least look like a soldier. Joseph's son, Ben, came home from town once proudly wearing a blue soldier cap that was two sizes too small! These were popular items despite the fact that they were taken from dead Union soldiers killed in battle and had been soaked first to remove the blood.

Joseph made maple syrup from the sap of his maple trees on the farm as many settlers did. This could be used as a sweetener on their food. However, he needed a way to better support his growing family. He decided that he would raise sweet potatoes. He traveled on the train from Morrow to Cincinnati to find a buyer. Once he found a buyer, he made arrangements to ship the sweet potatoes to Cincinnati by train every few days. Gradually he increased his production by building a hot house to start the plants. At one time he had 200,000 plants. Joseph went to Cincinnati periodically to collect his payment. Once before he boarded the train to come home, pick pockets had robbed him of one hundred dollars, and he came home without a dime. Samuel remembers going with his father to collect payment once as a boy. The streets were filled with people. He was in awe of the busy city because he had never seen so many people. While his father stopped to talk to a gentleman, Samuel took a few steps to view an auction in progress. When he turned back, his father was gone. He searched a bit but finally screamed in sobs. Some men settled him by telling Samuel that if his father didn't reappear, they would put him on a train to go home. Thankfully his father came, and Samuel stayed close by his side for the remainder of the trip.

During the Civil War, Samuel went with his father and James, his brother, by horse and wagon to Morrow to ship a load of sweet potatoes to Cincinnati. As they approached the town, they were amazed by the chaos before them. There were several tracks running through the town, and they were filled with stopped trains transporting 20,000 soldiers. Trains and soldiers were everywhere. The stores in town had closed, and the storekeepers and citizens were in the street. It was the Burnside corps which included Eastern men who had served for three years. Upon seeing the Watkins the soldiers called out in a raucous manner, "Gray backs! Gray backs!" President Lincoln had called for 75,000 volunteers in the first three months of war. The Watkins family knew of such volunteers in the area, lead by Captain Wallace, who trained at Camp Denison, near current day Indian Hill which is located north of Cincinnati, Ohio. They were known as the Company A Twelfth Ohio Regiment.

With all the soldiers in town, Joseph Watkins was puzzled about what to do with his load of sweet potatoes. The freight manager told him to put his load in the freight room, and they would be shipped out on the next train after the soldiers cleared. They began to carry the sacks into the freight room that was wide open. A throng of soldiers began to lend a hand making the task quick and easy, but James soon realized their intentions of taking the bags of potatoes right through the freight room and onto a train. He quickly jumped into their path and demanded they place the bags in the freight room. His brave action saved the load from being stolen!

Like many, the Watkins bought sorghum molasses to use as a sweetener that was shipped from New Orleans before the Civil War. It became too expensive like many other items once the war started. Joseph began to grow sorghum himself and sold it to folks nearby. Sorghum grows much like corn with a sweet, dark syrup in the stalk. At first he hauled the canes to a nearby wooden cane mill to be pressed. It was harder and dirtier work than sweet potatoes, but the profit was good. Eventually he bought his own cane mill. During one harvest Joseph's daughter, five-year-old Hattie, and his son, Ben, were operating the cane mill feeding the stalks into the press. It was late in the day. Ben was called to come and drive the cattle away. He returned to find Hattie screaming, and her arm was crushed in the rollers of the press. Three doctors were called in from a nearby town. They worked through the night in the Watkins's home to amputate the arm using no medication, and they saved her life. The whole family waited anxiously outside the bedroom while the doctors worked. Hattie became a rugged individual and quite a tough gal after that experience. With only a stump of an arm, she thrived and often rode a horse bareback on the farm. Hattie grew and became a teacher, but at the age of 23 she died of typhoid fever.

Samuel attempted to be a bookkeeper after finishing school. He scoured various businesses in downtown Cincinnati in search for a job for two days but found no one in need of a bookkeeper. He became a teacher four years after the Civil War. He taught in Ohio for awhile, but couldn't pass the teacher exam. A friend convinced Samuel to go along with him to

Missouri. There Samuel passed the teacher exam, and he went back to teaching again in Missouri.

He soon met Mary Ellen Harn, and they were married in 1871. He brought her back to the farm in Ohio where he grew up, and he returned to farming. For nine years he worked on the farm but could not make much of a profit. So, Samuel and Mary returned to Missouri with their three children, Edith, Wilbert and Henrietta, and Samuel worked on a dairy farm there. This meant that Samuel left his father in Ohio. Samuel's

Harriet Beecher Stowe Watkins

father was so sad to see them go somehow knowing he would never see them again as they boarded an early train.

Samuel's father was right in this premonition as he died the following May in 1882.

Mary Ellen Harn

Farming in Missouri was quite different. After farming in the hills of southern Ohio, he was amazed that he could plow for half a mile without turning around. In Missouri his earnings were not enough for his family, so Mary took in boarders to help pay for food and clothing. Samuel was soon in touch with his cousin, J.R., and he became a "Watkins Man" selling Watkins products door-to-door in Missouri. For twenty years he sold liniment and other elixirs. Samuel experienced various dilemmas where his team of horses and the wagon encountered a problem as he sold Watkins products. Many times they were stuck in the snow or mud. The horses were once spooked on a bridge and the wagon was jerked aside leaving it hanging from the side of

Wilbert , son of Samuel and wife, Nettie
John , son of Clinton and wife, Hattie

the bridge. Another time his load was engulfed in a swollen creek for two days causing all the doors and windows to swell shut. His

Samuel Watkins, "Watkins Man"

canvassing book with $1,200 worth of accounts was washed away. It was found downstream two months later by a sawmill hand in some driftwood. Such was the life of a traveling salesman.

Samuel died in March of 1919 at the age of sixty-six. He was amazed by all the progress he had witnessed in his lifetime. He remembered when threshing machines, similar to combines today, were run by horse power. Then steam engines ran the threshing machines that were pulled by horses. Of course, the steam engines later powered trains. He knew of a time when many believed that a steam engine could never be used to cross the ocean because it could never carry enough coal. They believed that a steam engine could never run on a road without a track. Both were proven to be wrong. Samuel witnessed the coming of electrical power, wireless telegraphs, air ships, automobiles and telephones.

Samuel, with brothers, Joe, Ben and Clinton

His life was one of hard work with prosperity and hardships always surrounded by a loving family who embraced the Christian faith.

Samuel and Catherine Watkins (niece)

Location of Watkins, Worley and McGuffey property along the Little Miami River in Bluechin

FAMILY CONNECTIONS TO SAMUEL WATKINS, JULIA WATKINS, AND J. R. WATKINS

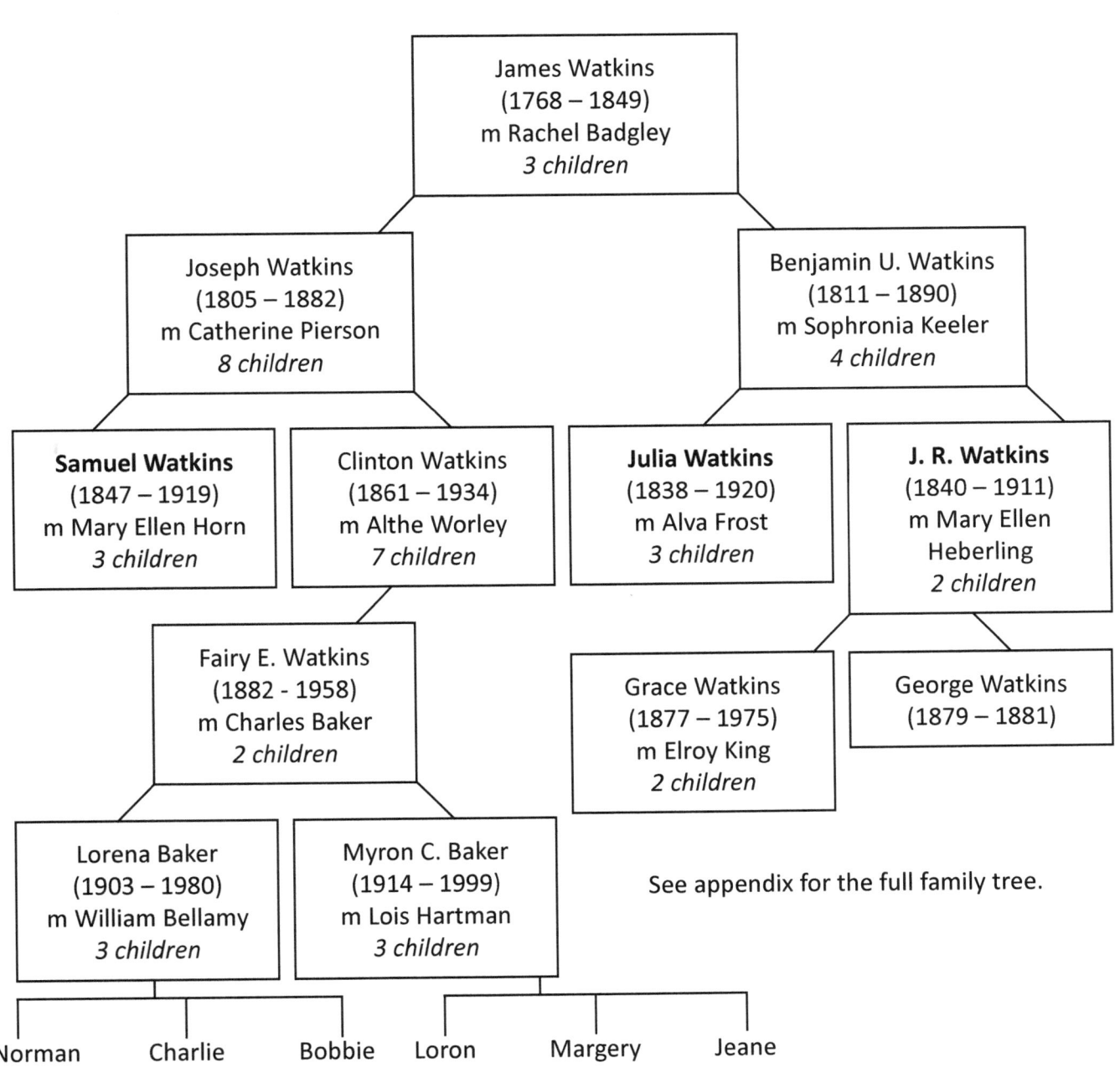

James Watkins
(1768 – 1849)
m Rachel Badgley
3 children

Joseph Watkins
(1805 – 1882)
m Catherine Pierson
8 children

Benjamin U. Watkins
(1811 – 1890)
m Sophronia Keeler
4 children

Samuel Watkins
(1847 – 1919)
m Mary Ellen Horn
3 children

Clinton Watkins
(1861 – 1934)
m Althe Worley
7 children

Julia Watkins
(1838 – 1920)
m Alva Frost
3 children

J. R. Watkins
(1840 – 1911)
m Mary Ellen
Heberling
2 children

Fairy E. Watkins
(1882 - 1958)
m Charles Baker
2 children

Grace Watkins
(1877 – 1975)
m Elroy King
2 children

George Watkins
(1879 – 1881)

Lorena Baker
(1903 – 1980)
m William Bellamy
3 children

Myron C. Baker
(1914 – 1999)
m Lois Hartman
3 children

See appendix for the full family tree.

Norman   Charlie   Bobbie   Loron   Margery   Jeane

GOING TO TOWN

One ordinary day Althe (Worley) Watkins decided to go into Lebanon to buy household items. Althe was married to Clinton Watkins, and they had seven children. They lived in the Stubbs homestead that was built near the mills. The trip to Lebanon was about five miles in distance traveling on Lebanon Pike which is now called Stubbs Mill Road. At this time it was hardly a road. It was more like a path because it was not heavily traveled. There were not much more than three bare lines on the ground that showed where the horse and wagon wheels traveled.

With few residents if any along the way, not much of the area was even cleared for farming. This road winds around and around and goes up and down hills much the same way it does now. One exception was just north of the Stubbs homestead. Instead of winding around the side of the hill as it does now, it went straight up the hill and continued in that path for quite a distance. When I was a child, this was pointed out to me by my father. He directed my gaze from the bottom of the hill looking up, showing me where the tops of the trees were not quite as tall as the other trees on each side of the line where the road once was. The original road passed right by the graveyard of the mill hands. Now the graveyard is quite a distance from the current road.

Unfortunately one cannot see any difference in the height of the trees now. In the mid 1900's the Stubbs homestead was where my great aunt and uncle lived, Blanche Watkins Sanford and her husband, Ford Sanford. Their son contacted my father when his parents were deceased. He asked if my father was interested in buying the property which is where the old road would have been. Donald Sanford quoted two prices – one price with the timber and one without the timber. My father thought it was over priced and rejected the offer. The land sold with the timber removed, thus causing the lower timber line at the tree tops to disappear.

The road also differed in the area where Interstate 71 crosses. Interstate 71 was built in a ravine. Stubbs Mill Road went down and back up this ravine rather than straight across and above the interstate as it does now. It's evident that this is an old road because it doesn't have any right angle curves. Later roads often had right angle curves because they were built between the property lines of the farms where square or rectangular fields butted against each other.

Althe set out for Lebanon in a horse and buggy with the house maid and her baby. Which child the baby was is not known. She left her older children at home for they were old enough to care for themselves. As they traveled into town, they noticed that a bear was following behind them. They were not too concerned because they reached town before it threatened them. They purchased their goods and headed home. Once they had traveled into the thicket

of woods, the bear reappeared. He had not forgotten the travelers. The bear followed for a great distance, and the women were hoping that the bear would become tired and eventually end his pursuit. But he did not falter. When they would speed up the buggy, the bear would increase his speed, too. It was difficult for the buggy to go too fast because of the condition of the road and the twists and turns and the hills of the road. The bear was relentless and would not give up. The women knew that the bear was hungry. They began to grow more fearful as the bear grew closer and closer closing the gap between them. They felt that they were doomed with no where to go to escape the bear.

There was no one within miles that could help them and no where to find refuge. They continued to coax the horse to go faster, but it didn't help. The bear was right behind them. At one point they considered throwing out a food item to appease the bear, but then concluded that it was not what the bear wanted. As conditions grew tenser, the house maid cried out in desperation, "Throw out the baby! Throw out the baby! You can get another one next year! That bear is hungry! Throw out the baby, and he'll leave us alone! Throw out the baby!" What an unbelievable remark for the house maid to make!

Althe did not throw out the baby. The bear never caught them, and they made it safely home. It's a bit overwhelming when one considers the threats and conditions they faced. They had to be strong people. I'm sure Althe continued to travel to and from Lebanon in the same way many times in order to get the household needs.

I heard this tale over and over from older relatives and especially from my great aunt, Blanche Watkins Sanford because Althe was her mother. Once the relatives had died, my mother told the story time and time again. When Aunt Blanche would tell the story, she would conclude by saying, "Nobody knows who the baby was, but just think. Some of us might not be here today if she threw out the baby. That baby might have been me or my sibling, and I wouldn't be here to tell the story." My mother, who married into the family, would end the story with the same words saying that our family might not be here. Boy, did I feel lucky to be alive.

Althe with all her children, except Stanley. Note: she did not throw anyone out.

Top right:
Clinton Watkins holding Margaret Brant, Hal Brant holding Harold Brant, Jane Brant, unknown, Adarene Watkins, Blanche Watkins, Dixon
Middle row:
Althe Watkins, Mills family, Charlie Baker (second from right) and Fairy Baker
Bottom row:
John Watkins, Hattie Watkins, Mills family, Kate Watkins, Lorena Baker

THE WATKINS LADIES

Clinton Watkins and Althe Worley were married in 1881 and had seven children. Clinton and Althe first lived on the Worley farm in Bluechin. They later lived on a farm on the corner of Waynesville Road and Shawhan Road, not farm from Stubbtown. Five of the children were girls and two were boys. The five girls were Fairy, Jane, Blanche, Adarene and Catherine. The two boys were Stanley and A. John Watkins. The five girls were very close and stayed in touch throughout their lives. My mother, Lois, found this to be a very interesting, and somewhat difficult situation when she married Fariy's son.

Lois Hartman married the son of Charlie and Fairy, Myron, and their first home was in a small house near the river where Stubbs Mill once stood. At first Lois felt a bit like an outsider because Fairy and her sisters had such a close relationship amongst themselves. Lois fondly remembers the girls, then grown women. As a wedding gift to Lois and Myron, the sisters made a knotted comforter for the newlyweds. Lois enjoyed their company and the feeling was mutual.

At one time Fairy told her sisters to not speak of it, but she was very fond of Lois. It was very important for Lois to feel accepted, and it is so sad to know that Fairy never told her.

The closeness of the sisters is evident throughout their lives. They all lived in the area. Fairy lived on Stubbs Mill Road. Jane lived on Miami Street in Morrow along the river. Blanche lived in the Stubbs homestead where her wedding was held. Adarene lived in Pleasant Ridge in Cincinnati. Catherine, or Aunt Kate as she was called, lived in Lebanon.

Fairy, Jane, Blanche, Adarene, and Catheryn

The women would gather once a month at Fairy's house to play cards. They had a wonderful time. Fairy would have a small inexpensive gift for each one every time they gathered. Lois remembers much later cleaning out Fairy's house and enjoyed seeing the mementos one more time before throwing them away.

After Fairy died, Lois would visit the women often. Jane had married Hal Brant and lived in downtown Morrow in a small one story house that had a small attic. The Little Miami River was right in her back yard. Therefore the house was raised off the ground to accommodate flood waters in the spring. Jane was a petite little woman. Almost every spring the Little Miami River would flood because of the persistent spring rains. Jane's son, Harold, along with Lois and Myron would plead for Jane to vacate the house before the water crept in. Most of the time, she refused. She was stubborn and determined to stay in her house. Eventually the fire department would have to take a row boat to get her and bring her to dry land. Many times this was viewed on television along with the news of the flooding. Sometimes she would be climbing out the attic window to get into the row boat with the help of a fireman.

Blanche married John Ford Sanford and lived in the Stubbs homestead near the Little Miami River. Fortunately that house was on higher ground. Lois's son, Loron, loved to go to Blanche's house and would run away from home to visit Aunt Blanche or sometimes his grandmother in the opposite direction up the road. There was a large gravel pit near the river. Sometimes the gravel trucks traveling on the road would pick up Loron and take him home. Lois finally had to tie Loron to the clothesline to keep him from wandering off. Today that would be considered as child abuse! Tying him worked most of the time, but one time Loron chewed through the rope and got away in spite of the rope. Blanche would sometimes have Loron and Margery, Loron's sister, sleep at her house. She would tell the kids ghost stories while the wind would be howling down the chimney or an owl would be hooting behind the house. It was so scary! The kids loved it. Blanche also made sock dolls for all the children. She would sew buttons and yarn on a sock to make a face and made clothes for the sock dolls to wear. Blanche and her husband were the last ones to live in the Stubbs homestead.

She held an estate auction in 1957 where she sold all of the original furniture that was stored in the attic. One particular bed was made by Henry Boyd, a well known cabinet maker in Cincinnati. He was a black man who had once been a slave but escaped slavery after crossing the Ohio River. She sold many of the Stubbs documents from the mill to the Warren Historical Society. They moved to a small house in Lebanon. Blanche had two boys. The oldest boy had diabetes. Because there was no true treatment at the time for diabetes, he died at the age of 37. The younger son, Donald, lived in Lebanon. A daughter, Charlene, lived in Lebanon, also.

Adarene married Dr. Leon Hunter and lived in Pleasant Ridge. Leon was an osteopath which Lois, a registered nurse, found hard to honor. They never had children. Lois would take Loron along when visiting. One time the Watkins sisters and Lois with Loron were there, and they were admiring some of the beautiful items that Adarene had in a curio cabinet. Lois had warned Loron that there were many lovely things at Aunt Adarene's house that he must not touch. Aderene always had fresh baked bran muffins for her husband. Leon, being a doctor, ate foods that were high in fiber such as whole grain foods. Adarene always offered a bran muffin to her guests. Eventually the ladies left the room probably to have a muffin and noticed Loron had not followed. When they returned to the curio cabinet, Loron had pulled a stool over to the cabinet and was standing on it with his hands clasped behind his back peering into the cabinet. The women were delighted to see a little boy resist temptation. When Leon retired, they moved to the Watkins home on Waynesville road. Later they moved to an old house built in 1829 north of Waynesville on Route 42. They left their estate to Blanche's son, Donald, who needed the aid.

Kate had curly hair and was musically talented. She played the piano by ear. Once she heard a song, she would play it. She used her talent at the movie theater in Lebanon playing along with the silent movies. When the plot became intense, she was known to bang out a tune. Kate married George Dugan and had one child, Audrey Dugan.

Oh, but Kate hated red hair. When Lois had her second child, Margery, and Margery had red hair, Kate was very displeased. Kate died of lung cancer, and Lois, who was a registered nurse, stayed with her many hours, day and night at the hospital in Cincinnati to comfort her. At that time, doctors would not tell their patients everything especially if their disease was fatal. Lois remembered that one time Kate had asked to see her recent x-ray. She told the doctor that she could tell that the tumor was larger in her lung. Naturally, the doctor could not argue. Lois believed that Kate knew that her death was near even though it was never discussed. It was unfortunate for Kate that she never lived to see her grandson. It was also fortunate that she never saw her grandson. He had red hair.

"Aunt Kate"

Lois Hartman Baker,
Christ Hospital School of Nursing,
Class of 1937

69

The five Watkins girls remained close and never ventured far from the area. They looked forward to their monthly gatherings to play cards and catch up with each other's lives. Below is a picture of some of their children at a gathering on the Stubbs homestead.

Watkins descendants:
Lorena Baker, Hal and Harold Brant, Myron Baker, Audrey Dugan,
Nyle and Dale Watkins

UNCLE JOHN – A. J. WATKINS

A. J. Watkins was born in 1885 in the Watkins home of his grandfather, Joseph Watkins. John was the son of Althe (Worley) and Clinton Watkins. He was the youngest brother to the Watkins ladies. The house where he was born was the house that James built himself out of native timber. This is mentioned in the chapter about Samuel Watkins. The house was one and a half miles northeast of Morrow in Salem Township. At the age of two, John and the Watkins family moved to the Worley house where Althe had grown up. This house was two and a half miles west of Morrow in Union Township. His family moved once again to the house which was across the road from the Stubbs homestead when he was five years old.

John and Mina—1958

John attended the Washington School District No. 3. At the completion of eighth grade, John passed the Boxwell Examination. The exam was very difficult, covering every subject. Only one in three passed the exam. One could only go to high school if they passed the exam. Their high school tuition would be paid by the township where they lived. John attended Morrow High school where he graduated as the salutatorian. He completed his education at The National Normal University in Lebanon. Once he graduated from The National Normal University, he met the requirements to teach which were he was more than sixteen of age, he graduated from high school and he passed the Boxwell Exam. John taught at two local schools. The first school was the Silver Grove Rural School. The second school was the Millgrove Rural School.

By this time he had met a lovely lady from Loveland, Harriet Ramsey, who was called Hattie. In 1906 they were married. That same year he quit teaching and became a brakeman on the Pennsylvania Railroad. The train ran between Cincinnati and Columbus, much of it along the Little Miami River. John would have the engineer blow the whistle of the train in a distinct pattern as the train traveled through Stubbtown. For many years the family would remark, "There's Uncle John on the train." Even in the dark of the night, John would swing a lantern as he passed the area. After John retired, Myron acquired a cabinet from the train with drawers filled with locks and keys for box cars. That was the job of a brakeman – to secure the cars on the train. The last few years that the train service was offered, Cliff Stubbs was the conductor.

Hattie and John had three boys Paul, Robert and Marion. Paul became a doctor. Robert had a career in the U.S. Air Force. Marion became a rear admiral in the U.S. Navy. John was very proud of his boys. Of the three Marion kept in touch with the family for many years.

In 1954 there was a flu epidemic which took the life of Hattie. A few years later, John retired, moved to Columbus, Ohio to be closer to his son, and he married Mina Byrd. John and Mina traveled often to see Charlie after Fairy died. Mina would scrub the large brick house from top to bottom. She would cook big meals. In the evening she would mend Charlie's clothes. Being just a child, I loved being with them. I would walk up the road to Grandpa Baker's house where they stayed. I was met with big hugs and warm greetings. I remember them being dressed in long pants and long sleeves in the heat of the summer when we went in the woods. Of course, I had on my everyday play clothes of shorts, a T- shirt, anklets and canvas shoes. Mina loved sassafras tea, so John would take a shovel, and the three of us would tramp through the woods until we found sassafras trees. John would dig up some roots, and Mina would boil them for tea back at the house.

John was an exceptional person and was dearly loved by the family. Everyone enjoyed having him when he came to visit. He had a great heart and could express himself with joy and humor. He spoke eloquently and had a great command of the language. His level of education was evident when he spoke, and yet he was never haughty. He was simply dear, but carried himself with distinction. John created a presence in the room that is difficult to describe. He cared about the family and in turn, the family cared for him.

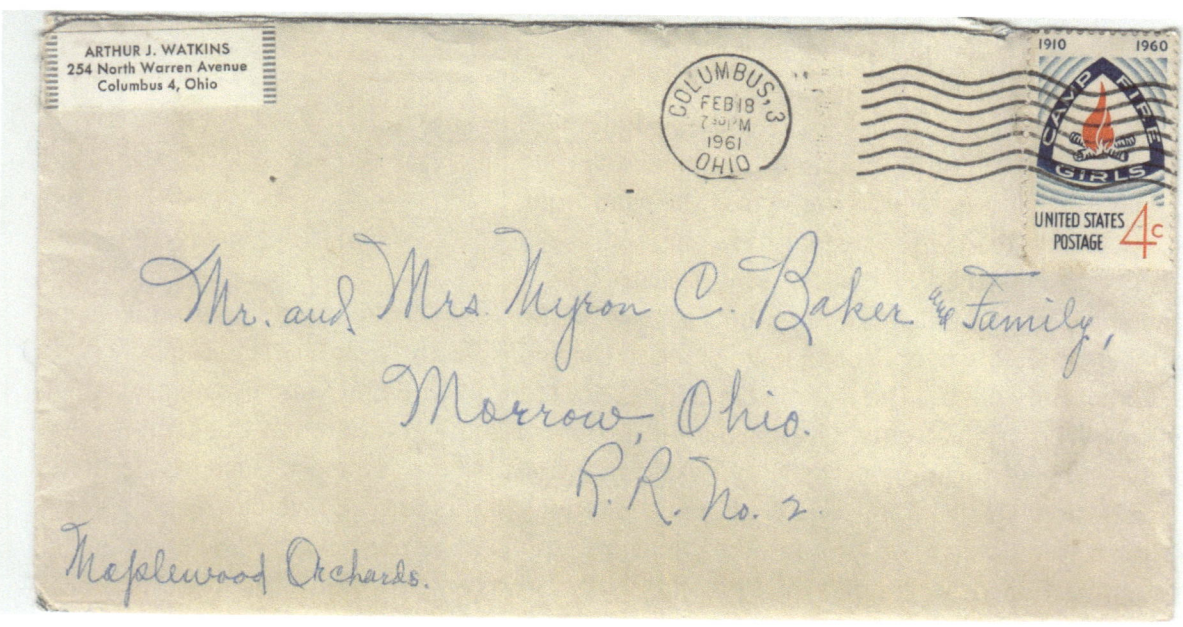

Above is the envelope from Uncle John's letter. In the letter (shown on the following 3 pages), Uncle John explains why he was not able to attend the wedding of Loron Baker and Dixie Amburgy. He also expressed his love and concern for Jean and her education.

Columbus, Ohio, February 17, 1961.

Dear Kin-folks:— At this time we may presume, that all the work, worry, excitement and fatigue incumbent upon those in any way a part of a Church Wedding has subsided; and relaxation and rest is the "Order of the Day." We have read and fully enjoyed the splendid account of the nuptial ceremony and activities. What a very happy affair, and in which all participants really were very much a part of the festivities.

We were much in regret that we failed to be present and make "hoop-lah" with the rest, but we confess cowardice in this winter weather and driving. Our Neighborly Neighbors' Club meeting on Feb. 11th at 1=30 P.M. did not close until 4=15 P.M. So for us to rest home, make preparation, and hurry to Lebanon, seemed rather too much for us two 'Old Cronies', so we played the game safe, and stayed home and lamented our absence.

We imagine the occasion demanded a whole church-full of relatives and friends. It is our hope that the life of the marriage may be as beautiful as the marriage occasion

2.

However we must admit that the greater part of the beauty of their married life will be framed by their own efforts; and come as a reward for those efforts. As God witnessed the ceremony, so may He be the pilot throughout its course in the coming years. May He smile upon them always.

It is reasonable to presume that the departure of our copious supply of snow has completely suited you. Yesterday the last of "the beautiful" faded away. It had long since outlasted its usefulness and welcome.

It is drizzling rain here today. We should like to see a heavy rain to wash away all the collection of dirt and mess of over two month's time.

Our imagination leads us to visualize the cute little lady we all love so much, Jean E. We know she enacted her part most splendidly, and really looked her part in grand style. Of course, you will have some pictures for us to view! After completing all the preparations, we should guess Mother and Father Baker looked and felt rather exhausted. You must not overlook the probability that, sometime in the future, there may be one or two daughters for whom similar preparations must be made. Such may exceed those of recent demand. Eh?

3.

Dr. Crane's letter in yesterday's paper caused me to think of our disappointment in the delay in Jean E.'s and Stevie's entrance into school. This piece by Dr. Crane rather heals the wound we suffered by their delay. I have read it and think an "honor student" (as Jean E. surely will be) is preferable to one whose social and physical development is far in arrears of her mental progress. So I feel we can rely up her progress being little delayed account entering school a year late. There is much of her education she already knows, and much is being learned each day. Her aptitude is great, so we shall watch her catch-up with the others.

We had a letter from Grandpa telling us of how he reached home in the snow-storm, and how he enjoyed his stay with us. We think it quite a stimulant for him to get out and around often. Change of scenery is always good for all of us. We enjoy having him and Jean E. You know, it rather raises our spirits too. Both of us are in usual winter health. My abdominal distress has somewhat subsided, feeling fairly good. We are waiting upon a chance of good weather, so we may run down to Warren County to see what transformation winter has wrought, and to chat with relatives. So if weather breaks, we shall come running. Tell Jean E. our little birds are wondering where their little friend went. She had a time with them.

Love and best wishes.

Aunt Nina and Uncle John

STRIKE UP THE BAND

Long ago music wasn't a part of the school curriculum. The family would usually encourage and teach their children to play various musical instruments. Sometimes they would take their children to private lessons. Communities would announce a concert and welcome anyone to come and play. Bands would just form independently and play at these community concerts on the lawn of a county building or some green space in town. In Lebanon the concerts would be on the side lawn of the Golden Lamb. Various places would hold competitions and award prizes to the better bands.

Charles Baker and his brother Jacob Baker, sons of John Quincy Baker and Mary Jane (Toms), were in the Knights of Pythias Band in South Lebanon. The Knights of Pythias was a fraternal organization that sponsored the band. Charles played the tuba and Jacob played the baritone. It was considered one of the best amateur bands in the county. It was organized in 1898 under the direction of Professor Hawley Clark. Their band played at concerts around Warren County. The band entered the Lebanon Fair contest and won second place which gave them a prize of fifty dollars. That was quite a prize in 1899. Much later, Norman Bellamy took the tuba leaving the case. Ty Baker now has the case.

Kate Watkins, daughter of Clinton Watkins and Althe (Worley), played the piano by ear. She played for the silent movies at the theater in Lebanon. She could easily play many forms of music to suit the mood of the movie. She also provided great entertainment at Christmas. A couple other family members would pick up an instrument and every one there would gather in the Baker homestead to sing Christmas carols.

Stanley Watkins, the son of Clinton Watkins and Althe (Worley), lived in the Worley home across the road from the Stubbs homestead. He spent his life farming and playing music which he loved very much. He was a music teacher in Lebanon. He could play woodwinds and brass instruments well. He attempted to give Myron Baker lessons on the saxophone. After three weeks of lessons, Myron showed no promise of being a musician, and Stanley gave up. In later years he worked for the state highway department. Stanley died at his home on 506 West Main Street in Lebanon in 1968. He lived to be 74.

Stanley and his wife, Martha (Connor), had two sons, Dale and Nyale Watkins. Naturally they inherited their father's gift of music, and they played in a band during the big band era. They played at dances in Warren, Clermont and Hamilton counties. Because Myron Baker was close in age to his cousins, Dale and Nyale, he would follow them to dances. Myron may not have had the talent to play music, but he sure had a talent to dance. He could swoosh

AGNES BELLE CHAMBERS
(wife of ANDREW JACKSON CONNER)
with her two Grandsons:
Dale Stanley Watkins & Nyale Watkins
(sons of Mary Conner & Stanley Watkins)

his partner as light as air across the floor with little effort. Dale and Nyale played in Loveland, Lakeside in Dayton, Castle Farm and Moonlight Gardens at Coney Island in Cincinnati.

One year they played on New Years at Spring Grove. Dale and Nyale loved the big band sound and whenever a famous band would come to town, they would go to hear them. Many times Myron went along. Some of the big bands they heard were Woody Herman, Duke Ellington and Glen Miller.

When Myron and Lois (Hartman) became engaged, they celebrated with friends at Castle Farm. Castle Farm was a supper club near Reading in Cincinnati that hosted swing bands and sometimes gambling.

Alfred Watkins was the son of Joseph Watkins and Mary Johnston. He grew up on the family farm in Morrow and lived there his entire life. He began his music career by playing the violin. He graduated from Morrow High School and continued his education at the University of Cincinnati where he graduated from the Conservatory of Music in 1916. He continued post graduate work at the Conservatory through 1918. For the next few years he taught in the public schools of Warren County. In 1921 he studied abroad at the Royal Academy in Munich and Leipzig and earned a masters degree. He traveled throughout Europe performing at concerts with various orchestras. He especially enjoyed playing for children's concerts. He returned home in 1923 and taught in all but two schools in Warren County. One year later he married Edith Trisler. He retired in 1937. His son, William lived in the Watkin's home later and his wife was a teacher in Lebanon.

Alfred Watkins

A little bit of the musical talent was handed down to me. I have had several years of voice lessons. I sang in ensembles and choirs in church and school. I sang the national anthem at sporting events. I sang at many weddings including my own wedding. I was in plays and musicals. I wanted so badly to play the piano, but after a few years of lessons, I wasn't very good. In high school I was part of a group selected by the chorus teacher called, "The Folksingers." The group consisted of two guitarists, a pianist and seven or eight vocalists. Not only did we perform at school events, but often we performed for organizations in the area. All of the organizations were very receptive with compliments and were delighted with our performances except for one. We performed twice for the inmates at the Lebanon Correctional Institute. After we would sing a popular song with an up-beat turn, the response from the inmates would be cold, hard stared and little applause. We learned to cope and go on through many uncomfortable moments. The response at Kings Island was just the opposite. We were hired to perform for the entire summer the year that the amusement park opened in 1972. We were even taken to a recording studio to perform the park's theme song that was used in their advertising. We learned a little bit about what it was like to be a professional singer and performer. It was a wonderful experience to entertain others no matter where we performed.

From playing various instruments to teaching music and singing, the family showed some talent. There is little evidence that the Stubbs were gifted in music. We only know that they had a piano. However, it was common for people to play instruments in the times before other types of entertainment appeared such as radio and television. Music was simply an enjoyable way to pass the time.

Band members (1898) Cornetist: Hawley Clarke
Musical Director: Victor Van Riper, Louis Dunn
Clarinetists: Gus Aste, Fred Watkins, Ray Brinkman, Ed Sears Altos: Fred Cox, Martin Holloway, Obe
Lucas

Trombones: Bert Baker, Jacob Baker Baritone: Wilber Snook
B Bas: Charles Sears Tuba: Charles Baker
Drum: Ellis Clark, Tom Karr

PART 4 – THE BAKER FAMILY

BUILDING WASHINGTON SCHOOL

Washington School was built in 1851 on the northeast corner of Stubbs Mill Road and Trovillo Road. An article in the local newspaper appeared on September 14, 1933 by Quincy Stubbs which was written much earlier. In the article he recalled what he remembered about the school. (See article at the end of the chapter.)

Washington School Teacher desk

He remembered going to the site one day when Elijah Trovillo was laying the foundation stone to the building. Elijah was a piano salesman in Warren County and lived close by. Zimri Stubbs, who was the brother to Isaac II, had donated one half acre for the building. At a later time he donated an additional one half acre for the school grounds.

The school was built with a hall across the front that was about six feet wide. At each end of the hall was a door that led into the classroom.

At one of the doors was a bell with a rope that the teacher would use to call the children inside to class. The seats and tables in the classroom were black walnut and white oak. There was a big box stove at the front of the room that was used to heat the room. The teacher's desk was oak with a stool behind it for the teacher. Charlie Baker bought the furniture along with the building years later. The teacher's desk is in the family possessions. In fact, it is the very desk that I'm using right now to write on my computer.

Two boys with a wooden stick would carry drinking water from Mathias Brant's farm that was a half a mile away. Sometimes they would choose to get water from the nearby creek. With a humorous slant, Quincy described the decorations in the room. There were paper wads on the ceiling and beech gads in the corner for whippings. Sometimes the boys would be asked to go gather beech gads, and they would gash or score the bark so they might break when someone got a whipping.

Out in the hall the children would place their dinner buckets or baskets on a low shelf. At times dogs or hogs from a nearby farm would raid the dinners leaving nothing for the children to eat. Other times the poor children would raid them.

The children were asked to bring goose quills to school. The school master would then take on the role of an architect trimming the ends to make writing pens. Chalk for the black board came in large chunks that were broken into smaller pieces for writing.

Stubbs Mill Road was originally behind the school. It was not uncommon to see oxen pulling wagons passing by. In the morning of many days, Zimri would use oxen and a wagon to bring the children who lived down the hill near the river to school giving them a reprieve from arduously walking up the hill. There was no gravel on the road until 1868.

Some of the games that the children played were town bail, paddle ball, bull pen and buck. In one of the games the students would stand in a circle with one in the middle who would recite a nonsense rhyme pointing to each student with each word. When he reached the end of the rhyme, the middle child would chase the other one until he or she was caught. The description of this game reminded me of "Duck, Duck, Goose".

Kids were not much different back then. Some enjoyed the challenge of learning new things and others did not. Sometimes a boy might prop his book on his desk and instead of reading it, he might take out his Barlow knife and drill a hole through the pages. Something like this would bring a stiff consequence. Most whippings were administered after school. The boys would stuff their pants with withes to soften the lashings. When the naughty boy was held after school, his friends might ring the bell out in the hall. This would distract the teacher causing the teacher to come to the hall, and then the bad kid would climb out the classroom window and escape his punishment. Other consequences for bad behavior included making scholars stand in the front of the room with a dunce cap on their head. Another master made the scholar stand in front of the room with his arms extended for a period of time.

The school master would teach in lengths of three months at a time. Some would leave after three months. Others would stay. Quincy couldn't remember well, but he thought the pay was forty dollars for three months. Quincy attended the school from September 4, 1852 until November 1866. He recalled having twenty-four masters. Four of them were Stubbs relatives. Jonas Stubbs was a cousin. Abias Stubbs was his sister. Jane Stubbs was also a sister. He remembered her whipping Quincy because he threw something at a bird. He was confused at the time because he didn't even hit it. Ellen Stubbs and John Trovillo were also masters. Joseph A. Dunham was a master who gave him the hardest whipping he had ever had. Lizzie Vestal taught in the school, and she cried over fiction love stories. Joseph Young had only one arm, and Quincy said that he should have been "in the pen". Washington Whitacre was a master who had "whiskers galore". Rose Clarige was a holy terror as a master. She whipped six students on her first day.

Washington School operated along with nearby Union Township School for several decades.

Washington School

Thursday, September 14, 1933

History of the Washington School -- by Quincy Stubbs

By QUINCY STUBBS, Cincinnati. (From memory in my 86th year.)

The first knowledge I had of the Washington school was in the year 1851 when I was nearly three and one-half years old. My father took me up to where Elijah Trovillo was laying the foundation stone for the old school house which stood a little north of this one.

I learned later that my father, Zimri Stubbs, gave one-half acre of land to revert back to the owner of the land when not used for school purposes. When the present school house was built another half acre was donated likewise.

The old school house had a hall nearly 6 feet wide across the front with a door at each end into the school room. The seats and desks were black walnut and white oak. A big box stove was up in front. Wood was burned all the time I attended, up to November, 1866. There was no well dug for a number of years after the school house was built. Two boys with a wood bucket on a stick would carry the drinking water from Mathias Brant's farm a half mile away, when they did not choose to get it out of a nearby creek.

The only decorations there were in the school room were the half dozen or more beech gads in the corner, the paper wads sticking to the ceiling, and the cross look on the master's face. Sometimes dogs and even hogs would raid the dinner buckets and baskets on the low shelves in the hall. Poor children would sometimes do likewise. We took goose quills to school and the master made our pens to write with. He had to be a mechanic as well as an instructor.

Chalk came in large lumps and had to be broken. There were wild turkeys in the woods. The road was east or back of the school house for a few years after the first school house was built. There was no gravel road past the school house until 1868 or later. Ox teams were a familiar sight. After a rain I would take the children from Stubbtown to school with a young ox hitched to a wagon.

A boy would set a book up on his desk and with his Barlow knife cut a hole through it. Boys that expected to get a whipping would put withs inside their pants. It was impossible for any to keep live stock out of their heads.

Masters and teachers were hired for a term of three months. I have a faint recollection that women teachers got forty dollars for the for a term of three months. I have a faint recollection that women teachers got forty dollars for the three months' term.

The bell rope hung at the side of the door in the hall. When a boy was kept in after school was out to get an introduction to the beech gads, boys would pull the bell rope. The master would run out to see who had rung the bell. The kept-in boy would jump out the window. Boys that were sent out to harvest a few beech gads would score or gash the bark, so they would break easily.

We played town ball, paddle ball, bull pen and buck. To play buck a ring was formed, a captain chosen, and he would call each one as follows: "One'ry, ora, icory on, fillison, follison, Nicholas, John, queva, quavy, English navy, stinklum, stanklum, buck." A scatterment followed, with buck trying to catch the nearest one. Some scholars would resent being whipped and would fight back. The whole school would watch very attentively the combat. I only remember of one master that made scholars stand out in front with a paper dunce cap on. Another master made them stand with an extended arm.

My mind often wanders back to my school days at old Washington and the many incidents that took place. One boy I often think about that lived on the old Paris farm, but later was known as the James Cook farm, moved with the folks he lived with away out west. The day they were loading their wagons for their long journey, this boy came to bid a last fond goodbye to his playmates. A short distance south near the road, he cut his full name and date on a beech tree which was visible for 25 or 30 years or more, until David Worley cut it down. His name, John W. Vananders, May 4th, 1854. In the 14 years I went to school I gazed on that name.

There were between 60 and 70 scholars enrolled prior to the Civil War. Statistics show there were more people in Warren County in 1850 than there were in the 40 or more years following. Out of the many that went to school, there are only 10 living, Francis Clark Adams being the oldest and past 91.

George Trovillo and Alfred Payne gave their all in the Civil War, also David Brant. F. W. Bryant is resting in an unknown Foreign Island. Three others are buried at Helena, Montana. Three or more found a silent abode in Philadelphia, three or more are sleeping at Independence, Missouri. Others are in Illinois, Indiana and in Ohio at Lebanon, Morrow, Waynesville, Clarksville, Mason and West Chester, Hamilton county.

In the rapidly passing years the 10 of us yet living will soon behold the Pale Rider on the white horse coming around the bend for his final call. But such is the way of life.

The Dead Past

From memory in my 86th year. ..Rt i palL

Masters and teachers I went to school to from September 4, 1852 to November 1866, at Washington School in Warren County, Ohio. About one half of the instructors I went to were called masters.

1. James Young, an oldish man, blind in one eye. He was my first master. If a scholar was violating one of the iron bound rules, he would throw a big beech gad at them, big end first. They would have to take it up to him and most times feel its power. He drew me a bird on a bush and wrote on it Quincy Stubbs, January 26, 1853. I have it yet.

2. Jonas Stubbs, my second master. He was my first cousin.

3. Joseph Robertson. He taught longer than any other.

4. Abiah Stubbs, my sister.

5. Jane Stubbs, my sister, whipped me for going out to throw at a bird, and I did not hit it either.

6. Ellen Stubbs, last survivor, about 90 years.

7. Lee S. Dunham, was county treasurer.

8. Joseph A. Dunham, gave me the hardest whipping I ever had.

9. Kane Graville, was too lenient.

10. Mary F. Wright, large woman, with eyes like an owl.

11. John F. Kibbey.

12. Rose Clarige, a holy terror, whipped six the first day.

13. Thomas Platt, a swell dresser.

14. Julia Saunders, called the bloomer girl. She wore bloomers.

15. Mary E. Fall, small in stature, but very neat.

16. Washington Whitacre, with whiskers galore.

17. (—) Fisher, had one short leg.

18. Rebecca R. Bovey, she got closer to the scholars than any other.

19. Alfred N. Rich, Loveland, Ohio.

20. John C. Trovillo, a former scholar.

21. John Milton Dunham, next last survivor, about 88 years.

22. Joseph Young, only had one arm. He should have been in the Pen.

23. Lizzie Vestal, enjoyed crying over fiction love stories.

24. Sarah Compton, my last teacher, she wore boots.

I was told I went to a Miss Johnson, but I cannot recall her. I went to school a few days as a visitor to the old log school house in 1852 that was on the Peter Drake farm. They only had slabs for seats, there were no desks, I remember a cold, rainy day the Master tried to start a fire in the big stone fire place with a flint.

Washington School. There is not a list of students, but Myron Baker is seen in the back row. Picture is around 1922 as best can be determined.

WASHINGTON SCHOOL

When public schools were first established in the Northwest Territory, it was decided that every township would have sixteen acres set aside for their school. This acreage would be farmed, and the school would be built on it. The responsibility of the school was laid upon the residents in the township to build the school and maintain it. Most of the residents were farmers at that time, so among them they would decide what was to be planted on the acreage and share the burden of growing and harvesting the crops. The profit from the crops would be used to maintain the building, buy books and supplies for the school, and pay the schoolmaster. Most schools were one room classrooms including the Union Township School which still stands today as a church on Stubbs Mill Road. Before being a church the old school was owned by Dallas Worley where he operated an Allis Chalmers farm implements dealership.

There was also Washington School in Union Township. Most of the students attended these schools through eighth grade. Some would continue their education at a nearby high school. At first Morrow High School did not accept students outside of the village since the people in the village funded the school. Later they accepted students from the surrounding area who paid tuition. Many could not afford the tuition, and therefore their education was not continued. It was common for most people to only have an eighth grade education.

As the population grew, the small one-room classroom could not accommodate all the students. In addition some people residing in the township worked in other fields other than farming as time progressed. Therefore these people did not contribute to growing crops which funded the school. Eventually the one-room classroom and the acreage would be sold, and the profit from the sale was used to buy other land to build a much larger school. When this happened, usually townships would join with other townships to build a school with several classrooms and several teachers. That's what happened, and eventually there was no longer a school in Union Township. Slowly the one-room classroom disappeared, but the concept of funding schools continued. Just as the one-room classroom was funded by the sixteen acres of real estate, the larger schools were funded through real estate taxes on the residents.

The Washington School was named after the first land owner, George Washington. He surveyed much of this area and claimed the property. He later sold the property to John Cleves Symmes, and then Symmes sold the property to Jonathan Dayton.

Symmes paid one fourth of a cent per acre for the land.

Washington School after a recital. Alma Baker in right window and Jake Baker in the left window. Teacher was Mary Irons. Other individuals, not in any order: Norma Phillips, Althe Watkins, Raleigh Popps, Mollie Baker, Kate Sparks, Raymond Sparks, Adarene Watkins, Isabel Murphy, Grandpa Phillips.

The photo above shows Washington School with many children gathered in front of the building. The inscription on the back states: "April 13, 1906 with a handwritten note stating, "Jake Baker and I are in the window. F.B. March 1, 1966". It is not known who "F.B." might have been as Fairy Baker had died before 1966.

John Q. Baker

Mary Jane (Toms)

The children of John Q. Baker and Mary Jane (Toms) were Alma, Jacob and Charlie. Their children attended and graduated from Washington School. Charlie graduated with three other students. Each student was required to give a speech at the graduation ceremony. According to the program, Charlie's speech was entitled, "The True Dignity of Labor". William Shawhan was the treasurer, and John Q. Baker was the clerk. Those names are familiar to the area. Charlie went on to the next level of education at the Normal School, in Lebanon which was built in 1844.

Charlie married Fairy Watkins and purchased a farm 1/2 mile south of the school. Charlie and Fairy's children, Lorena and Myron, attended the school through the eighth grade. A copy of a report card exists which reflects the success of Myron in school.

A story of Myron's birth was shared by Leonard Micheal. When Myron was born, a messenger came to the school to announce to the class that Myron had been born. As Lorena was twelve years old at the time, she was needed at home and dismissed from class immediately. Myron was born in the house where Charlie and Fairy lived.

After completing eight years at the Washington School, Myron continued his education at Lebanon High School. He often spoke of making the journey in a Model T Ford. He was just

a kid, but the school paid him for transporting some of the neighbors' children to school. This was before the state required a driver's license. He wasn't big enough to push the accelerator and see the road at the same time. Therefore he would alternate between the two – crunch down to push the pedal and then pull himself up to see through the steering wheel. Back and forth this went on for the whole trip to school and back home!

Myron, aged 6, his first day of school

It is uncertain if tuition was paid for him to attend high school. Myron had a desire to play sports, but his father was against the idea for Myron's help was needed on the farm after school, and therefore Myron could not attend practice after school. Because of his father's opposition, Myron became a cheerleader at Lebanon High School. Of course, this didn't involve practice after school, so how could his father deny him of this activity? This allowed him to attend all the games and proudly don the maroon sweater with a large "L" on the front. It also meant he could go to the games free! There were two cheerleaders, so Myron enthusiastically cheered on the team along with a girl. Myron said that at first being a cheerleader was a joke. Some boys had started cheering at the games, and eventually Myron began to lead the cheers. Myron said that he enjoyed becoming acquainted with the fans, and naturally he liked talking to the pretty girls.

Myron graduated in 1933 from Lebanon High School. He should have graduated a year earlier, but because of a case of pneumonia, he could not attend school most of his junior year. Myron became very ill and nearly lost his life. There were no antibiotics at this time. One had

to simply suffer through the disease. Myron spent weeks in a hospital in Cincinnati. Doctors determined that in order for him to survive, part of his damaged lung needed to be removed. This meant the lung needed to drain so a tube was placed from his lung through his ribs. Myron began to recover. It was a long journey for his parents to make when visiting Myron in the hospital. Their car had to travel back roads at limited speeds. Myron would lie in the hospital many days alone. The tubing was left in his side for quite a while after he returned

home. As a joke Myron would sometimes blow in the tube and his chest would make a strange noise causing others to laugh. Thankfully he returned to good health. When the following school year began, he repeated his junior year.

After high school Myron attended Ohio State University studying agriculture. He roomed with a guy from the area whose last name was Casto. Casto studied dentistry, and later had an office in Morrow as a dentist. Casto's practice was not always ethical. He was known to pull teeth when it was not necessary. He did this in college also which gave him ample spending money for him and Myron. Needless to say, they were known to have some good times in college at the expense of other's teeth! Myron left Ohio State during his sophomore year. He had flunked English his freshman year, and when he flunked it again in his sophomore year, he dropped out. He was also frustrated with his classes, and decided he would not pursue a career in farming.

In the 1940's Charlie Baker was approached by a married couple from Cincinnati about building a house right across from the Washington School. By then Charlie owned a significant amount of property, 115 acres to be exact. The couple expressed they were ready to get out of the city. Plans were drawn up for a two-story home with a separate two-car garage behind the house. It was to be a lovely home for its time with a large basement, a full attic, and on the first floor a large kitchen with a separate dining room, a large living room with a fireplace, a half bath, a screened-in porch on the side and a small porch in the back. The second floor had four bedrooms and a full bath. This was around the

same time that the school was sold. Charlie Baker bought the school building, one out house (there were two out houses) and a shed, but not the acreage. His idea was to use the bricks to build the house across the road. That's what he did. To this day if one looks at the back side of the house closely, it is apparent that there was not quite enough bricks from the school, and new bricks had to be bought to complete the house. The match of new bricks to the old bricks is very close. The school had been painted white so the bricks were laid with many reversed and only some showing the white paint. There are two broad steps of solid limestone leading to the front porch. These stones were part of the school. The original steps to the school were tossed behind Charlie's barn because they were cupped from the wear and tear of students entering the school. Charlie also kept the schoolmaster's desk. This was the desk that Charlie's son, Myron, remembered the schoolmaster sitting behind on a stool.

In the middle of the construction, the couple from Cincinnati decided that moving to the country might not be as grand as they once thought. They no longer wanted the house because their original plan had included building a restaurant in the home.

By the time the construction was complete, they felt there was too much competition. So, Charlie completed the house and moved in with his wife, Fairy. When finishing the construction, he did omit some of the frills in the plans such as the decorative railing along the roof top of the side porch and the bay window in the dining room. It did have many modern conveniences such as central heating, electricity throughout including an electric refrigerator and electric stove. He also took some old flooring from the old bowling alley in Lebanon and used it to build two sections of the kitchen countertop. The wood was light colored in thick, skinny strips that were about one half inch wide. It was great for preparing food because it was the perfect surface for a cutting board. As modern as it was, Fairy was not quite ready to subject herself to totally adopting modern appliances. A brand new large cooking wood stove was also added in the kitchen. This was the way Fairy had learned to cook and bake for she baked a fruit pie almost every week. The kitchen table always had a pie and dish of applesauce along with salt, pepper and sugar covered by a linen towel between meals.

The house was quite a place for the empty nesters to occupy. They decided to open a restaurant, serving Sunday chicken dinners, for Fairy was quite a cook. The large living room was converted to a dining room. Of course, the meals were prepared in the kitchen and the original dining room was used as a waiting area for guests before they were seated. There were two swinging doors in the back area of the house: one between the kitchen and hallway, and the second between the hallway and the dining room that facilitated moving the platters of delicious food from the kitchen to the dining room. This lasted for a time until the couple decided to close the restaurant.

Charlie would peddle his produce from door to door at times. There is an old hand bell that he used when he entered a neighborhood to announce his arrival. He also went to estate auctions from time to time to sell his produce. He would set up a small stand and sell to the people who would attend the auction. Many times when the auction was over, Charlie would buy furniture that was left from the sale. His house was soon filled with nice pieces that were bought at low prices. Such pieces included a roll top desk, a bearclaw dining room table, a china closet, a curly maple bedroom set with a matching rocker and desk. In one bedroom rockers and chairs were stacked that Charlie had bought at auctions. Many of these pieces of furniture are still in the family.

The house then became a great place for gatherings of family and friends because of its size. One such celebration was for the golden wedding anniversary of Charlie and Fairy in 1951. Many pictures were taken for the joyous occasion. Many fond memories were made from holidays and birthdays. Also, Fairy cooked a large meal at noon and fed the hired men every work day.

Charlie and Fairy spent some of their later years in Florida during the winter. It was hardly a season of rest and relaxation.

He never stopped working. Charlie would buy a farm and grow oranges, strawberries or vegetables during the winter months.

Many times he would renovate the house on the premises only to sell the farm and buy another one. This continued for several years. In Florida, Fairy died of heart failure in 1958. Loron, who was eighteen, flew to Florida and then rode the train back with his grandmother's body. The funeral was held in Morrow. The community abundantly showed their respects to Fairy. So many flower bouquets were sent to the funeral home that they spilled out onto the front porch of the building and onto the steps.

Charlie developed ulcers and decided to sell his farm to Myron. He continued to live in the brick house until he could no longer physically reside there. While Charlie was in Pinecrest Nursing Home in Morrow, Myron's daughter, Margery and her husband moved into the house for two years. Then, they moved to Arizona in 1974, and the house was rented for several years. In 2000 the house was totally gutted and renovated by Myron's son, Loron and his wife. When the chimney was dismantled in order to be rebuilt, a brick was found with the name TROVILLO stamped on it. The Trovillo family was one of the families that helped to build the Washington school. Elijah Trovillo and Charlie Baker had been life-long friends.

The beautiful home still stands across the road from where the old Washington School house once was. Its appearance easily fools those who pass by as being much older than it truly is because of the old brick from the school house. Family and friends still gather there in the stately house to socialize, for celebrations and holidays. Loron often tells tales to the family on holidays of the days he remembers gathering there with the Baker family and friends. The celebrations continue, and Dixie, his wife, being a good cook, prepares wonderful meals just as Fairy once did.

Charlie Baker's Graduation from Washington School — May 22, 1897

School District of Warren County, Ohio

J. C. Jordan **District Superintendent**

TO THE PATRONS

1. This report is sent to parents or guardians soon after the close of each school month. Please sign, as evidence that you have inspected the grades, and return PROMPTLY.
2. The grades are based upon attention, application, class work, and reviews given by the teacher or superintendent.
3. Below the high school an average in all grades of at least 80 is required for promotion, with an average in no one of less than 68. But low grades the last months of school indicate that the child is not ready for the next grade, even though the average is barely 80.
4. You can help materially by commending, admonishing, or encouraging and assisting the pupil, as the grades seem to require.

VALUE OF GRADES

Over 93 excellent; 87 to 93 good; 80 to 87 medium. An average below 80 indicates failing.

As each month's report is complete in itself patrons can easily determine the pupil's standing at any time. While regular promotion each year is most satisfactory all round, it is UNJUST to the child to promote it when not able to do the work of the next grade, and parents are warned against such practice. It is unfair both to the pupil and the next teacher. In the long run the "slow" child is just as likely to "make good," as the one too precocious.

We have the interest and well being of the children very much at heart and ask your sincere and hearty cooperation.

Respectfully,

F. B. HARRIS, County Supt.

September	Mrs. Chas S. Baker
October	Mrs. Chas S. Baker
November	Chas S. Baker
December	Chas S. Baker
January	Mrs. Chas S. Baker
February	Mrs. Chas S. Baker
March	Mrs. Chas S. Baker
April	Charles Baker
May	Mrs. Chas Baker

WARREN COUNTY HIGH SCHOOLS

Washington School .... Report of
Myron Baker Grade 2

School year of 1921. 1922.

Months	1	2	3	4	5	6	7	8	9	Ave.
Days School	18	20	17	20	19	18	20	20	19	20
Da. Present	18	19	16½	20	15	15	20	20	19	
Times Tardy	0	0	0	0	0	0	0	0	0	
Min. Tardy	2	0	0	0	0	0	0	0	2	
Deportment	94	95	94	94	95	95	95	96	96	
Reading	95	96	93	92	92	91	92	93	94	93
Writing	94	95	95	96	96	97	97	97	98	96
Numbers	96	98	96	98	99	99	99	99	99	98
Spelling	95	96	90	92	92	91	93	94	96	93
Average	95	96	93	94	95	95	95	96	96	95

Rea Stacy ....Teacher

May 18 1922

Myron Baker .... having

completed the work of the 2nd Grade, is *promoted* to 3rd Grade.

Rea Stacy .Teacher.

Myron Baker's report card for the 2nd grade—Washington School 1921—1922 school year, front (left) and back (right).

MAPLEWOOD FARM

Jacob Baker was born in 1778 in Saluda Township, Indiana. This area is along the Ohio River downstream from Madison, Indiana. Not much information is known about him such as who his parents were. He married Adiamy Sipes, and they moved about from state to state. They had nine children, four girls and five boys. Their first two children were born in Pennsylvania. The next four children were born in Sycamore Township, Warren County or Hamilton County, Ohio. The last two children were born in Indiana. John, their eighth child did not live beyond infancy.

Back row: Joseph Baker and Charles Q. Baker Front row: Alva, Charles, Mary Kate, Mary A. Baker and John Q. Baker Picture taken about 1870.

Their sixth child, Charles Baker, was born in 1818 in Hamilton County, but his family must have moved to Warren County sometime after his birth. Charles married Mary Ann Phillips on December 19, 1843. They had six children, two girls and four boys.

Mary Ann Phillips was the niece of Jabish Phillips who sold his mill on the Little Miami River to Isaac Stubbs. Once again, one can see that people didn't travel far from home and married someone who lived in the surrounding area. One of their five children was John Quincy Baker who was born in 1852.

It was the Stubbs who first started growing apples on Stubbs Mill Road in the early 1800's. John Quincy Baker, the son of Charles, also grew apples on Stubbs Mill Road.

Mary Ann Philips.

She was the daughter of Joseph Phillips and Margaret Hines. Her grandfather was Jabish Phillips who had sold his mill to Issac Stubbs.

John Q. married Mary Jane Toms, and they lived in what was a log cabin approximately two miles north of the Stubbs homestead. Before coming to America, Mary Toms was born of royalty in England. John Q's father, Charles, lived in an area just north of Lebanon around U.S. Route 42 called Avalon Heights. Charles worked as a carpenter in town and rode a bike where ever his job would take him. He once built a barn for a farmer who lived north of Lebanon on Route 122. The barn was built of large timbers which he bore holes into. In order to attach them, he would

drive pegs into the timber. He was paid twenty-five cents a day.

Right beside John Q's house also on the west side of the road is where his youngest sister, Kate (Mary Kate Baker) and William (Bill) Sparks lived. Her mother, Mary Ann, died when Kate was twelve years old. Kate was placed in the guardianship of John Shawhan who lived close by and was an attorney in Lebanon. Kate and Bill's house still stands and is a bit Victorian in style. Bill would often visit Charlie and Fairy by simply hitching his horse to a wagon and traveling a mile or so to Charlie's house. Bill was an alcoholic and was often drunk. Sometimes Charlie would simply pick up Bill after he fell in a drunken stupor, put him in the wagon, give the horse a swift smack, and the horse would find its way home.

Mary Jane Toms, John Quincy's wife, was the daughter of William Toms and Mary Jane Goe. Mary Jane and John Quincy lived in a house even closer to the Stubbs homestead on the west side of Stubbs Mills Road in a log cabin that still exists. Lois Baker asked Alma Baker Harris once what she remembered about her grandmother, Mary Jane Toms Baker. Alma said that there was a porch wrapped around the house. Her grandma would often sit on the porch and smoke a corn cob pipe. It's not exactly what most might remember about their grandmother! Our family has a large framed charcoal portrait of Grandma Toms with a very solemn expression. (See picture above).

As Grandma Toms aged, she developed dementia or Alzheimer's and was easily confused. She could not be left alone for she would wander aimlessly. On one occasion John Q and his wife asked Lois and Myron if they might watch Grandma Toms while they went to a Grange meeting. They brought Grandma Toms to Myron's house. At the time Myron was living in the small house at the top of the hill on the west side of the road. Sure enough, within an hour or so Grandma was missing. They found an open window in the back of the house where she had climbed out. They searched about, soon found her and brought her back into the safety of their house.

John Quincy's father was named Charles, and John Quincy named his son Charles Stanley (my grandfather). Not only did John Quincy grow apples but he also had a forge. For a long time the family owned his anvil. Myron remembers watching his grandfather making horse shoes and shoeing horses in the barn behind the house. Myron also remembers him making pop guns for the kids in the family. Mary Jane didn't appreciate her husband making pop guns for a few reasons, but mostly because he made them of elderberry twigs. The elderberry branches were suited well because they had a pithy inside that could be easily removed. The outside of the branch was hard. This made a perfect tube for inserting spitballs as ammunition. Mary Jane thought it was such a waste. She wanted the branches to be left on the tree allowing more elderberries to grow, so that she could make lots of elderberry jam. Myron also remembers going to visit his grandparent's house and playing in the basement of their home. In the winter John Quincy would take an ice saw and go down to the river near the mill. In the mill race of the Little Miami River the ice would form sooner than in the river. He would cut large chunks of ice out of the mill race and take them to his basement to be used as needed in his ice box. He would also collect heaps of saw dust from the saw mill with the goal of preventing the ice from melting. The saw dust would be used to cover and insulate the ice chunks in his basement. Myron would often play in the heaps of saw dust around the ice in their basement.

Charlie Baker married Fairy Watkins, the girl next door in 1902. They first resided at the

Watkins farm near Morrow. Fairy was eighteen, and Charlie was nineteen. Fairy was anxious to marry since she was the oldest of her six siblings. She was tired of taking care of her younger brothers and sisters. She and Charlie had decided that they didn't want children. That didn't quite work out for them. One year later they had a daughter, Lorena. They thought that one child would be enough since originally they wanted none. That didn't exactly

work out either. A son, Myron, was born twelve years after Lorena. By this time they had moved to the house on Stubbs Mill Road. Three generations of the Baker men are together in the photograph above. While Myron is playing, his father Charlie, and his grandfather, John Quincy, are building a shed. The axle of the vehicle has a belt around it which is used to power the saw that they were utilizing to cut the boards. The shed was erected within fifteen feet behind Charlie and Fairy's first house. The shed had a dirt floor and a pot belly stove for boiling water. The shed was also used for butchering animals that were raised on the farm. Hence, the butcher block table, constructed from a tree stump, as pictured to the right was an essential part of the shed. Later, the

butcher block table was converted into a display table and used in the apple market along with other antique items, including a brass cash register. A statue of Johnny Appleseed is also part of the display.

In 1916 Charles Stanley planted apples trees by first clearing a thicket south of the farm house on top of the hill. He had bought thirty-three acres there on the east side of Stubbs Mill Road. His down payment was a turkey hen. The purchase was made before Thanksgiving, and the owner was hungry. The previous owner was quite pleased with this agreement even if it wasn't a gobbler but merely a hen. The apple trees, just little whips, were only three or four feet tall. He bought a big barn for $300 in Lebanon that was a lumber company. It was between U.S. Route 42 and the railroad tracks. He took the barn apart and brought it about five miles to his farm on Stubbs Mill Road and put it back up. That barn still stands today and was considered the apple barn. In the late 1960's Myron had purchased a large apple grader that went where the east wall stood between the barn and an adjoining garage. When he removed the wall for the grader, Myron had steel beams placed in the structure for additional support.

Close by on Morrow-Mason-Millgrove Road toward South Lebanon was the Hayner farm. John Hayner purchased the farm in 1862 and made a living by raising and drying corn. John Worley also produced dried corn around this period. When there was no longer a demand for dried corn, Hayner converted his barn to a cannery. Charles Stanley worked at the cannery soldering the lids to the cans after they were filled. Much later in 1955 he raised sweet corn for the cannery and was paid eighteen dollars per ton for the corn. The Hayner house was a beautiful home built 1852 in the Greek Revival architecture style. It was dismantled and later rebuilt in 1967 in the Heritage Village in Sharon Woods, Cincinnati where it now stands.

Myron had a pony named Buster while growing up. He would ride his pony to the top of the hill, but it would go no further. Myron would coax and coax his pony to go down the hill jabbing his heels into the pony's sides. The pony wouldn't go. Myron decided that he would race the pony as fast as he could before reaching the top of the hill. Surely that would make the pony go down the hill where his grandparents lived in the Stubbs homestead. The pony galloped ever so quickly, and just as it reached the crest, it stopped abruptly. This caused Myron to lose his grip, fly over the pony's head and roll a few feet on the ground. Ouch! His plan failed in getting the pony down the hill. After that Myron simply walked down the hill to visit his grandparents. His grandparents never minded a visit from Myron, but they refused to babysit him. He was too ornery. If Charlie and Fairy needed a babysitter for Myron, they would take him across the road from his grandparents to the Worley's house. Apparently they never minded his antics.

Lorena Baker married Bill Bellamy at the early age of fifteen in 1921. Lorena married young. It was

Lorena and Bill Bellamy

said she uttered the same words as her mother once had. She wanted to get out of the house because she was tired of taking care of Myron. Bill was from Kentucky, had helped a friend move to the area, and he stayed. They were married in Kentucky, then later the marriage was celebrated at Fairy and Charlie's house. Charlie bought Lorena a farm on the west side of Stubbs Mill Road just north of Shawhan Road. The house still stands. Lorena and Bill had some issues and were divorced only to remarry later for a second time. Lorena and

Bill lived on Stubbs Mill Road for several years until they moved to Bradenton, Florida.

Lorena had three children, two boys and a girl. Once they grew up, Charlie, their grandfather, promised to see that they received money to have a career. One of their sons was Norman. Norman was a big guy and played football for Lebanon High School. No one messed with him. As a prank, one time some teenagers blocked the road with corn stalks. Norman came along on the road, and this angered him, so he beat them up. By today's standards, this would be considered an extreme reaction. Norman joined the Air Force out of high school. Later Norman married but was in a terrible car accident. It took him many years to fully recuperate from the accident. After serving in the military he became a liquor license inspector.

The other son was Charlie. He joined the Army where he acquired the skills of an electrician and plumber. While he was in the Army, he smuggled guns home. He would

disassemble guns, and put them in a food tin can that he sawed in two. He would solder the can back together and glue the label over the cut. Fortunately he was never caught doing such an act. When Charlie Bellamy returned from the service, he was a county plumbing inspector. In time his grandfather, Charlie Baker, bought property for him where he built laundromats. One laundromat was in Miamisburg near Dayton. Charlie Bellamy married Alice, who he met at a restaurant near Lebanon. Alice had moved from Kentucky to Waynesville, Ohio to live with her sister in order to attend high school. Charlie Bellamy and his wife, Alice, built a house almost directly across the road from where Charlie Bellamy grew up on Stubbs Mill Road. Eventually he formed his own business, Bellamy Alarm Company. Charlie Bellamy had two boys. They both graduated from the University of Cincinnati. Duane went to medical school and became an anesthesiologist. Glen went to medical school plus law school and became an attorney in intellectual property law and patents. Charlie Baker financed the education of Bill and Lorena's youngest child, Roberta or Bobbie. She went to the University of Cincinnati and graduated in chemistry. Her first job was with Procter and Gamble in research. She grew tired of that and later became a flight attendant. Then, she moved to California. Not one of Lorena's children slipped by without a career.

Myron Baker met Lois Hartman on a blind date. Lois had a friend named Verna that dated Joe Worley, a cousin of Myron's. Lois was not keen on going on a blind date, but Verna insisted. It seemed that Myron was not too keen about the idea either. Lois said that she did not like

Joe Worley, Miriam Worley, Myron Baker, Lois Baker and Elizabeth "Franke" Conway.

Myron at all on the first date. When asked why not, she first replied, "Oh, I don't know." As the story continued the truth was that Myron had a little too much to drink that first time, and Lois was very uncomfortable even admitting it. On the second date on New Year's Eve, he was more like himself. He had a new car; it was a 1933 Pontiac Straight 8 with a rumble seat and spoke wheels. Myron had purchased the car from his friend, Leonard Michael. The fenders rolled down to a step on each side. On each side of the fenders was a spare tire with flashy spoke wheels. It was a sporty car that would impress any girl. They married the following year in 1937. They had three children, Loron, Margery and Jeane.

Charlie believed that there was no need to help Myron's children with an education. Myron would see that his kids were educated and set for a career. Loron attended Wilmington College and Ohio State University. Without completing a college education, he worked his way up in banking from a teller, to a bank examiner, to president of the bank in Brookville, Indiana. He married Dixie Amburgy. They had two children, a girl and a boy. Kathy graduated from Miami University in finance. Ty graduated from Indiana University in business.

Myron's daughter, Margery, graduated from The Christ Hospital School of Nursing and later earned a college degree in nursing from Arizona State University. She had three girls. Elizabeth graduated from Arizona University in art education and continued earning a masters degree in education from Chapman University. Melanie earned a doctorate in dentistry from Missouri University. Laura graduated from Duquesne University in physical therapy. Myron's second daughter, Jeane graduated from Wittenberg University with a degree in education and later earned two masters degrees in school administration from Wright State University and Xavier University. Jeane had two children, a girl and a boy, Susan and Richard. Susan graduated from Emory University in art history and earned a masters degree from Columbia University in museum administration. Richard graduated from Purdue University with a degree in electrical engineering. It was important to Charlie Baker that his grandchildren had an education and career. Unfortunately he didn't live to see how his influence would carry onto his great grandchildren as well.

In the early 1900's, Charlie tapped the maple trees in the virgin woods behind his first

house and the barn. The maple trees in those woods had to be at least forty years olds in order to tap. Down by the creek there was an old maple sugar cabin used as the plant. After the second thaw in February the sap would start to run. Taps were placed in the trunks of the trees with a bucket hanging beneath them to catch the sap.

In the old maple syrup cabin there was a huge metal vat that was raised and lots and lots of buckets. Some of the buckets bore the word "STUBBS" in large letters. These were saved from when the Stubbs made maple syrup. The vat had baffles on the bottom to distribute the heat in order to prevent burning. Beneath the vat would be burning wood that was all hand cut. The buckets of sap would be collected and eventually poured into the vat. The thawing of the land would cause a muddy mess in the woods. It was hard to walk up and down the hills or drive a tractor in the soft ground. Even with two work horses and a wagon it was difficult to move without getting stuck in the mud. On the east side at the top of the hill, they built a large cistern to deposit the sap. The sap would be poured through a large metal sieve above the cistern to remove debris. From the cistern the sap would travel into an underground pipe that would bring the sap down the hill to the maple syrup cabin. This replaced carrying the sap to the cabin. The

sap would cook down until it was a heavy syrup. It was a slow process. According to the sugar content of the sap, it would take as much as eighty-six gallons of sap to make one gallon of syrup. The sap would have to have a constant fire beneath it for a very long time. In shifts the men took turns stoking the fire through the day and night. Unfortunately, one night Myron fell asleep and burned the whole vat. Lois remembers making sandwiches for Myron and the other workers in the middle of the night. It was a bit eerie as she carried a lantern with a basket of food down the hill to the maple syrup cabin through the cold, black of night.

During this time the farm was named Maplewood Farm. Once World War II began, production ceased. Many of the workers went off to war. Maple syrup production occurred at the same time as the pruning of the apple trees. There simply weren't enough hands to do both. With that, Charlie relied on farming and began to expand the apple business. The old maple syrup cabin stood with tall stacks of metal buckets and the old vat empty until it fell to ruins.

For many years Maplewood Farm continued as a typical farm with various crops and livestock. There were fruit trees and vegetables, sheep and cows and chickens. The focus would change in time. The apple production would gradually begin to dominate.

Copied from an old family Bible 1898

Parents Record

Father, Charles Baker was born near Cincinnati, Ohio on the 14th day of May 1818. Moved to Scott County, Indiana when two years old. Remained there until 21 years of age then moved to Ohio and remained in Warren County until his death the 1st of May 1880. Buried in Lebanon Cemetery.

Mother, Mary A. Baker (NEE) Philips was born 6th February, 1825 in Warren County Ohio living Warren County all her life never out of the state but twice. Then only on a short visit was sick with consumption for two years. Past away on the 18th of September, 1878. Buried in Lebanon Cemetery lot.

Joseph Baker, born 1844, died 1872. He was the son of Charles Q. Baker and Mary Ann Philips

Marriages
Charles Baker and Mary Phillips were married December 19th 1843.

Joseph Baker, born 1844, died 1872. He was the son of Charles Q. Baker and Mary Ann Philips
The sugar cabin is to the left. It was not uncommon for the Bakers to gather with friends

and have a chicken dinner down at the maple sugar cabin. The picture above is of such a dinner. Charlie Baker is pouring coffee and Fairy is in the center with her cup in her hand. The gentleman to the left of Fairy is Ernest L Hern (1882– 1948). Kneeling to the far right is Myron Baker. The lady behind Myron with the fur-trimmed coat is Dollie Barkalow (1882– 1979). She is the daughter of Robert Finley Hearn and Alice Belle Toms (1859—1924). Alice Belle Toms was a sister of Mary Jane Toms, John Q. Baker's wife.

For the dinner, they would take cut-up chicken, wrap it in foil, then wrap it in wet newspaper and place in the hot coals that came from the maple syrup fire.

Charlie Baker spraying fruit trees.

Apple customers at the orchard

OBITUARY

MARY JANE BAKER

Mary Jane Toms was one of ten children to bless the home of William Toms and Mary J. Goe and was born July 11, 1862 and departed this life May 4, 1944 at the age of 81 years 9 months and 23 days.

On September 16, 1880 she was united in marriage to John Q. Baker and to this union were born four children: Maud Cecil who died in infancy, Charles Stanley, Jacob Earl and Alma Eva.

The greater part of her life was spent in one vicinity of Warren county near Lebanon, where she endeared herself to a wide circle of friends, neighbors and relatives, by her devotion, consideration and helpfulness to those she loved. Several years ago she became a member of the Methodist Church, and was faithful and constant in attendance, and active in it's several organizations, until recent years when health denied her this privilege and source of so much comfort and happiness. Very important in her life also was her Charter Membership in two local Organizations: Lebanon Grange and Lebanon Farmer's Club where she was ever ready to lend her usual helping hand and to enjoy to the fullest, their ritualistic and social activities. Mr. Baker having passed away February 24, 1924.

Courage and strength to meet the many phases of life encountered through the years, were hers from Trust and Faith in Him who doeth all things well. Her love of music and the words of God are evident in her choice of the following hymns:

"Will there be any stars in my Crown." and "Someday I'll understand."

Leaving to mourn their loss are, two sons Charles S. of Morrow, Jacob E. of Middletown and one daughter, Mrs. Alma Harris of Lebanon also six grandchildren and five great grandchildren as well as other relatives and a host of friends and fraternal associates.

EXPRESSION OF THANKS

We wish to thank all our friends and neighbors for the kindness extended us at the time of the death of our dear mother, Mrs. J. Q. Baker. We also wish to thank the honors of the many beautiful floral offerings. Rev. Chiles and the Johnson Funeral Home for their efficient services.

Mr. and Mrs. Charles Baker
Mr. and Mrs. H. R. Harris.

$2.00 a Year, in Advance.

PROMINENT FARMER SUCCUMBS WHILE AT WORK MONDAY

John Q. Baker, Aged Farmer Of The County Dies Of Apoplexy

ILL TWO HOURS 1924

Was Charter Member Of The Grange And Active In Community Life

John Q. Baker, 72, one of the most prominent farmers of Warren County, died suddenly Monday at noon two hours after he had suffered an attack of apoplexy while sawing wood on his farm a quarter of a mile from the house. John Wright, a neighbor was with Mr. Baker when he was overcome. He hastened to the house and informed members of the Baker family. Mr. Baker was removed to the house where he lingered two hours. He did not regain consciousness.

The deceased is survived by his widow, two sons, Charles Baker, living on the old home place, and Jacob, of Middletown, one daughter, Mrs. Henry Harris, of Red Lion, one brother, Henry L. Baker, of Arkansas, and one sister, Mrs. Will Sparks, of Lebanon. Funeral services will be held at the late residence at 2 o'clock Thursday afternoon in charge of Rev. Mr. Levitt, of Mason Universalist Church. Burial will be made in the Lebanon cemetery.

Mr. Baker has been in very fine health for the past 25 years and during this winter had enjoyed his duties about the farm. On Monday he went with Mr. Wright to cut down some trees for fire wood. Two trees had been felled and they were working on the third when Mr. Baker became dizzy and fainted. He was born and reared on the farm three miles southeast of Lebanon on the Stubbtown road and has made his home there throughout his life time. He was a charter member of the Grange and an active worker in the Farmers' Club. He was of the Universalist faith and always interested in the welfare of his community.

THE LOVE LETTER

In the papers of my family, I found a faded letter from September 10, 1878.
As I read it, I was struck by what was recorded…. A broken date, a young man watching over his dying mother and the love of his life as the recipient of the elegantly penned letter. I was not sure who "Mollie" was and could not figure it out with what I knew.

The young man was my great-grandfather, John Quincy Baker (JQB) and my great-grandmother was always known as "Grandma Toms". Was she the woman of this letter?

Mary Ann Toms came from England to the United States in the 1870's, and her family settled in Warren

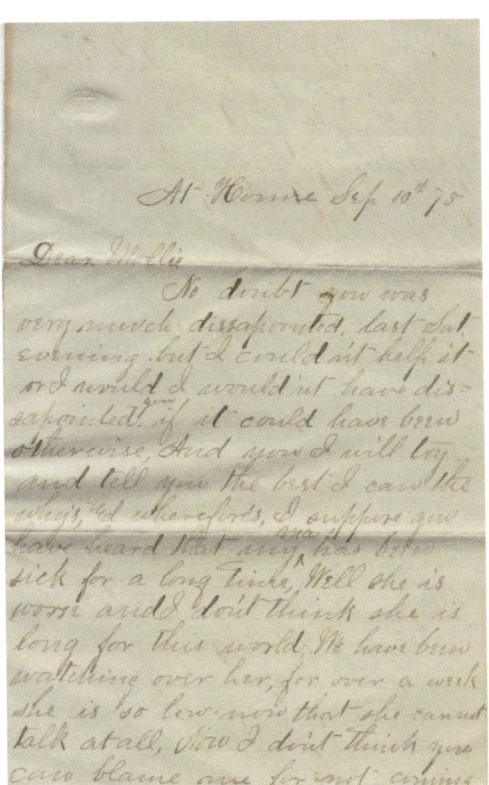

County. There she met John Baker. The details of their courtship are lost to history, but this letter survives. And, she is in fact, "Mollie". She and John were married on September 16, 1880 and lived in the log cabin on

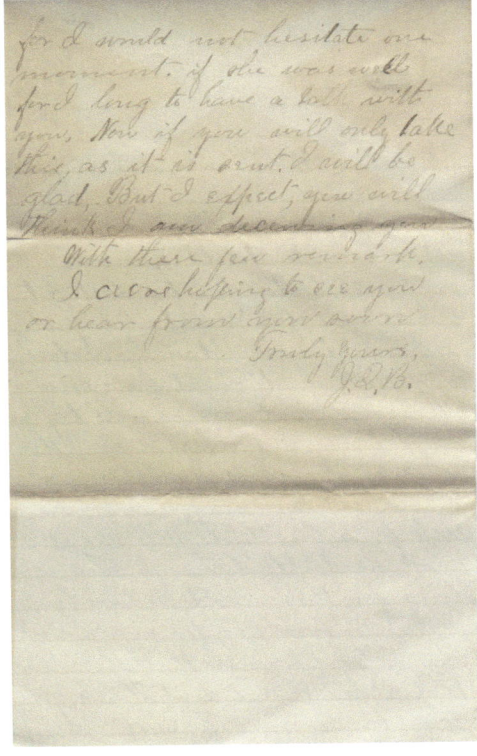

Stubbs Mill Road near Shawhan Road. They were blessed with three children. Their oldest son, Charles is my grandfather.

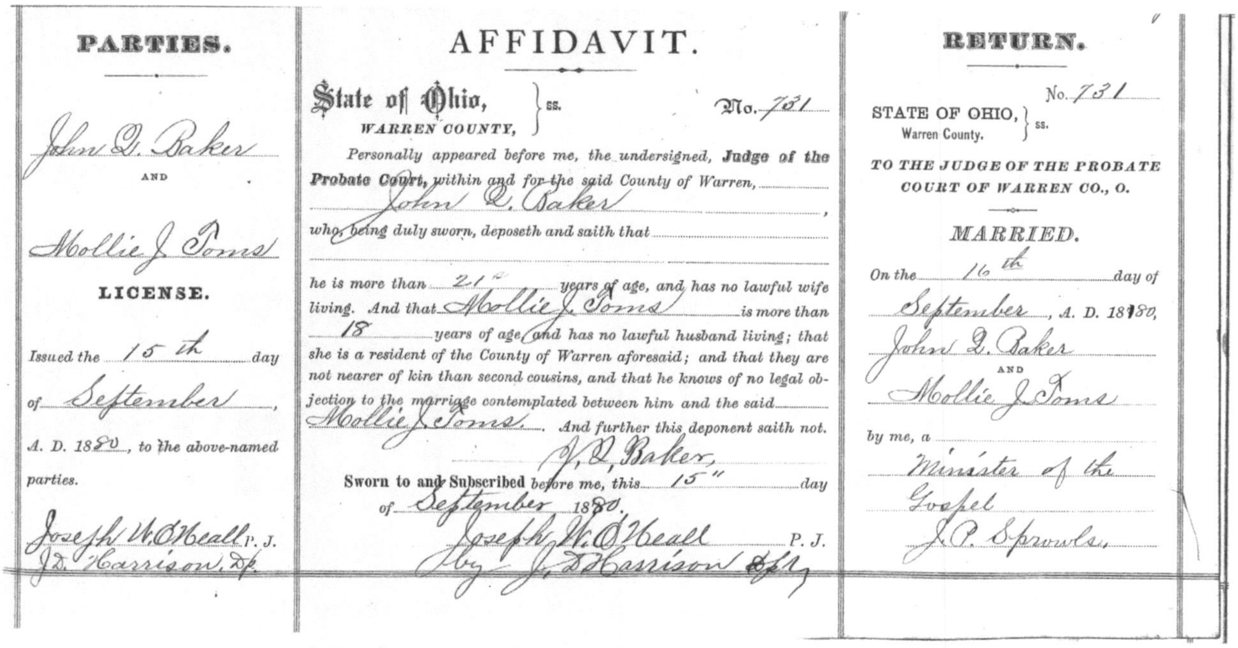

PARTIES.	AFFIDAVIT.	RETURN.

PARTIES.

John Q. Baker

AND

Mollie J. Toms

LICENSE.

Issued the *15 th* day

of *September* ,

A. D. 18*80*, to the above-named

parties.

Joseph W. O'Neall P. J.
J. D. Harrison, Dp.

AFFIDAVIT.

State of Ohio, } ss.
WARREN COUNTY,

No. *731*

Personally appeared before me, the undersigned, **Judge of the**
Probate Court, within and for the said County of Warren, _____
John Q. Baker _____,
who being duly sworn, deposeth and saith that _____

he is more than *21* years of age, and has no lawful wife
living. And that *Mollie J. Toms* is more than
18 years of age, and has no lawful husband living; that
she is a resident of the County of Warren aforesaid; and that they are
not nearer of kin than second cousins, and that he knows of no legal ob-
jection to the marriage contemplated between him and the said
Mollie J. Toms . And further this deponent saith not.

J. Q. Baker,

Sworn to and Subscribed before me, this *15"* day
of *September 1880*.

Joseph W. O'Neall P. J.
by J. D. Harrison Dp.

RETURN.

No. *731*

STATE OF OHIO, } ss.
Warren County.

**TO THE JUDGE OF THE PROBATE
COURT OF WARREN CO., O.**

MARRIED.

On the *16 th* day of
September , A. D. 18*80*,
John Q. Baker
AND
Mollie J. Toms

by me, a

*Minister of the
Gospel*

J. P. Sprowls.

Wedding Affidavit of John Q. Baker and Mary Jane Toms, known as "Mollie"

THE UNCATCHABLE COWS

The Great Depression started in 1929 and lasted through 1939. Stock market prices took a major fall, personal income and profits dropped and unemployment rose to 25% in the United States. Both urban and rural areas suffered. Many industries were brought to a halt which denied many in the urban areas a job and a source of income. A drought in the heartland of the United States and lower food prices affected farmers in rural areas. Americans were faced with hard times. Many could not afford to pay their rent or mortgage nor could they afford food and clothing.

Charlie Baker's son, Myron, graduated from high school in 1933, right in the thick of the depression. He attended college for a year and a half and then dropped out. For a short period of time, he worked at a gas station in the Cincinnati area. He was paid 25 cents a day. He spent a nickel of his earnings each day on lunch. He would go to a nearby diner and order a bowl of chili and a glass of water. With a bottle of ketchup nearby, he would eat his chili. He would take a couple bites and then add a couple dollops of ketchup to the bowl and stir. He would take a couple more bites and then add a couple dollops of ketchup to the bowl and stir again. He would continue this, stretching the bowl of chili as far as it would go until it was mostly ketchup. At that point he would stop eating. His meal was over. This is an example of just how dire conditions were at the time, and yet the affects were not as severe for farmers as other people. They suffered by not earning as much from their crops, but they did not experience a drought like in the plains. Farmers in this area could grow their own fruit and vegetables and can them for the winter. They could also butcher their livestock for meat. Their fear was how long the depression would last. They wondered how long they could survive with little or no cash.

During the depression Charlie Baker was approached by a nearby farmer. This farmer owned land beside Charlie's farm at the top of the hill on the west side of the road. He wanted to know if Charlie would be interested in buying his cows. Charlie agreed and a price was set. Charlie attempted to catch the cows and move them to his property. The cows were wild and could not be caught. No matter what he tried, they could not be herded and moved. Faced with such a dilemma, Charlie decided that he would shoot the cows one at a time, butcher them and sell the meat. That's what he did. Once he butchered a cow for meat, he would take the meat to South Lebanon or another nearby town and go door to door selling the meat. He built racks on the back of his Model T Ford pick up truck and hung the meat. He also built a slatted board for the bed of the truck on which to place the meat. It took some time and some work, but Charlie bought the cows from his neighbor and made a profit. In the end it was a good deal, for he had more cash in his pocket than he started with.

Another neighbor who owned land behind Charlie approached him. This farmer was Jimmy Hatfield, and he had a farm on Shawhan Road. The farm is still owned by his son, Johnny. He asked Charlie for a loan. Jimmy had no cash, no money at all and needed money for the mortgage on his farm. The bank was threatening to repossess Jimmy's farm. Jimmy was fearful that if he didn't make the payments, he would lose the farm and become homeless. Charlie took the money for the payments on Jimmy's farm to him in a shoe box for a period of time until Jimmy could make the payments himself. Jimmy was forever grateful to Charlie and would often comment on how Charlie saved his farm and his livelihood.

The Great Depression was a horrible time for Americans. It challenged the people and showed just how strong the people of this country were. They survived, and this country soon thrived again. In Charlie's case it showed the determination of not only helping yourself to survive, but helping others so that they would survive as well.

Charlie Baker

MAPLEWOOD ORCHARD

Fairy Baker was very interested in growing fruit and vegetables. A green house was attached to the farm house on the south side. That was Fairy's green house. She and Charlie loved to enter samples of their harvest of fruits and vegetables in local county fairs each year and won many first place ribbons.

A fruit display at the Ohio State Fair

Charlie would climb up into the apple trees to find the very best fruit for several nearby fairs and the state fair. He would place the fruit in wooden trays that held about twenty apples. Sometimes their fruit would be displayed on a small plate. Quite often he would win first prize which would earn him $1.50.

Charlie won first place so many times at the county fair that the fair board decided that it wasn't fair to the others who entered their fruit. Others growers were dropping out of the competition knowing that they didn't stand a chance to win against Charlie Baker. It was decided that first prize would be given to a different grower each year to encourage more growers to enter their fruit samples at the fair. With that ruling, Charlie decided to quit taking his apples and fruit to the county fair.

Myron with trays of apples

Fairy began to graft more apple trees as time went on. She acquired most of her grafting tree branches from the old Stubbs orchard. She would plant apple seeds which would naturally produce a generic variety and watch them grow. When they were big enough, she would slash the small trunk and graft a piece of a twig, say, perhaps a Red Delicious onto the trunk, cover it with bees wax and wrap it.

The trunk and the branch would eventually grow together. That would create a Red Delicious apple tree to plant in the orchard. She made many, many trees this way.

109

They advertised their orchard as having sixty-five varieties of apples. Myron, who was just a kid, would tell of driving the truck while his dad, Charlie, would go from door to door to sell his apples.

Charlie would also sell to customers on the weekend in the barn. They grew other farm crops as well. They had a few pear trees, plum, cherry and peach. They had a huge chicken coop filled with chickens behind the house. From time to time they had sheep, cows and pigs. They had a cow which ran freely about the barn yard that the hired hand milked in the morning, and they milked in the evening. The cow had a bell around its neck. As a child, Loron was asked once to get the cow for milking. This was usually an easy task for one only had to listen for the bell. He listened and listened for the bell but heard nothing and searched and searched all around the barn yard. She was hiding! He finally found her lying in the woods and brought her home. There was another cow that decided to suck on her own tits. She was hungry! Charlie finally made a harness for her head that prevented the cow from reaching her belly. Now the family had milk.

One weekend Charlie's brother, Jacob Baker, arrived while Charlie was selling apples. Jacob was drunk and asked Charlie for money. Charlie was very displeased and embarrassed that such an incident would occur in front of customers. When Charlie realized that Jacob was intoxicated, he said, "Can't you see I have customers! Don't ever come here drunk!" Unfortunately the brothers never spoke again.

As the years rolled on, Charlie and Fairy moved into the new, big brick house up the road. Myron and Lois moved into the farm house that Charlie and Fairy vacated. To a home designer, this house would be considered a disaster. It had started as a four room house with two rooms on the main floor and two rooms above. A stone walled foundation was on the lower level which made it easy for mice to enter. Seven additions were added to the house through the years. The living room had one large window. The other three walls had a total of six doorways. The main bathroom was off the kitchen. Upstairs were four bedrooms, one which was entered through another bedroom. One time when Myron went to grab his shot gun standing upright in the corner of the kitchen, it accidently went off. The shot went through the ceiling in the kitchen and the floor upstairs before stopping. The kitchen ceiling was easily patched and repaired. The hole in the wood floor upstairs was simply covered by the metal lid of a Mason jar. The house may have been designed horribly, but it was ahead of its time when Charlie lived there. It had electricity. However, no electric lines ran from the road to the house. Charlie simply made electricity by the means of a generator. He lined the basement walls with large batteries that held the power from the generator, and they powered the whole house. This was the house Myron was born in, and he never moved.

The house had a coal furnace in the basement. Sometimes Lois would burn trash in the furnace. One time the debris floated out the chimney and onto the roof making the wood shingles on the roof start to burn. A neighbor, who lived at the top of the hill, saw the fire and ran up to the house to tell them of the fire. Lois called the fire department. She had just purchased two new mattresses for the twin beds in one bedroom. In a panic she opened the window in the bedroom and wedged the mattresses out the second story window and onto the ground below. Meanwhile, Myron got a garden hose and

Sue, Margery holding Jeane and Loron

a ladder and put the fire out. The fire department was sent back to Morrow. Lois felt a little foolish as they carried the mattresses up the stairs and back onto the beds.

Myron and Lois also raised a teenage girl along with their own children. She came from a poor family in the area. Lois became acquainted with the family when the PTA asked for donations to help the family. Lois donated a coat for Sue, one of the children. Sue's father was soon hired to work at the orchard, and they lived in the small house at the top of the hill where Myron and Lois had once lived. Working on the farm was okay, but Ernie Poston was a small man and not well suited for heavy farm work. He was eventually hired as a janitor at a convent in Martinsburg, Ohio. Sue was very unhappy when she realized that she would attend another school for her high school years. Myron and Lois offered to let her live with them which worked out well. Sue Poston was a cheerleader in high school. She was attractive and full of personally. She was even the mascot at the school, a black panther. After graduating, Myron and Lois offered to continue her education. She considered a program to be a flight attendant or go to business school. Instead she married. Unfortunately her husband was abusive, and the marriage didn't last long. She continued to live in the area, and the family stayed in contact with Sue.

Myron became serious about growing apples. As he planted more and more trees, many

grafted by his mother, he developed a scheme. He decided that while planting trees, he would be sure to plant an orchard for each of his children. He compared the growth of a tree to educating a child. A typical apple tree would not really produce many apples until it was about five years old. That's when his child would start school. The tree's production would increase as it grew until it was about eighteen or twenty. At that time production would peak. That's when the child would go to college. The tree would continue to produce at its peak until it was about forty. Myron would sum up his story with a grin and explain that for the kid and the tree once you hit forty, it's all down hill.

In 1936 Myron also built six ponds on the farm near six of the orchards. This would provide water for spraying the trees. He had a 1935 Caterpillar that pulled a slip to dig the ponds. Eventually he expanded the orchards until there were seventy-five acres that contained about four thousand trees. He also had about four hundred peach trees. Myron and his father worked together, but more help was needed. All of those apples had to be picked by hand. Frank Alderson was hired to work year round. Frank was from Kentucky and had an eighth grade education, but worked hard. He did everything from picking to grading to making cider and mowing while Myron marketed his product and worked on machinery. Frank earned a salary and was given free rent at a two story house just up the road that Myron's father owned. His wife, Ruby, also worked grading and bagging apples along with other women that lived nearby on Trovillo

Leonard picking apples and Myron at the bottom of the ladder

111

Road. Myron hired a few men from time to time who lived in Kentucky to pick apples. Virgil and Leonard were the last two pickers who left their families in Kentucky right after Labor Day and stayed until every apple was picked late in October. Most pickers were paid by the bushel at the end of each week, but Virgil and Leonard didn't collect until they were finished. Those two men picked hundreds of bushels of apples from dawn to dusk. Each fall they walked away with one big check and headed back to

Original Barn and storage

Kentucky. They lived in either an old tractor trailer or a hunting cabin back in the woods behind the barn. The hunting cabin was built by Charlie and his friend, Art Rust, who would visit from Pleasant Ridge, Ohio.

New addition is the white structure to the left of the red barn.

Charlie became acquainted with Art after making several purchases at Art's hardware store. Charlie had bought used tobacco boxes at an auction. He and Art took them apart and built a two-room cabin with a covered porch. Art used the cabin when he came hunting on the farm. Pictured below is Art and his wife (couple on the right hand side) hunting with another couple.

Another place where the apple pickers lived was the trailer which was once parked in front of the barn and was painted with a big

apple as a sign identifying the farm as Maplewood Orchard. Later it was parked down the road at the intersection of Stubbs Mill Road and U.S. Route 22. Both accommodations were very primitive with two cots and a wood stove. There was drinking water and restrooms in the apple barn for them to use. Occasionally the two men went to town for groceries, but otherwise they picked apples, ate and slept.

The business grew and soon the old cider mill near the chicken coop simply couldn't keep up with the demand. Myron built an addition onto the back of the big barn in 1950 that would house a new cider mill and a large cold storage room for the apples and cider. The cold storage room was lined with thick cork to insulate the room. Three large refrigeration units were installed. It would hold about ten thousand bushels

Frank Alderson jugging cider

of apples. He upgraded the cider mill so it would produce a thousand gallons a day. Many years it made 150,000 gallons. Each bushel of apples would produce three gallons of cider, so there was dry apple pulp that was left over. This was fed to the cattle on the farm, so there was no waste. The cider mill had a more sophisticated way of filtering the fresh juice. It first went through a screen and then a round plate and frame filter. Thick pieces of paper were placed between each metal plate. The cider would be pumped through the filter with the paper filters removing the tiny pieces of apple pulp making the juice clear with no residue at the bottom of the jug. It was a beautiful clear amber. The cider only improved in flavor through the fall as the harvest continued. It was always made with no less than three varieties of apples. As more varieties ripened, it improved the flavor of the cider. One of those varieties needed to be sour and one sweet. Cider making always started on Labor Day. That was the day that the whole place really came to life for the harvest. The problem with starting on Labor Day was that there were no sweet apples ripe until mid September. The cider started out rather sour. Eventually Myron froze some of his sweetest cider from the previous year and added it to the new cider in early September. It was deliciously tart and sweet. When he built onto the barn, he made a loading dock for shipping in and out. That also allowed other fruit farms to

bring their apples to be made into cider. As production increased, he sold his cider to local farm markets, Frisch's restaurant chain and to a local chain of dairy stores, United Dairy Farmers. He contacted Meier's Winery in Silverton outside of Cincinnati and sold cider to them for their

Ben Browning and Myron Baker

"Grandpa's Apple Wine". Meier's bought 100,000 gallons of cider a year. This lasted until President Johnson enacted "The Great Society Welfare Program". The poor no longer bought the cheap apple wine for they now had more money from the government. They bought whiskey in place of the wine.

In the 1960's the foreman, Frank Alderson, developed back problems which eventually lead to surgery. Frank was a rather small man in stature which didn't help his back when lifting bushel crates of apples. The surgery was successful, but Frank filed for disability compensation with the government. Frank quit work, bought a house in Morrow and moved. My father was angry and so disappointed. When he discussed this with my mother, I would hear him say, "My back hurts every day, but I'm still working. I think Frank is just taking advantage of the government." They parted in not the best of terms. In the previous fall my father had hired a couple young guys to help with the harvest. One of them was Ben Browning who had relatives nearby on Shawhan Road. Myron tracked Benny down and offered him a full time job. Along with a salary he offered him housing in the small house across the road from the apple barn. Carl Roberts had lived in that house when he worked on the farm with Frank. Benny had dropped out of high school and had spent time in and out of jail. None of his crimes were violent. Many times he was simply drunk and rowdy or drunk and driving. His record had prevented him from securing a steady job. Benny worked many years at the orchard for he loved living and working on the farm. He stocked a couple of the ponds with fish and hunted in the woods. Occasionally he would share his catch with our family. We ate fish, rabbit, squirrel, frog legs and turtle. However, one time we ate ground hog. The pesky varmint was eating the wires on the tractors and farm trucks until my father shot him! Occasionally Benny would have a party on the farm with his friends. He would cook and serve a menagerie of items from his hunting escapades.

Sometimes he even served snake! He called his party "A Taste of Morrow!"

A few years after Benny was hired, my sister was home for the weekend. She attended the Christ Hospital School of Nursing which was held year round. It was a Saturday night, and my parents were out with friends leaving my sister and me home alone. We were upstairs getting ready for bed when a car pulled in the driveway, and someone knocked on the door. They said that the house at the top of the hill was on fire. My dad had just recently rented the house to new tenants, and they had moved in that day. My sister called the fire department, grabbed a flashlight, and together we ran through the orchard toward the burning house. Faintly in the distance we could hear sirens. When we approached, smoke was rolling out from the eaves of the roof. A young couple was stumbling down the front steps in a sleepy daze wearing their night clothes and wrapped in blankets. The man was a few years older than my sister and had grown up nearby on Trovillo Road. She knew John Downing. "Are you alright? Is there anyone else inside?" she asked. "Yes. Yes. There's a baby in the front bedroom!" My sister covered her nose and entered the smoke-filled house. I stood in the dark and feared for her safety as flames appeared at one edge of the roof. In minutes she came out with the unharmed baby in her arms, and the couple was united with their child. The fire department put out the fire, and we all went home. Minimal damages to the house were contained mostly in the attic area. My parents were home by then, we told them of the fire and went to bed. We were all surprised that the couple had exited the house without their baby. We awoke in the middle of the night to the sound of pounding on our door. We all arose and as we approached the stairway to go down, the blazing sight visible through the window of a fire at the top of hill immediately told us what was wrong. The once charred house was totally engulfed in flames. It was gone. The fire department was able to save the detached garage. The house was razed and totally rebuilt in much the same fashion as before. Benny had a wife and a child by then and could use a bigger house. The rebuilt house became his new home.

Through the sales of apple cider, my father became acquainted with Henry Sauderman, the owner of Meier's Winery, and in a few years my father decided to plant grapes for wine. He planted eight acres of vines along each side of the air strip where he kept his airplane. Some of the varieties had common names such as Concord or Niagara. Others had numbers for names. One of the favorites was ten-eight-seven-eight. Myron loved growing grapes. They were just smaller and required far less muscle power to grow than apples. Women could easily prune and pick the harvest. A small sprayer could be used to fight disease and blight. As the vines matured, the yield increased. In 1970 the grape harvest was sixty-five tons.

With so many apple trees, a couple hundred peach trees and later grapes vines, Myron had become a distributor of Niagara Chemicals, and he had a small warehouse in a separate barn where the Washington School once stood. He didn't handle the money, for the billing was through the company. Many times a whole train car of spraying material would arrive down the hill near the river. There was a side track where the car would sit until Myron unloaded it onto a truck. One time they brought large bags of fertilizer up to the farm from the train tracks and stacked them in the hay barn at the end of the driveway. It was a hot, humid night when they heard a big boom with a thump. They looked in the barn yard and saw nothing unusual. The next day when Frank went to milk the cow, he realized that the floor had collapsed taking the fertilizer onto the ground floor. It had become damp from the humidity adding more weight than the floor could handle. The cows had entered the lower level from the back side of the barn to eat hay. One cow was killed and six others were injured. That day was spent slaughtering the cows for beef. The beef from the surviving cows was very tough because they had struggled to free themselves from the debris.

There were about two dozen fruit growers in the area who would buy their chemicals for spraying from Myron. He became very knowledgeable about using them. Often the farmer would not only get what he needed, but he got free advice in growing his crops. Myron also made dusters to sell after World War II which were a new idea at the time. Dusters were used to apply dry pesticides on the wet tree before damage was done. Dust was much better than applying liquid lye and sulfur which could burn the leaves if the outside temperature was warm. On apples it prevented scab, a rough brown area on the skin, from forming on the apple. When building a duster, he would use the chassis of a Model A Ford and a Willis engine which ran at a high RPM.

Duster to apply dry chemicals to the crops. Myron built this model.

One man would drive a tractor which pulled the duster. A platform on the back of the duster is where another man stood holding a hose which would blow the pesticide onto the trees. To Myron this was just the beginning of building machines.

The representative of Niagara Chemical from Marietta, Ohio, would visit three or four times a year to check on the inventory. Bob Stacy, the company rep would come overnight and stay at the Golden Lamb. Many long conversations were held at the kitchen table over coffee or dinner about growing fruit or most any crop. Eventually he started to bring his wife, Pat, and they became good friends with Myron and Lois. The government added a restriction to using insecticides (insect control) and pesticides (fungi and insect control) in the 1960's. Farmers could not buy chemicals for their crops unless they passed an exam. Myron would drive to Columbus every year or two to take the exam. It was just an expense and a chore for him. Others might have studied, but Myron felt no need. It was always so easy for him, and he aced it every time.

In the 1950s, the use of clear plastic bags became popular. Myron began to pack apples for grocery stores in three or four pound clear plastic bags. That was a new concept for its time. He

"Pick your own" orchard.

sold bagged apples to Kroger and A & P grocery stores. He decided to open one of the orchards in the fall to the public. It was the orchard closest to the house and didn't have a pond which eliminated the threat of an accidental drowning. So, another new concept was born. He called it "Pick Your Own Apples". With so much going on during the week, pick your own was only open on the weekends. This is when the retail market was its busiest. No longer did Myron take apples to the wholesale market in Cincinnati or Huntington, West Virginia, because he could sell all the apples in the market.

The market expanded in time to offer not only apples and cider but honey, popcorn, jams and jellies, pumpkins and gourds, Amish cheese and other county store items.

The cider fountain originally offered "all you can drink" cider for a penny. The sign said, "You pay for the cup, we give you the cider." As prices increased, it was offered for a small fee, but it continued to be "All you can drink". It was a sure way to sell gallons of cider. The retail market drew crowds of people on the weekends. It was so popular that many times a policeman was needed to direct traffic. A gentleman from Morrow would come on Sundays and make Dutch apple flappens. The peeler machine would peel and core the apples. By hand the man would horizontally slice apples into a doughnut shape. The slice would then be dipped in yeast batter and then deep fried and served warm sprinkled with powered sugar. They were tasty. Hayrides were also offered on the weekends. It was the Baker family members that chipped in along with a few hired people that operated the retail business. On Sunday nights after closing, the family would all go out to eat exhausted from a busy weekend.

Myron acquired the peeler machine which would automatically peel, core and slice three apples at a time. It was amazing. He sold fresh sliced apples to two of the big bakeries in Cincinnati, Busken Bakery and Servatii's. Many times he would bring back a few fresh pies and sell them in the market on the weekends. Busken Bakery also made a whole apple dumpling that was delicious.

He contacted Blue Bird Pie Company in Dayton and sold them fresh apple slices. I went with him one time on a delivery, and he took me into the factory. They were making lemon meringue pies that day totally by machine. Not one person ever touched the pie from the beginning to the end. It was fascinating.

Myron approached food trailers at the county fair who sold candy apples in an effort to drum up business. He soon supplied apples for several of them. One of his favorite customers was Mrs. Cody. She took her trailer to most of the fairs in southwest Ohio. I particularly remember going with him every year when he delivered apples to the Montgomery County Fair in Dayton. Mrs. Cody would always give me a cotton candy. One year we actually saw Bobby Darin perform at the fair from her location. I was little and had to stand on a large crate to see the entertainer over the crowd. Myron began to ask Mrs. Cody about how she made the red, hard candy apples and the caramel apples. He came home and asked Margery, his teenage daughter, if she would like to take on a project. Before you knew it, she was making candy apples in the basement of the house and selling them to three or four local high schools at their football games. Margery would rise at four AM on Fridays to start cooking the candy in a small copper pot heated with propane gas. Margery profited well and was the best dressed girl in high school.

Myron became active in the area. He was a member of the Lions Club in Morrow. He served on the school board at Little Miami Schools for sixteen years. He supported the Morrow Fire Department, and they in turn came to the rescue when there was a fire even though the farm was in Union Township. He attended the Lincoln Day dinner every year held by the Republican Party. He was always pleased to see his high school friend, Corwin Nixon, who was a state representative. At the county airport, Myron served on the Warren Country Authority board along with Neil Armstrong. Myron knew of some Flying Farmer friends in Neil's hometown. Myron also served on the Western Water board. He also stayed in contact with Ohio State University agricultural department as they developed better ways to farm. He was a member of the Ohio State Horticultural Society and served as president. That group sponsored the Ohio Apple Queen. My parents encouraged me run for the spot. In 1973 I toured the state appearing at fairs and festivals as the state apple queen.

My family will never forget the spring of 1967. There was a beautiful blossom that year with all the apple trees filled with bloom. Imagine seventy-five acres of flowers. The aroma alone was heavenly. It was early May when the trees were in full bloom. After a streak of warm days, the weather prediction was for a cold front to pass through bringing night time temperatures down to the upper twenties. The fragile blossoms could never survive a harsh freeze. Myron had heard of fruit growers hiring a helicopter to hover over the orchard stirring the air, keeping it warm when they faced such a dilemma. He could not possibly afford that. Myron was no stranger to the community, and he came up with another plan. The lumber company in Morrow brought a couple truck loads of saw dust. The gravel company brought old used truck tires. The school collected empty large tin cans that once held canned fruit or vegetables from the school cafeteria. The Ashland Oil Company in town brought a truck load of oil. By late afternoon the barn yard was filled with all that was collected and volunteers. They distributed the tires throughout the pick your own orchard and doused them heavily with oil. They filled the tin cans with saw dust and then doused them with oil. The cans were distributed throughout the eight acres of grape vines in the vineyard. They waited and watched the temperature fall that night. In the wee hours of the morning, they began to light the tires and the cans. My mother came and gently woke me from sleep. She whispered, "Jeane, get up. You've got to see this." I crawled out of bed and in the dark went to the window at the top of the stairs with my mother. This window faced south overlooking the yard and beyond that the "pick your own" orchard. All the tires had been lit and the orchard glowed in an orange hue. It was an amazing sight. The emotions around the sight were one of fear, doubt and pain. Nobody knew if it would work. When I went to school the next day, the orchard and nearby area was filled with a black smoke and a sharp odor of burning tires. There was a smoky silence in the air. For the next few days, my father would walk in the orchard. Sometimes I would walk with him. He would pluck a dried blossom from a tree, and just below the blossom there would be a bump. He would split the bump with his thumb nail. That was the apple which should have been a bright lime green. It would be black. He would drop it to the ground and say, "Dead." The entire crop was lost.

That summer the trees became very full and bushy. Their energy went to their leaves instead of their fruit. Myron sprayed them rarely, just enough to keep the leaves healthy. Myron diligently searched that summer through every ad that appeared in his Fruit Grower magazines. He made lots of calls. He found a grower in northern Ohio and one in Indiana that would sell him apples for the retail market. He found another grower in North Carolina that would sell him two semi loads of apples for cider making. I remember the trucks coming late at night in the fall. Myron operated the fork lift relentlessly until all the skids of apples were in the cold storage. Money was tight that year, but we made it. The toaster broke and would only toast one slice of bread on only one side, but we ate toast. My clothes were all hand-me-downs, and I worked in the school cafeteria to pay for my lunch. We made it. More profitable times would return in another year.

Myron also sold apples to a potato chip factory in Cincinnati called Husmans. To one side of the factory there was a small piece of machinery that made caramel apples that the company

operated in the fall. The owner would distribute the caramel apples along with his potato chips. Myron would often return from a delivery with a big red can filled with yummy potato chips. After supplying the apples for a few years, Myron bought the machine in 1968. Along with buying the machine, he had to buy a recipe for the carmel. He bought the recipe from a German caramel maker in Chicago for $12,000. Myron paid him $3,000 a year for four years. Myron contacted

other potato chip manufactures to distribute the carmel apples with their potato chips. A couple years later Myron had to turn down orders. He just couldn't keep up with the demand. He needed a bigger machine. The following spring he tackled the task. He sold the old machine to an apple grower in Newcomerstown, Ohio. He also realized that he needed space, so he put an addition on the front of the barn for his caramel apple factory.

The caramel apple machine was in two parts. There was a sticker and a dipper machine.

The new sticker required two people to operate rather than one. The sticker machine processed fifty-two apples a minute. The operators would simply place two apples at a time, stem down on horizontal rotating arms with springs that would bounce when hit. Automatically a stick would drop vertically onto the apple and a hydraulic hammer would tamp the stick into the apple. A conveyor

would move the apples with sticks up to the dipper area. The dipper ran vertically. It would dip the apple on a stick into a skinny vat of hot caramel, spin the apple to remove excess caramel, tip it sideways to roll in chopped peanuts, then the machine would release the apple from the conveyer onto a large rotating table of chopped peanuts. The dipper processed eighty apples a minute. To make up the difference in the timing of the sticker and the dipper, initially the stick machine would make a stock pile while the caramel was cooking. There were two moving lines of apples on the dipper. Two people placed the apples on the dipper conveyer in chucks that would lock, and two people picked up the caramel apples at the end and placed them in boxes. Myron made the entire machine with only a small help from his friend, Leonard Michael, who had a machine tool shop in Maineville. Myron was approached by companies in California, New York and Virginia to produce machines like the one he used. He refused their offers in an effort to eliminate competition. He may have been an

apple grower, but he considered himself a mechanic at heart. One never saw him pick apples, prune or spray the trees, make cider, or mow an orchard. He was always repairing a tractor or a piece of machinery; he was welding to make something or he was out and about marketing his product.

When making the caramel apples, one person was designated as the cook. That person and my dad knew the secret recipe. The ingredients of the caramel were evaporated milk, sugar, corn syrup, vanilla and a vegetable oil, which came in flakes. This would give the caramel a shiny coat. The corn syrup and evaporated milk were bought in large metal drums that a fork lift would pick up and place on each side of large scales where they would empty into a large copper kettle. The milk was shipped from Rondelac, Wisconsin in thirty-five gallon barrels. The sugar was bought in one hundred pound bags. The ingredients were measured in pounds. I remember the vanilla was measured with a shot glass and the flakes were one scoop. (Actual recipe is located in the Appendix.) Myron made a motorized lift that would pick up the copper kettles and place it on an open stove. The mechanism that grabbed the handles of the kettles was made with two old car steering wheels. A motorized arm of large paddles with a thermometer would gradually fall into the kettle. The paddles would stir the mixture constantly until the caramel reached 220 degrees. At that point everyone would stand clear because it would boil and splatter onto the floor. The lift would remove the copper kettle, swing over to the dipper and would tip pouring the steamy hot caramel into an insulated holding vat that released caramel into the dipper vat with a release handle.

Each box held twenty-eight caramel apples. At its peak years, Myron sold 30,000 to 40,000 boxes. Sales reached more than a million caramel apples in a year. The caramel apples retailed for fifteen cents. The machine ran for two shifts, sixteen hours a day. I would fall asleep at night hearing the t-ch–t-ch of the air hammer putting the sticks into the apples. The best apples for making caramel apples were Jonathan. They were tart and flavorful with a thin skin that was easy to bite through. Just like the cider, the best combination was to have a sour apple with the sweet candy. If you remember, my dad planted an orchard for each child. The apples in my orchard were close to reaching their peak in production at this time. There was some assortment of apple varieties in every orchard, but most of them in my orchard were Jonathan unlike the other orchards. It was perfect for filling the needs of the caramel apple business.

The assortment of varieties planted in every orchard would enhance pollination. Certain varieties would pollinate better than others. One such variety was the Banana apple. Another was Cortland. The Banana apple got its name because the skin was a bit oily like a banana. That variety was not very tasty to eat, so most of them went into cider. But at least they helped the other varieties produce. Myron never had bees because the orchards were surrounded with woods where wild bees lived.

In the late 1960's a new type of fruit tree became available. It was the dwarf tree. Myron thought this type of tree would be perfect in the pick-your-own orchard because people would be able to reach the fruit more easily. Most nurseries would guarantee their trees for one year, but that was not enough time for the tree to bear fruit. One might think they were buying Red Delicious trees only to find a few years later that the trees were another variety. Myron found a reputable nursery in Maryland to buy fruit trees. He ordered two hundred trees. These would be the first trees not to be grafted from the older trees on the farm. I had had my driver's license for about six months when he sent my mother and me in the station wagon to pick up the trees in the spring of 1971. My mother preferred not to drive, so I drove there and back. We decided to go a bit early and take in some sights in Washington, D.C. The cherry trees were in full bloom when we arrived. We took Kathy and Ty, my niece and nephew, along with us to see the nation's capitol. We laughed at the remark of seven-year-old Ty as he marveled at the Lincoln Memorial. "All my life I have looked at a penny and hoped that some day I could see the Lincoln Memorial." The apple trees we picked up were mere whips as the nursery loaded all two hundred in the back of the car before we headed home. Those trees were a great addition to the orchard, and they bore beautiful fruit like my father had never grown before.

Meanwhile, through all this time of business growth, Myron's wife, Lois, was conducting school tours. Every week day morning and afternoon she led school groups from southwest Ohio through the apple barn. After school she led scout groups on tours.

They walked into the big cold storage, saw the grader that washed, dried and sorted apples by size. She would show them the apple peeler and how it worked. They saw cider and caramel apples being made, tasted cider and picked an apple in the orchard. Many years she had to turn down groups as available tour dates would book quickly. Hundreds of children toured the orchard every year. My sister believe that her first grade teacher contacted my mom and that class was the first to tour the orchard.

There wasn't much work that could be done by children on the farm. Most of the tasks required adult strength. It was hard labor. My brother mowed all the orchards in the summer when he was a teenager. My sister and I would occasionally help on the grader after school. As soon as we were old enough to count, each of us, my brother, sister and I, were handed a cigar box with some quarters in it and told to sell pumpkins on the weekends in the fall. Not only did this sharpen our math skills, but we learned to deal with the public. We learned to talk to

people. It built confidence within us. It was a fun experience for a kid to be in charge.

When I was a teenager, I was checking a car out of the "pick your own" orchard.

They had their apples in the back seat of the car and happily paid for what they had picked. I asked if I could please check the trunk of their car. They refused to allow me to look inside. I explained that we look in every trunk before our customers leave. I calmly asked that they pull aside to let others through while I got another employee. They pulled up on the driveway where there was a slight incline. With my father at my side, when they opened their trunk, a cascade of loose apples fell to the ground and rolled across the driveway. We bagged the loose apples which came to more than two bushels and asked if they would like to buy them. They weren't interested in purchasing the apples. Rarely were there problems like this one. Most of our customers were great people looking for a day out in the country in the fall.

The caramel apple business lasted for about ten years and then dwindled and died. Inflation hit causing the price of a caramel apple to rise from fifteen cents to fifty cents or more, and the demand dropped. Myron was contacted by an apple grower in Nova Scotia, Canada about buying the caramel apple machine. Myron and Lois flew to visit them, and a deal was made to sell the machine. Myron had always been honest in other deals and was far too trusting of others. The price was set with a schedule of payments to be made. The machine was shipped to Canada but never did the buyer make a single payment. Because it was out of the country, it was nearly impossible to legally collect the money due. Myron took into consideration that the machine he made had paid for itself over and over many times. It was a tough lose, but the machine no longer had a value to him.

The rest of the apple operation continued through the years. In the later years Virgil and Leonard no longer picked apples each year. It became harder to find pickers. Even after a transition from bushel containers to eighteen-bushel bins that moved the apples by fork lift, no one wanted to climb a ladder with a bushel bag on their shoulders. Myron closed the biggest orchard of forty acres on the farm. He arranged to bring in Mexican workers and started to build housing for them, but at the last minute the deal fell through. Right before he died of heart failure in 1999, the government added a restriction that apple cider must be processed. The equipment for that machinery started at $35,000. This was very discouraging to Myron at the age of 83. The idea of putting a small sticker on every

individual apple was being introduced. Myron expressed his concern.

More restrictions since then have been made on apple growers. One might have noticed that very few apple orchards around this area still exist. Most have disappeared. Maplewood Orchard has disappeared, too.

The orchards are gone and in their place are corn and soybean fields. Two of Myron's children, Loron and I, and a grandson, Ty, still live on the farm.

From the Stubbs through eight generations, apple growing was a part of farming in this location. One thing for sure, when Maplewood Orchard existed, Charlie and Myron worked to make it a profitable enterprise.

Label for the pure maple syrup

Myron talking about the apple business in the barn with many bushels of apples. The cider mill is in the background.

"HOME, SWEET HOME ON THE RANGE" FOR BAKERS WHO COOK ELECTRICALLY

While Mrs. Baker watches little Jean-E's expression, Margery Baker removes a delicious fresh apple pie from the electric oven in the Baker all-electric home.

Warren County family learns secret of clean, convenient kitchen range, on which daughter earns money for trip

Cooking is both fun and profitable in the farm home of Myron Baker on Stubbsmill Road near Morrow, in the heart of Warren County (near Serpent Mound).

Mrs. Baker's favorite recipe is for apple pie, and a good thing, too — since Myron Baker's farm is known as Maplewood Orchard, and his important product is apples! The family agrees that her apple pies are wonderful!

"Chief advantage of an electric range," says Mrs. Baker, "is that it is so clean, automatic and economical." With some planning for short cuts and better methods of using the automatic features of the range, Mrs. Baker finds time to be PTA President, Sunday School teacher and chief promotor of the Future Nurses club.

Meanwhile daughter Margery, a 4-H member, makes candied apples which she sells — hoping to earn enough money for a trip to Alaska next summer. Father gives her the apples; mother lends her the stove; Margery buys the sugar and all other ingredients — does the work — and makes the profit.

HOUSEHOLD HINT FOR IRONING:

Other electrical equipment helps Mrs. Baker do her work, too. The washer and dryer are her favorite work-savers. For example, she removes clothes from the dryer before they are fully dry, then stores them in the washer. The washer is clean and holds the necessary moisture for proper ironing.

For additional hints on using electricity to make your work easier, and for estimates of cost, ask the farm representative of your local power company, or write for information on electric cooking. Address: Ohio Electric Utility Institute, 50 West Broad Street, Columbus 15, Ohio.

Margery has a specialty all her own: candied apples, from which she makes a nice profit; hopes to finance a trip to Alaska.

Neat trick is to keep clothes damp in the clean washer — until it is time to iron them . . . thus no added sprinkling is necessary.

TIME AND LABOR SAVING IDEAS FOR FARMERS FROM THE OHIO ELECTRIC UTILITY INSTITUTE

The Baker Family was featured in an article about electric stoves on May 16, 1959 in "The Ohio Farmer". Myron Baker, Margery, Jeane and Mrs. Lois Baker.

A spray today keeps the blight

FMC's agricultural chemicals control rot and pests on apples, peaches, and grapes

A full spray program with FMC agricultural chemicals and *Bean* sprayer is utilized by Maplewood Orchard to protect fruit from diseases.

Good management and innovative ideas have paid off for the Maplewood Orchard of Morrow, Ohio, some 32 miles northeast of Cincinnati. Among the retail-oriented ventures of the owners, Myron and Lois Baker, are the coating and selling of caramel-coated apples.

The Bakers have also developed a brisk pick-it-yourself trade which attracts hundreds of people from miles around each weekend during the apple season. They press and sell over 150,000 gallons of cider a year and bag their apples for direct grocery-store sales and distribution to roadside markets.

The specialty of the house, however, is caramel-coated apples on a stick. Now the biggest part of their business, it got its start only seven years ago when the Bakers' older daughter, Margery, wanted some to sell at high school

The Bakers grow peaches and grapes as well as apples on their 75-acre orchard.

12

away

football games. Distribution has now expanded to retailers throughout southern Ohio, and in 1972 sales were more than 43,000 boxes, 28 caramel apples to a box—almost 1¼ million apples.

Despite limited rainfall in the area and below-average growing conditions, the 75-acre Maplewood Orchard produced 30,000 bushels of apples.

As usual, special attention was given to a full, multi-functional disease and pest control system developed over the past 25 years with FMC's Agricultural Chemical Division. A regular *Polyram* fungicide schedule is followed from petal fall through the growing season. Other chemicals are used to combat special pest problems: copper sulfate to curb fire and blossom blight, *Kolodust* fungicide to halt apple scab, and other chemical controls for insects and mites.

continued

Apple-coating equipment designed and adapted by Myron Baker is used to insert sticks, dip apples in caramel coating, and coat with nuts. The wheel dips 80 apples a minute.

1972

In addition to apples, the Bakers devote part of their 75-acre orchard to peaches and to French hybrid grapes for sale to Ohio wineries. Mr. Baker plans to promote a greater regional wine business, which has suffered in the past from damage to the grape crop from black rot diseases. Now, he says, modern FMC fungicides can control these rots and make commercial grape production more practical in the area.

As local apple queen (and state runner-up), Jean Baker rides in parade of queens at Lebanon, Ohio, Honey Festival—another boost for Maplewood Orchard.

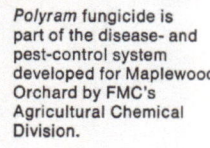

Polyram fungicide is part of the disease- and pest-control system developed for Maplewood Orchard by FMC's Agricultural Chemical Division.

FLYING FARMERS

Myron Baker was always intrigued by flying. When he was sixteen, he forged his mother's signature on a release form so that he could ride in a hot air balloon. He knew that his parents were not excited about flying like he was. They firmly discouraged him from choosing a career in flying. In spite of their attitude, Myron convinced them to allow him to take flying lessons at a nearby air strip from a private pilot while he was in high school. He became a licensed pilot in 1938 at the age of 24. He probably would have joined the military to fly airplanes if he could. Because of his lung issue with pneumonia in high school, he could not enlist.

A year after dropping out of college, Myron and Lois married and lived in a small house on the Little Miami River for a year. It was very close to where Stubbs Mills had once stood. The house had no running water, and Myron didn't have a job initially. Charlie paid Myron two dollars a week to work on the farm until he found a job. Lois remembers her mother coming to visit and being overjoyed when her mother would bring her a pair of silk stockings. It was quite a luxury for Lois. Myron eventually landed a job with the Crosley Corporation before World War II. Myron and Lois soon moved to a nicer house at the top of the hill on Stubbs Mill Road. One day in December Myron and Lois looked at an airplane that was for sale, but didn't buy it. They decided to think about it. Later they were happy that they didn't make the purchase. The very next day Pearl Harbor was attacked, and all aircraft in the U.S. were grounded. If they had bought the plane, they wouldn't have been able to fly it.

During the war Myron worked at Aeronca Aircraft in the experimental department in Middletown, Ohio. This fulfilled his desire to learn more about flying and aircraft. He left that job when the war was over because aircraft production dropped, and he started working on the farm again with his father. In his spare time he decided to build an airplane himself. He built the frame of the wings but progressed no farther. The wings are still in the attic of the apple barn up in the rafters.

Myron's first plane.

After World War II the flying restriction was lifted, and he bought a plane. His first airplane was a used Piper Cub. He bought the plane in Wilmington and flew it to Attaway's air field south of his residence. It was a single magneto plane meaning the engine had one device to start the engine. A single engine generator used permanent magnets and coils to produce a high voltage pulse which would fire the aircraft's spark plugs. This technology is more than one hundred years old and is still used in lawn mowers and chain saws along with small aircraft. Models produced after Myron's plane, were equipped with a battery along with the magneto making it safer. For this reason he purchased his second airplane from Attaway in 1946. It was a new

Taylor Craft. Attaway also was a Buick dealer, so Myron bought a new Buick at the same time.

My parents joined the Air Ranch Club at Attaway's air field which was located on Fields Ertel Road in the Mason area and they met socially and flew about the area. The Club held a "Family" day once a year and the kids were allowed to have soda which was a rare treat.

Myron made an airfield in the middle of a meadow on the farm and built a hanger. Since the farm was mostly rolling hills, it was difficult to find an area long enough and flat enough. The air strip was near the corner of Shawhan Road and Stubbs Mill Road. Flying

Myron with his family and his second plane (about 1946).

in and out was a little tricky but doable. At one end there were electric wires. It had a slight grade going down to a pond on the opposite end. Myron tried to persuade the electric company to bury the wires, but they refused stating that they couldn't justify that expense for a private

strip. Flying a small plane was such a rare thing to see that when we flew in or out of the air strip, cars would often park along the side of the road to watch. When he first started flying, sheep grazed on the air strip. This proved to be a nuisance because many times when he would try to land, the sheep wouldn't move off. He would buzz them and buzz them flying low to the field, and they would only move up or down the field but not off. The sheep were soon sold. He also painted on the green roof of the apple barn in yellow-gold block letters, "MAPLEWOOD".

Flyers could easily find the farm when they came to visit.

Before the end of his flying career, he had owned four airplanes. His third plane was a new Piper Tripacer, and his last plane was a newer Piper Tripacer that had a bigger engine. I remember distinctly when he bought the last airplane. When flying friends came to visit, they would first fly around our house and the barn with the bold letters, "MAPLEWOOD". That would alert my parents to drive up the road where the air strip was. One beautiful afternoon when I was playing outside, a plane buzzed the house. I went in the house to get my mom. As my mother had a book listing the license numbers of all their friends, she picked up her book. We read the unfamiliar license number on the bottom of the wing having no idea who it was because it wasn't in the book. We climbed in the car and went to the airfield to pick up whoever it was, and to my mom's surprise, my dad climbed out of his newly purchased airplane!

In 1946 a new organization was forming in Ohio called the Flying Farmers. Myron and Lois became charter members. The first president of the organization was Dale Studebaker from Dayton. Myron became the second president in 1947. The organization would have "fly-ins" at various airports and the private strips of farmers in the state throughout the spring, summer and fall. The meeting would usually be held in a hanger where tables and chairs were setup, and the wives would bring dishes for a pot luck meal. Sometimes they would have a guest speaker. Other times they would just socialize and talk about farming. In 1959 Myron was named "Ohio Flying Farmer of the Year". In 1960 Lois was named "Ohio Flying Farmer Queen".

My father had trouble saying the word "pizza". Instead of pronouncing it, "pitza" as most people do, he would say, "pissa". He also had trouble saying, "Lois". It came out more like "Lows". Her middle name was Matilda, and so he started calling her "Tillie" . It caught on, and people started calling him "Bake", so they were soon known as "Tillie and Bake" at least around the Flying Farmers.

For a few years in the 1950's, Myron and Lois would host a fly-in at their air strip usually on a weekend in July. Flyers would throw a tarp over the wing of their parked airplane and camp at the side of the air strip. The area was named Hot Dog Hollow where a bon fire was made for roasting hot dogs. My dad purchased a large open tent where the flyers could place the food items on tables that they brought for the evening meal and breakfast. There was a huge barrel filled with ice tea, sweetened with sugar and orange slices near the tent. My mother would arrange for a local assistant minister to lead a brief worship service on Sunday morning before the flyers left. It was an event well attended by Ohio Flying Farmers. (See flyer on next page.)

The organization started with chapters in nearly every state in the U.S. Eventually it grew to have chapters in Canada and Mexico. It soon became the International Flying Farmers. Myron made many trips helping to form a chapter in Ontario. Once a year the organization would have a convention for five days in the summer. Myron attended every convention except the first one which was held in September. Being an apple grower prevented him from leaving the farm during harvest. The early conventions were usually held at a college campus because most hotels weren't large enough to hold the group. When their grandson roomed in Carey Hall at Purdue University, Lois said, "Oh, we stayed in that dorm during a convention." The conventions were a hubbub of activities. Each year a few states would choose to present their attributes for holding the convention the following year. A committee would choose a state, and it would be announced on the last night. Hundreds of planes would fly into the host city the day before the convention. Buses would be arranged to transport people to and from the convention site. Myron and Lois flew all over the country going to the conventions. My mother raved about the Teton Mountains when they returned from the convention in Jackson Hole, Wyoming. She told about eating dinner in the Space Needle when they returned from Seattle, Washington. I flew

OHIO FLYING FARMER
OVERNIGHT FLY-IN

Saturday Afternoon, July 13 21

Maplewood Orchard Air Strip
Morrow, Ohio

If you cannot land on 1200 feet go to
Fred Field - 4 miles north - and trans-
portation will be furnished.
Maplewood is located on Cincinnati
Sectional Map.

Bring -
    Weiners & Buns, Potato Salad, or
    Baked Beans for a Weiner Roast.
    Blankets or Sleeping Bag So You
    Can Sleep Under The Stars.
    Your Fishing Pole if You Like To Fish.

We will furnish a tent, plenty of straw
on which to sleep, and breakfast.

If you plan to come - drop me a card
and I will send you a detail map of
the field.

                    Myron Baker
                    Morrow, Ohio

Warren County's Flying Orchardists

Bakers Active In Flying Farmers
Myron A Director, Lois Was Queen

BY SUSAN DAHL
. . .Star staff writer

One of the "pioneer" flyers in Warren County is Myron Baker, owner of the Maplewood Orchard near Morrow.

Myron acquired his student permit for flying in 1931, but didn't become a licensed pilot until after World War 2. During this time, farm duties and the fact that individual p i l o t s were almost unheard of kept Myron's flying to a minimum. On December 7, 1941, Myron and Lois Baker were returning from looking at a plane they were interested in buying when they heard the news about Pearl Harbor. They had decided against that particular plane and were grateful for it, since all private planes were grounded for the duration of World War 2. Immediately following the war, the Bakers bought a Piper Cub 2 seater and flying became much a part of their life.

Maplewood Orchard covers 201 acres and produces from 10,000 to 15,000 bushels a year of apples and peaches. Most of the fruit is sold to the Kroger Company and the A and P chain in Dayton and Cincinnati. Myron is the third generation of Bakers to run the orchard and Loron Baker, Myron's son is now actively engaged in helping his father. Having a plane at his disposal, plus a landing strip just a short distance from the farm is a great convenience for Myron's business. He uses it mostly for picking up supplies in nearby cities where driving would be more costly and time consuming. The suppliers are most cooperative about meeting the plane and arranging either for the supplies to be at the airport or for transportation to the supply house. The Bakers do not use their plane for dusting t h e trees in their orchards because it is not practical for small farms and would be dangerous for surrounding farms.

The airstrip which the Bakers built after World War 2 at one time was the only private airstrip in the county. Lois states that it was a real novelty at that time and that people used to line the road to watch the plane take off and land. She says that most of the people secretly thought that they would never see the Bakers again

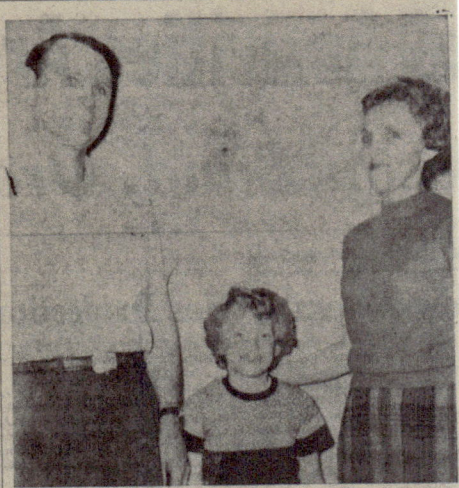

VETERANS AMONG WARREN COUNTY FLYERS are Mr. and Mrs. Myron Baker of Maplewood Orchard near Morrow. Myron started in 1931 and his wife has been an enthusiast for many years. She has recently received the Land-it Award. Their six-year-old daughter Jean joins them here in front of a United States map they use to chart their flight plans.

(Star photo—Susan Dahl)

when they took off on an excursion.

When the Ohio Flying Farmers was formed in 1946, Myron Baker was a charter member as well as serving as their first secretary. Since that time he has been one of their most active members and avid supporters. He served as president in 1947-48 and is now the regional director. His duties as such are to act as a representative between the National Flying Farmers organization and the clubs in Michigan, Kentucky, Ohio, Indiana and Illinois. This position entails quite a bit of traveling to the five states which he represents a n d that makes it even more enjoyable for Myron and his family.

Lois Baker is just as enthusiastic about flying as her husband is and takes an active part in the Ohio Flying Farmers too. She received an award given by the Ohio Flying Farmers called the Land-it Award. This shows that Lois has

learned how to land a plane, an women are encouraged to lear just in case something should hap pen to the pilot while they are passenger. She was chosen as Ohi Flying Farmer Queen in 1960 an just r e c e n t l y relinquished he crown to the new Queen. Lo i feels that her term as queen wa something she will never forget not only for the honor, but becaus of all the wonderful people she me during her reign. The Queen mus serve as hostess at all fly-ins i her state, write a column of loca organization news for the nationa magazine and also a newslette each month which is sent to a Ohio Flying Farmer members.

The Bakers have attended ever Flying Farmer national conventio since the inception of the organiza tion except one, which was held i September, their busy season. The are making plans now for the 196 convention in Tucson, Arizona.

The Bakers office in their home has a most unusual wall covering on two walls. They have created a map of the United Staes with aviation maps they received from the U. S. Government. Although this makes the room very attractive, it is not only decorative, but useful as well. With this giant map, they can figure the distances for trips they make and decide before they leave how far they will travel in one day as well as the most convenient route and landing strips on their way. In all, there are 44 maps.

Lois Baker, not only shares her husband's interest in flying, but she also takes time to serve as Mother Advisor for the Rainbow Girls. Their daughter Margery is active in the organization and Jean, 6, who starts to school in September will keep Lois busy with school activities for another few years.

with them to Norfolk, Virginia for the convention and then onto Tangier Island where there were no cars and could only be reached by plane or boat. I flew with them to Miami Beach. From the plane only a faint line would distinguish between the blue ocean and the blue sky which revealed a slight curve of the planet. I went with them to Edmonton, Alberta, Canada for the convention and saw the Canadian Rockies from the air. We also visited Banff and Jasper and of course, Lake Louise. On our journey there, my dad surprised me while flying across the Bad Lands. He flew up from behind and then tilted the wings to bank around the faces of the presidents at

Mount Rushmore. He did the same thing when we flew to Ontario banking the wings above Niagara Falls. The Flying Farmers organized a trip to the Bahamas and my parents flew their little plane to the island.

Winning the Teen Talent Contest, 1967

When arriving at the convention, people would register and buy a booklet full of tickets. The tickets would admit them to banquets, a luncheon, events, and group tours in the area. There were usually vendors set up in the lobby to promote farm machinery or airplane equipment such as radios. The week would have guest speakers who talked about farming or flying. When the women had a luncheon in Dayton, Erma Bombeck was the speaker. In New York City the women were given plenty of time to shop. In Richmond, Virginia the men toured the Marlboro tobacco plant. On opening night there would be a teen talent contest sponsored by Beechcraft Company. I entered when I was thirteen singing Second Hand Rose in Little Rock, Arkansas and won first prize of one hundred dollars. I had rehearsed with Claudine Fogle, a Flying Farmer, for months at her home in Dayton. On the last night a formal dinner dance with a live orchestra was held and the queens from each state were presented on stage in their beautiful gowns. The queens who chose to contend for international queen were introduced with more personal details. Not every queen wanted the expense of traveling the following year all over North America. Earlier in the week they had been interviewed, and one was chosen. The end of the evening was celebrated with dancing as the new queen was crowned. At some time in the evening, each state would gather their members for a group picture. It was not unusual for Ohio to have two or three hundred members there.

The next morning a meteorologist from the airport would be in a banquet room with a big map of the United States. He

Aeronautical Map on Myron's wall

would specifically review the weather across the country warning the fliers of possible storms and advising them of where they shouldn't fly. When we flew from Edmonton such a warning was given. Sure enough, we were grounded before reaching the United States. We landed on a small grass field in Canada where the one lonely guy at the airport took us to a small motel in town. We soon realized that other flyers were there from the convention that we didn't know. After eating supper at the diner across the street, we sat in one of the motel rooms talking and telling jokes. The Canadians told Newfie jokes (about people from Newfoundland) that were similar to our blonde jokes or hillbilly jokes.

Myron had a large aeronautical map in his office that covered two whole walls. It was forty-four maps put together. On the map was a tack on our home location that held a string. We had to move a piece of office furniture when we flew to Florida because that map was close to the floor. The night before we left for a big trip, he would take the string to the point of our destination and hold it, then swing the string to a clear horizontal tape that measured miles.

That would tell him the length of the trip in miles. He would calculate the time for the trip and where he would need to refuel. He enjoyed refueling at Charleston, West Virginia and Billings, Montana. Both of those airports were situated on a bluff. He could simply glide onto the runway on the edge of the bluff. When leaving, he wouldn't have to lift the nose. He could just fly off the edge of the bluff. It was like flying off the edge of the world.

He would take a separate map from the one on the wall and draw a pencil line on the path of the trip. That was for my mother who would follow the line as his navigator. The map showed towns, railroad lines and interstates that she would look for on the ground. The map would also show the altitude of mountains. When we were flying to Virginia, the clouds became very, very thick over the Appalachian Mountains. They don't call them the Smokey Mountains for no reason. I could barely see the wheels of the plane out of my window because of the thick clouds. Every time my father pulled the nose up to gain altitude in order to cross the mountains, the wings would rock from side to side, and he would quickly level the plane. This happened several times which seemed to be an eternity. My mother would look at the map and call out the altitude on the map above the roar of the engine. Immediately our three sets of eyes would direct their gaze at the altitude meter. We were above but not far from the top the mountains. It was frightening to me, but my dad was calm. Eventually we broke through the clouds and the Shenandoah Valley was beautiful!

My parents made friends with farmers all over the country. Lock and Nan Norton were great friends and raised cattle and grain in New York. Pete and Joyce were peach growers in Georgia. Bill and Ruby Sheets were orange growers in Florida. They also made friends with orange growers in Tucson. Leslie and Charlene Combs owned Sprendthrift Farms in Lexington where they bred race horses. Tex and Betty Anderson were ranchers in Texas. They made friends with corn growers in Iowa. Of course, they became great friends with the farmers they saw most often at Ohio fly-ins. For many years Myron was the district three director of the organization which put him in charge of an area including Ohio, Indiana, Illinois and Michigan. He traveled to those states to motivate members and help with any issues. He also met with the other directors once a year at the Flying Farmers headquarters in Wichita, Kansas. He had many conversations with William Piper, C.G. Taylor and Clyde Cessna during these meetings.

Myron would generalize by saying that the air east of the Mississippi was hazy and humid, and the air west of the Mississippi was clear and dry. That was true, but one day proved his statement to be wrong. We were returning home and traveling west. We had just crossed out of West Virginia. It was an unusually clear day; I mean crystal clear, as clear as a bell. My dad pointed ahead to the left. In the distance the tops of the skyscrapers in Cincinnati were peaking above the hills. We looked ahead to the right and we could see a few buildings in Dayton. When we looked farther to the right and beyond Dayton, we could faintly see in the distance the buildings of Columbus! That was a rare sight.

In the spring of 1966 my parents flew to Michigan to a fly-in in their Piper Tripacer. It was

Myron and his parents, Charlie and Fairy

a cold morning when they left. As they were taking off to return home, the engine stalled in mid air. There was ice in the carburetor. They were above ground at the end of the field. In front of them was a ditch below and wires above them. My father banked the plane to the side and rolled the aircraft crumpling the wings. It eventually landed upside down with my parents strapped to their seats dangling. As this was a four-seater, the plane only had a door on the passenger side in the front. The back of the plane had a door on the pilot's side.

Fearful of an explosion my mother quickly released her seat beat, landed on her head then opened the door and ran. She screamed at him, "Get out! Get out!" while she ran. She glanced back at my dad at one point, and there he was hanging upside down flipping switches on the dashboard to turn everything off including the gas tanks. My mother had a bruise on her arm where she was holding her basket purse. My dad had a cut on his ear where his head went through the side window which is where my mother's purse flew out and its contents blew across the field. They were lucky to escape harm. They sadly returned home the next day.

The plane was totaled. It came home on a flat bed tractor trailer a week later in the dead of the night when no one would see it. My dad had it unloaded behind the barn. He later sold it for scraps. That was his last airplane. He had no insurance, so it was a true loss. His explanation was that having an airplane was just a luxury, and that he was fortunate to have flown for so many years. Yes, that was true, but it was also his passion. Many of his happiest days were when Myron Baker was flying.

He continued to fly to conventions for several years renting a plane at the Blue Ash airport near Cincinnati where he knew the mechanic, Moose. Each year the airport required that before renting he would have to go with an instructor who would test his skills. It was a breeze, literally and figuratively. He could handle a stall, a loop or whatever situation the instructor proposed. They continued to stay in touch with their Flying Farmer friends. In retirement Myron and Lois drove from town to town in Florida visiting snow birds who were long time friends and retired farmers that they met through the Flying Farmers organization.

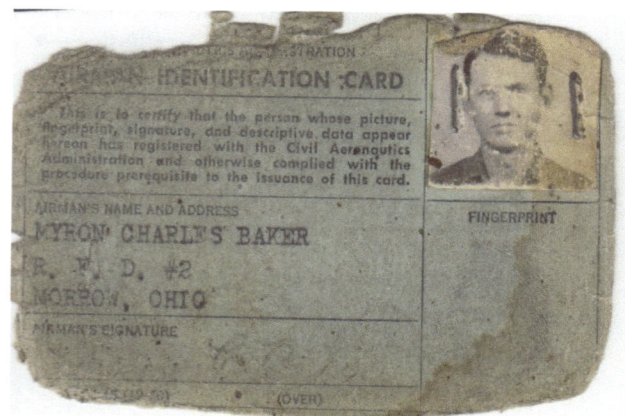

Pilot license issued 1951

THANKSGIVING IN NEW YORK

On a traditional Thanksgiving Day the men would go hunting in the morning while the women cooked a grand turkey dinner. The patriarch, Charlie Baker would go out with his son, Myron and his grandsons, Norman, Charlie, and Loron in search of squirrels, rabbits or perhaps wild turkey or pheasant. One year they decided to hunt in the woods just north of the apple barn on the east side of the road. They were creeping slowly in the woods with their guns in hand and eyes peeled for any movement. Within a few moments up popped a rabbit. It quickly scampered across the dried leaves on the ground. Immediately each man shot at the rabbit. Over each other's voices they cried, "I got it! I got it!" After each one had made their claim, they bickered, "No, I got it!"

Each one was sure their marksmanship was the fatal shot to the rabbit that now lay dead beside the wire fence. Charlie walked over and examined the rabbit for gun shot wounds. "No one got it!" he exclaimed while laughing. "The rabbit broke its neck trying to get through the fence!" That story was repeated many times at Thanksgiving dinners with great joy.

Thanksgiving Day was not celebrated in the traditional way in 1956. Myron and his family were invited to Loc and Nan Norton's house for Thanksgiving. The Nortons were great friends in Elba, New York whom they had met through the Flying Farmers. They had a big cattle and grain farm in an area that had rich, dark soil known as muck. Loron remembered them growing peas, and I remembered them growing onions. Nan Norton was a fourth grade teacher at a nearby school. The Nortons were wonderful people and fun to be around. They had a son, Dennis, who was one year older than Loron and a daughter, Candice, who was Margery's age. Myron set off with the family – Lois, his wife, Loron who was seventeen, Margery, who was twelve and Jeane who had just turned two. Loron had a basketball game on Wednesday night before

Margery, Jean and Loron

Thanksgiving, so the plan was to leave around four A.M. on Thursday and arrive at the Nortons around noon. Without interstate highways the trip would take eight hours to reach the area just west of Rochester. That would allow the Bakers to arrive at the Nortons on Thanksgiving Day.

When the Bakers left, there was light snow on the ground, but it soon cleared as they headed north. At Willoby, east of Cleveland, it began to snow quite hard, but there were plenty of snow plows to keep the roads clear. They turned onto U.S. Route 20, a four lane highway, as the snow began to increase causing them to lower their speed to between twenty and thirty miles an hour.

The snow was thick, making it difficult to see well. At 7:30 A.M. on Thursday they stopped in Ashtabula to eat breakfast. After breakfast they were heading for Erie, Pennsylvania which was forty-four miles away, and they hoped to reach Erie by 10:30. The snow was about eight to ten inches deep making it difficult to see the road as they traveled down the highway following the tracks of other vehicles. For several miles they were able to follow an Ohio snow plow until they reached the state line. Going into Pennsylvania they were on their own, traveling through thick snow on the Pennsylvania Turnpike. The turnpike was a modern road with two lanes going in each direction with a grassy median. They had traveled down the highway for about four miles when traffic stopped.

They waited an hour in a line of traffic and then attempted to travel on going around the cars and trucks when they were stopped again. It was nine o'clock. This time they sat for three hours with the car off and on, running the heater in an attempt to keep warm. Luckily Myron had fueled the car when they stopped for breakfast. Myron left the car to speak to other stranded drivers including a couple of big rig drivers about the conditions. Being stuck in the car for a long period of time meant that eventually someone in the family had to urinate. They would take turns using their bodies as a privacy screen while the other would relieve themselves at the side of the car.

The area around them was very rural with open fields used for farming. One driver had ventured to a farm house and convinced the farmer to pull his car out of the snow with the farmer's tractor but had little success. The tractor was soon stuck in the snow. It was snowing hard and the wind was blowing around twenty miles per hour. A few cars had pulled out of the line, so Myron followed only to stop again in half a mile. Loron decided to venture to the crest of the hill ahead of them to possibly see if there was an accident. He was wearing his engineer boots, which were popular footwear at the time for teenage boys. They were black leather with a buckle on the side that hit the leg at mid calf. He had on jeans and a sweater under his thick wool coat that he pulled up around his neck. Lois offered her wool plaid muffler which he used to cover his head. The rest of the family waited anxiously in the car for his return. Myron was concerned when Loron had not returned for almost an hour. How could he have missed our car? It was difficult for Loron to trudge in the deep snow and get his bearings as he returned to the car. He felt lost with everything covered by the heavy snow, so he was quite relieved when he climbed into the warm car. He reported that he had walked for about a mile to the top of the hill. Beyond he saw nothing but cars and trucks facing in all directions in all four lanes. There was no accident, but the situation was not good. They were caught in what one calls "lake effect snow". Myron calculated that they had enough gas to idle until midnight. They had a half bushel of apples intended to give to the Nortons and a box of peanut brittle to eat if they became hungry.

Their car was quickly losing its identity as the heavy snow blanketed the hood, windows and roof. They were surprised when an unseen man tapped on the driver's window. He informed them that help was behind them in the small village of East Springfield – population,

300. The family was to leave their car, walk and go right at the first road. The fire house would give them shelter for the night. They bundled up with hats and gloves. Even though Jeane was potty trained, there was still an emergency cloth diaper in the glove compartment for Loron to wear on his head covering his ears as much as possible. It was unusual for Lois to not wear a dress, but she had on wool pants and a sweater. She had a long coat and a pair of thin, fold up, plastic boots that she pulled over her loafers. Myron had a long coat, gloves and a hat. He put on some pull over galoshes that were in the trunk. Jeane had on a cute winter outfit which was a wool coat with matching leggings, mittens and a bonnet. Lois grabbed a brown bag to carry a dozen or so apples and some food for Jeane along with a couple pillows and blankets they had in the car. Margery was only wearing saddle shoes. She had no mittens or boots, so Lois grabbed two pairs of bobby socks from their suitcase in the trunk. Lois instructed Margery to put one pair on her hands and save the other pair to replace her wet socks after walking in the snow.

They began to trudge through the blinding snow as it was beginning to grow dark. Myron took long strides as he carried Jeane. It was hard for them to see one another through the snow in the semi-darkness. Margery became very tired and sleepy after continuously lifting her short legs in the deep snow. When she fell, she dozed off in the snow. She thought that if she could rest, she would have more energy to walk. She was covered instantly with falling snow. Thankfully a man by the name of Roger, who was several paces behind them, stumbled on Margery and picked her up even though Margery protested saying, "No, let me sleep. I'm tired." Without Roger's assistance, her absence might have gone unnoticed for quite a while. Roger was from Connecticut driving alone, heading home and was stuck behind the Bakers on the road. They soon came to a firehouse and stopped there to warm up, but it was packed with people, so they were told to move on to the school a few blocks away. Myron was fatigued from driving all night and handed Jeane over to Loron. She was cold and began to cry as the family set out once again. Loron fell in the deep snow a couple of times, but she hung on never releasing Loron from her grip. The street lights gave little light as the snow continued to fall heavily. The four room school was down a long lane. Lois grew weary and was having trouble staying upright, so Myron helped her down the long lane. The brown bag with apples had become wet, and the apples fell to the ground. They managed to pick up a few and put them in their pockets. Loron tripped on the blanket that had been around Jeane just as they reached the first step going into the school. Someone opened the door and helped them up, taking Jeane from his arms. The Bakers were finally out of the storm which still raged.

More and more stranded people began to arrive. The "lake effect" snow had taken so many travelers by surprise. The people were from all walks of life. A few people had been on their way to a wedding. The men were dressed in suits, and the women were in nice dresses with only nylon hosiery and heels. One woman had on strapped heels with a short fur coat. Some were very poor. Many were truck drivers. In the restroom was a woman with a baby rinsing out the baby's diaper. The baby had a diaper rash probably because the baby had worn the diaper too long. Lois gave the woman the diaper that Loron had used to cover his head which was fairly dry. A quiet black man offered his shaving powder to sprinkle on the baby's red bottom. Among the travelers was a bulldog, a French poodle, a Pekinese, a mutt and a boxer. There were also two people from Life magazine, a reporter and cameraman who later submitted an article that was published about those stranded in the storm. Among all the discomfort there was no complaining in the group of stranded travelers. They were satisfied to be warm and safe.

The local women prepared beef gravy on bread with green beans, coffee or milk and canned peaches. In an empty pie pan donations were accepted for the food. Most of the stranded people simply emptied their pockets of loose change or a dollar as a donation. Myron gladly dropped a twenty dollar bill in the pie pan. A line was formed with Lois being twelfth to use the one telephone in the school. She called the Nortons at 1:30 A.M. to explain the circumstance. The Nortons encouraged the Bakers to proceed for they had very little snow accumulation. More than one hundred people were bedded down for the night in the school. The Bakers slept on their blankets in the corner with their coats draped over them. It appeared to be a primary school with little desks and chairs. Lois found a play table that was about two feet high for Jeane to sleep on. It would keep her above the draft of the cold floor.

The next morning there was a small amount of scrambled eggs, coffee and a biscuit for each person. The travelers gathered around the radio to hear the weather report. It had stopped snowing, but it was cloudy. Twenty-seven inches of snow had fallen the previous day with winds that caused drifts up to seven feet tall. More snow was expected around 3 P.M. The high was twenty-six degrees, and the low was sixteen degrees. No one was leaving the school. A meeting was held at 10 A.M. A "caller" was nominated among them, and it was decided that a telegram and a call should be made to the governor of Pennsylvania. By noon a state of emergency was declared and the National Guard was authorized to assist where needed. Vice President Nixon was called and asked to give help. The executive Secretary of Ohio and the commissioner of Public Health in Harrisburg, Pennsylvania were also called. The water supply was running out. The toilets were not flushing well in the rest rooms. One group reported that a hundred people had slept in a private home for the night. It was reported that five hundred travelers had spent the night in the small village of one gas station, a hardware store, a grocery store and a general store.

At 1 P.M. a few travelers were directed to go outside and make a large X in the snow. This would serve as a marker for the National Guard to drop food. They all gave thanks that evening at their meal of Spanish rice and peas. There was bologna, too. Everyone was warm and fed. They were thankful for that. Another helicopter arrived and dropped bread. Army trucks had been sent with supplies, but they rolled over in the snow. At 7:30 P.M. two Army trucks arrived with food. It had taken the trucks with ten wheel drive five hours to drive twenty miles. More and more people arrived who had been stranded. Marine trucks arrived late in the afternoon to help people move out. Only thirty could fit in a truck that was designated for women and children. Lois refused to separate the family. When the trucks drove away, there were more men than women and children who remained.

Many of the men began to talk of getting out. The Lyons Truck Company had brought in some bulldozers to get eight of their trucks out of the snow. A few men including Myron and Roger decided to dig their cars out after dinner in the dark. The rest of the family waited in the school. When the men reached the car, the snow was up to the windows with a foot of snow on the top.

They borrowed a shovel from one guy and started to dig . The area was lit by the headlights of the car behind them. Roger had chains on his car which helped him greatly in getting his car out. The men helped each other as they pushed several cars out of the snow. Myron was able to go to the school and pick up Lois, Loron, Margery and Jeane. Myron crossed the median of the highway where it had been plowed and headed out in the east bound lane going west because it was the only direction they could go. Roger followed. Within miles they passed though a blockade created by the National Guard preventing cars from entering the area. They were finally out of the area where the snow storm had hit, but there was one problem. They were almost out of gas. It was close to three A.M., and all the little gas stations were closed. After passing through several towns, they found a police officer in his cruiser who awoke the owner of a station to open up, so they could purchase gasoline. Now it started to snow. They were traveling right outside of Lewisburg when they approached a right angle turn. Myron was driving very slowly, but with the fresh snow the car refused to make the turn. The car landed in a deep ditch on its side. No one was hurt thankfully. The family climbed into Roger's car and went to the firehouse in the town. A fireman contacted a wrecker which pulled the car out. The car was not damaged. It was four A.M. They all spent the remainder of the night sleeping in the firehouse. They made the most of the couch and recliners while Margery and Jeane slept on the pool table.

With a new day ahead, the family was optimistic about reaching their destination. They climbed into the car, but it wouldn't move. Oh, no. Now what? The right front tire was frozen. It wouldn't turn. Myron walked to a nearby gas station, bought some chains and borrowed a torch to heat the wheel. The torch did its job, the chains were on, and they set out on snow-covered roads.

Eventually they hit the throughway to New York City. They stopped and ate an early lunch, and bid farewell to their friend, Roger, who had followed them. They followed Roger for a while on the turnpike until they reached their exit ramp. Then the Bakers honked their horn and waved to Roger as he traveled on to his destination. He had been a great back up and possibly had saved Margery's life when he stumbled upon her in the snow. They were grateful for his help. He had left a soft place on their hearts. For a couple of years they exchanged Christmas cards then eventually lost track of him.

They arrived at the Nortons at three o'clock on Saturday. It had been a very, very long trip. The Norton's son, Dennis, had decided to go skiing. They had no idea when the Bakers might arrive, and the snow storm had given the area ideal skiing conditions. Loc Norton decided to contact Dennis to tell him to come home. He climbed into his airplane along with Loron, and they headed for the ski resort. They identified Dennis on the slopes, and Dennis waved when he recognized the plane. Loc wrote a note telling Dennis to go to the Buffalo airport. He swooped down near Dennis and dropped the note out the window. Dennis picked up the note, read it and waved. No one can deny, that is literally "dropping someone a note"! Loron and Loc met Dennis at the airport and brought him home.

The Nortons and the Bakers enjoyed a wonderful Thanksgiving meal on Saturday night. The Bakers were full of stories from their adventure in traveling through the snow to New York. They could now reflect and all laugh about the many trials along their trip.

On Sunday morning everyone enjoyed a leisurely breakfast before The Bakers headed back home. Myron called the state highway patrol to get an update on road conditions. Some roads were still closed. They would have to travel further south than expected in New York to get home. They made it home safely without an incident, but they witnessed stalled vehicles, cars in ditches and one accident which occurred right before their eyes. It wasn't an easy trip. The roads were slick with ice and snow. The Bakers arrived home at 2:30 A.M. on Monday morning.

The Nortons remained good friends of the Bakers. In the summer of 1959 the Nortons decided to take a road trip to Alaska with their daughter, Candice. Margery was asked to go along as a friend to their daughter for the adventure. The Nortons would be gone for four weeks in their station wagon and camp for the entire trip. As they entered Alaska with its vast wilderness, they were stopped at a checkpoint where they had to show two hundred dollars in cash and a gun. The Nortons were going to visit a young man, Buddy, who had once worked on their farm. He had joined the military and was stationed in Alaska. He fell in love with a girl in Alaska and married her. He decided to reside in Alaska. He bought a town which was named Circle because it was near the Arctic Circle. The town housed scientists who were planning the pipeline. It had a bar, a restaurant and a few cabins. The only paved roads were in Anchorage.

The roads were so rough on their trip that they went through five tires. They also went through three head lights, and they needed a new fuel tank before the trip was over. Alaska had just become a state on July 4th while they were there, and it was truly an adventure to visit.

Thanksgiving of 1956 for the Bakers would not be forgotten. So often when it was told, Loron was thankful to have a diaper to cover his head. Margery was thankful that a man stepped on her. They were all thankful for the people who gave them food and the little school that gave them shelter in East Springfield, New York. It was truly a thankful Thanksgiving unlike all others. In 2018 Pennsylvania had another terrible, terrible snow storm. It was reported that the storm was worse than the one which held the record in 1956.

Author's note-

The information of this event was written by Loron as a writing assignment and was later submitted to his high school newspaper.

EXPEDITION ERIE (HTTP://HISTORY.GOERIE.COM)

EXPLORE THE HISTORY OF ERIE (HTTP://HISTORY.GOERIE.COM)

 War of 1812 (http://history.goerie.com/erie-timeline)

EXPLORE A TIMELINE OF MAJOR MOMENTS IN ERIE'S HISTORY

Remembering the snowstorm of November 1956

There are probably a quite a few Erie old-timers that can remember the Thanksgiving storm back in 1956 that was so bad they had two helicopters from Pittsburgh drop food supplies to West Springfield. So when you hear from the older folks those "back-when-I-was-a-kid" stories, believe them! The below article tells the story.

ARMY EQUIPMENT USED TO DIG ERIE OUT OF BIG SNOW

Erie, Pa., Nov 24 (AP) — Army tanks, bulldozers, snow plows and hundreds of men with shovels stepped up efforts today to dig out this lakeport city of 130,000 and adjacent areas from one of the heaviest local snowfalls in history.

Thousands of citizens joined in "operations snow removal," trying to clear side streets and roads of the drifts which buried autos and snarled transportation.

The Thanksgiving Day storm which dumped from 22 to 33 inches of snow in this immediate area tapered off last night into only occasional snow flurries.

Similar conditions also were reported east and west of Erie where the storm also snarled traffic. The snow belt extended roughly 150 miles along the lake front, 50 miles west of here into Ohio and about 100 miles east to Buffalo.

While the big snow removal job was under way two helicopters flown from Pittsburgh dropped food supplies at West Springfield, a community of 1,500 about 30 miles west of Erie. More drops were planned for today if roads couldn't be opened.

West Springfield was only one of the many communities cut off completely by the storm which marooned hundreds of motorists and truckers. Many vehicles remained bogged down in the snow and are handicapping efforts of the weary snow-plow crews.

Army tanks were called into action to help pull big tractor trailers out of highway snow drifts.

In Erie 500 members of the National Guard pitched in with civilians. The Red Cross gave a hand to those who needed emergency food supplies and various welfare agencies also helped.

Mayor Arthur Gardner said he hoped that he would be able to end the state of emergency within 24 hours.

UNEXPECTED GUESTS

"Rinngg! Rinngg!"
"Hello. Maplewood Orchard."
"Hello! This is Don Holmes. Is this Tillie?"

That day, Sunday, September 14th, 1958, started out very typical until this call. Lois and the children had gone to church, and Myron stayed home to sell apples and cider to customers. It was a sunny, crisp fall day. The other employees were off for the day. It was still a bit early in the season. Leonard and Virgil, who normally picked apples every day, were probably off as well.

They had probably picked all the Jonathan, Cortland, Grimes Golden and Banana apples on the farm and were waiting a few days for the Red Delicious and Golden Delicious to fully ripen. Lois and Loron might have helped Myron bag more apples in half pecks, pecks, half bushels and bushels in the afternoon as more customers arrived. Margery might have been working on homework or playing with Jeane who was nearly four.

It was an unexpected call late in the day. Unexpected guests were coming for the night. It was Don and Ruth Holmes, Flying Farmer friends from New York. They had dropped off their son at the University of Missouri and were on their way home. He was a freshman and had received a scholarship through ROTC (Reserve Officer Training Corp). They didn't leave the university as early as they had planned, and there was not enough daylight for them to fly back to New York. My father and most of his other flying friends did not have the skills needed to fly after dark. The Holmes refueled their plane in Hamilton, Ohio and gave us a call. Flying from Hamilton to our farm would probably take no more than ten or fifteen minutes. My father spoke to Don on the phone and reminded him of the conditions as he did every time a visitor flew in. He was to fly in from the south end of the air strip because the north end was near the road where there were electric wires. Don had flown in before to visit, so he was familiar with the air strip. It was not too unusual for flying friends to drop by occasionally. The farm was easy for others to find with the bold letters across the barn roof in bright yellow gold, "MAPLEWOOD".

Myron and Lois were excited to see their friends. Lois pulled out some potatoes and began boiling them for mashed potatoes and prepared a couple of fresh chickens (she had received them from her inlaws earlier that day) and started frying them. Margery added a leaf and set the table and husked a few ears of corn.

Just as expected the plane with our guests soon buzzed around above the house. We all went out and waved our arms broadly to welcome our guests. My dad went to the car and drove up the road to the air strip. Lois and Margery returned to the house to check on the dinner in preparation for the Holmes. Lois told Margery to get Jeane in the bath tub. There was only one full bath in the house which was adjacent to the kitchen. It was easy to keep an eye on her from the kitchen as she bathed and played in the water. Giving Jeane a bath early would make the bathroom available later for the guests.

Strangely, Myron soon returned in the car without the Holmes. He was puzzled because the plane was circling the air strip again and again but wouldn't land. The sun was down, and it was becoming darker with every minute that passed. He urgently told Lois to call another nearby air strip about ten miles away that had lights on their field and tell them to turn on their lights. Maybe the Holmes would see that strip and land there. He told Loron who was nineteen to get in his car and follow him back to the air strip. Loron could park his car at the south end of the strip and light the field with his headlights. Myron could park his car at the north end of the field near the road and shine his headlights on the field. Myron also had some flares to line along the side of the strip. In desperation Myron hoped to light the field so that his friends could land safely.

Lois and her daughters stayed home. They sensed that something was very wrong. So many times other flyers had landed with no problem. With fear in their hearts, they prayed. Eventually they heard in the distance what they were hoping could not be. It was sirens. As the blaring noise increased, they soon saw the Morrow Fire Department trucks roar by the house with a life squad (now called EMS) following. Their stomachs sank, and Lois began to cry. Margery fetched Jeane from the bath tub without dressing her, frantically getting her arms through the arm holes of her thick, white terry cloth robe. She whisked her up quickly into her arms and went out the door. Meanwhile Lois was getting the truck, and off they went up the road. As they traveled up the road, they turned the curve to see the flames and smoke from the accident. The Morrow Fire Department and the Lebanon Fire Department were frantically pouring water onto the wreckage. The fire was huge. After all, they had just refueled the plane. The fire was particularly difficult to extinguish because of exploding magnesium.

Lois parked the truck in the driveway of a house across the road. Jeane distinctly remembers being there "in just her robe".

They left her with stern commands to not move; stay there. Jeane was told, "Don't you dare leave the truck." Jeane sat there in horror watching the firemen run about with hoses attaching them to water tank trucks, spraying the fire and shouting to one another. As Jeane looked around, a bright flickering light danced on everything from the blaze of the fire as if it were day. Cars were lined along the road as far as one could see. People were gawking at the horrible event. Loron's '55 Chevy was at the far end of the air strip with its lights on. Myron's Oldsmobile was at the opposite end close to the wreckage with its lights on. Fortunately his car avoided damage from the flying debris of the fire. The airplane had wrecked in the adjacent field right before reaching the air strip. The plane had hit the power lines. Lois and Margery ran about until they found Myron. He had witnessed the crash and was first on the scene. He tried desperately to save them. He heard them screaming, and he tried to pull them from the crash, but the fire was too intense. His face was anguished with sadness, and his hands were burned. He cried out to Lois, "I told Don about the electric wires, and he hit them anyway. He said that he remembered. Why did he hit the wires?" Lois tried to comfort him to relieve him. As they looked about, they realized that there were live electric wires hanging near the road. The electric company needed to be informed before someone was accidently electrocuted. It appeared that no one in the house across the road was home, so Lois, Margery and Jeane returned home in the truck and called the electric company. Lois sat and cried.

It was past 10 o'clock before Myron and Loron returned home. In a frantic rush to leave the house, Lois had left the chicken on the stove on low heat. It was black from being over cooked. She asked with little hope of a reply if anyone was hungry. Myron took one look at the chicken and said sadly, "No. There's no way I could eat that. That's what they looked like when rescue workers pulled them from the wreckage." Lois cried.

Lois felt that relatives of the Holmes should be contacted, but she had no phone numbers and really didn't know who their closest relatives might be. She called their good friends, the Nortons, who were Flying Farmers in New York and gave them the task of reaching their family. Hopefully, they would contact other New York Flying Farmers if necessary, and together they would be able to reach the family with the news.

The back door swung open wide and in came some dear friends of Lois and Myron. It was Frank and Virginia Bolanger who lived in South Lebanon a few miles away. Frank was dressed, but Virginia was in her night gown, slippers and robe. Virginia was crying. They had heard the news that there was a plane crash at Maplewood Orchard. Virginia hugged Lois tightly and admitted through tears, "I thought it was you." Frank had told Virginia that Myron would never land over those power lines, but Virginia had to see for herself that the Bakers were alive and well.

Loron had nightmares for quite a while about the burning plane. It wasn't easy to forget what he had witnessed. It was hard to shake. In his nightmares he would see his father desperately trying to pull people from the flames of the airplane.

For many days there was a discussion at home and among friends about the crash. Why? Why? A conclusion was finally drawn from their discussions. Don must have suffered from some medical illness that prevented him from landing the plane after leaving the airport in Hamilton. Perhaps it was a heart attack or a stroke or a seizure. Ruth couldn't land the airplane. She probably attempted, but didn't have the skills. That was why the plane kept circling and circling above the field. It made Lois think. It made other women in the Flying Farmer group think, too. A crusade began to train women on how to land a plane. Many of the women went to flying instructors for lessons. The certificate they earned wasn't a license to fly. It was called a "Land-It". From then on about once a year, Lois would say to Myron as they approached their destination, "Let me land it. I want to practice." Myron would draw back his feet from the pedals and draw back his hands from the wheel. Lois would land it. Hold on. Usually it was a bumpy landing unlike the ever so smooth landing Myron made as they skimmed onto the runway. But it was a safe landing. It was one that might prevent a fatal crash and save their lives some day.

A few years later Loron married Dixie Amburgy whose home was also a few miles away near the Bolangers. She remembered hearing of the fatal crash, and her family drove to the scene on the night it happened.

About fifty-two years passed, and one day a car pulled into Loron's driveway at the Baker homestead. Bob Short, whose wife was the librarian in Morrow, appeared from one car. An unknown man and his grandson appeared. Bob introduced the man and his grandson. This man had graduated from the University of Missouri. He was retired from his profession as a veterinarian. He had traveled with his grandson and gone to the library in Morrow to seek information on his parent's death in 1958. All that he knew was that their plane had crashed at a friend's farm in Morrow, Ohio. When he asked the librarian about finding more information on the crash, she replied with surprise, "Oh, I remember that. I was fourteen and was a good friend of Margery Baker." She said that he should talk to Loron Baker. They talked of the fatal event, and Loron showed him the location of the crash. It was a somber conversation, but important. For him it was what he had wanted for a long time. It was closure.

The fatal crash was a tragic event that left a scar on the minds of many who were friends and relatives of the Holmes. As it is said so many times at such an incident, hopefully they died happy doing what they loved, flying among the clouds in their small plane. The silver lining to the cloud is that many spouses of pilots learned to land an airplane to prevent such a tragedy from happening again.

Newspaper article on front page of The Western Star, September 18, 1958

Trapped In Cabin After Craft Hits Wires, Bursts In Flames

An upper New York state couple, Mr. and Mrs. Donald F. Holmes died in the flaming wreckage of their single-engined, four-seated private plane Sunday evening along Stubbs Mills Rd. just south of Shawhan Rd. as they prepared to land at the home of Mr. and Mrs. Myron Baker for an overnight visit.

LHS Band Show Friday Honors U. S. Constitution

The Lebanon High School marching band will present a pageant of re-dedication to Our American Heritage at the Wilmington football game this Friday evening. Featured at the half time presentation will be the American Legion. The American Legion, Auxiliary, and the Veterans of Foreign Wars 'Auxiliary color guards. The half time activities are in observance of the 171st Anniversary of the adoption of the constitution by the congress.

The ninety member marching unit is under the direction of William Donovan. The head Drum Majorette is Ann Vest. The band officers are Douglas Corwin, president; William Hatfield, vice president; Carol Rufner, secretary; and Brenda Wilson Treasurer. Game time is 8 P.M. Friday.

The Holmeses apparently misjudged their altitude and distance from a landing strip on the Baker farm, striking utility wires along Stubbs Mills Rd. with the plane coming to rest nose up about 25 yards from the road. The craft burst into flame and was almost completely consumed by fire by the time the Morrow and Lebanon fire departments could arrive at the scene.

Mr. and Mrs. Holmes had been visiting friends in Iowa earlier Sunday and had flown into Hamilton to refuel, calling ahead to the Baker residence.

Mr. Baker placed flares along the landing strip.

The Holmes' plane arrived in the area just before dark, but started circling the area until after darkness had settled.

Then they began their descent, hitting the wires and crashing a short distance from the landing field.

The couple was trapped inside the burning wreckage as firemen battled the blaze and exploding magnesium for almost an hour.

Mr. and Mrs. Holmes were from Lawyersville, N.Y. a community of about 300 residents located miles west of Albany.

DOLLAR DAYS
The annual Lebanon Dollar Days celebration of the Retail

A BAKER IN CALIFORNIA

Charles Stanley Baker had a first cousin who lived in Chattanooga, Tennessee. His name was Warren Baker, the son of Jacob Baker, and he sold New York Life Insurance. He was quite a distinguished man and convinced several members of the family to buy insurance. Charlie's wife, Fairy, bought insurance for several members of the family as gifts especially at the birth of a child. Fairy bought a $1,000 policy for Loron. That was a generous gift. It concerned Loron when he thought of how hard his grandmother had to work in order to make the eighteen dollar monthly payments. Loron cashed his policy which was worth $18,000 when he purchased his first house in Morrow. Margery and Jeane also had a policy. Margery cashed her policy when her husband, a doctor, opened his medical office. She spent it on equipment. Jeane cashed her policy when she went to college.

Warren had three children, two girls and a boy. The boy was James Baker, and he eventually lived in Baton Rogue, Louisiana. One of his daughters was named Margaret and she was rather eccentric. Information on the other daughter is unknown.

Margaret graduated from college with a degree in interior design. At the time of her graduation, there were few jobs available in that field. She took a job working for Powell Crosley and became his personal secretary. Crosley was an inventor and a pioneer in broadcasting. Through his manufacturing of cars, appliances and radios and his creation of WLW radio and television, he became a millionaire. He also became the owner of the Cincinnati Reds profession baseball team. Along with her salary, Margaret earned a considerable amount of stock in the Crosley Corporation. Margaret remained single during her years of employment for Crosley. Crosley was married and had two children. However, some members of the family were suspicious that Margaret was also Crosley's mistress. Margaret would celebrate Christmas with the Baker family during this time at Charlie and Fairy's house. She worked for Powell Crosley until he retired. Margaret was independently wealthy and moved to California. She married a widower who had two young girls but never had children of her own.

Margaret built a beautiful home on the side of a mountain in a remote area in Concord near San Francisco. She loved the outdoors and had a large tall fence around her property to prevent the deer from entering and destroying the vegetation around her house. On one of Myron Baker's many trips, he and his wife, Lois, visited Margaret. Margaret graciously showed them around the city. She showed them many of the interesting attractions including the Golden Gate Bridge. She was a lovely host to her family guests.

Margery, Myron's daughter, moved to Arizona long after Margaret retired. Occasionally

Margery would be in the San Francisco area and would visit Margaret. She enjoyed their visits because Margaret was unique. Margaret traveled the world often and would have not pictures of her trip but mementos that she would show Margery. The last time that Margery saw Margaret, Margery ignored Margaret's generalization about older people not having a reason to live. A few months later Margery received a package from Margaret. In the package were many of the souvenirs Margaret had collected in her travels. At the time Margery thought that was very odd but thought nothing more even though Margery's mother-in-law was suspicious. Soon after the package arrived, Margery learned that Margaret had taken her own life. Margaret was eighty years old.

Stanley's 75th Birthday Left to Right:
Myron Baker, Alma Baker Harris, Warren "Stanley" Baker (Charlie's cousin), Lorena Baker Bellamy, Margaret Baker

FAMILY LIFE ON AN APPLE ORCHARD

In the 1950's my parents had settled into their own lifestyle. They had two active children, an apple business that was growing, a life in the community through various organizations, activities through the Methodist church and a means to travel, quenching my father's passion for flying. In the beginning of 1954 my mother became ill. In the coming summer she and my father would be forty years old. My brother would be fifteen and my sister would be ten years old. My mother couldn't keep food down, and there was a swelling of her abdomen. One might have thought she was pregnant, but she was still experiencing monthly menstrual periods. She went to the doctor fearing that there could be a tumor. Needless to say, to her own surprise as well as the whole family, she returned home from the doctor to announce that she was indeed pregnant. My sister was ecstatic for she had begged for a little sister for the last few years. My brother's response was, "Oh, no." The baby, who was me, was due at the end of the apple season. My mother continued to be sick throughout her pregnancy, getting by mostly with the only thing she could keep down, chocolate candy. Despite her illness, I was born at a healthy eight plus pounds. My hands were wrapped initially because I had no fingernails at birth which was attributed to my mother's lack of proper nourishment.

With older parents and older siblings I grew up somewhat like an only child in an adult environment. Living out in the country with no close neighbors prevented me from having lots of playmates. However, I was perfectly happy. In the winter months I played with dolls and toys. I loved to play my sister's records and sing along. My cat had kittens every spring which I played with throughout each summer. The foreman, who lived in the next house up the road, had a son just three weeks younger than me. Steven and I roamed the farm everyday that the weather allowed us to venture. Along with my grandfather's property across the road, we had about 250 acres to explore. There were creeks to wade in and logs to carefully walk on across the creeks, and plenty of apple trees which were perfect for climbing.

Jeane, sitting in the back with Steve Alderson.

One day Steven and I came in the back door of my house to get a drink on a hot day. I began to explain to my mom that Steven and I had explored every bit of the entire farm – the woods and creeks, the orchards and fields, the back forty acres, everything. I suggested to her that we should move to another farm so that there would be new places to explore. She found great humor in my request as she repeated my suggestion to my dad and close friends. I didn't understand the humor at the time. To a kid like me, it only sounded like a logical request.

Jeane and her sister, Margery.

When my sister, Margery was home from school, she gave me her full attention. We danced and sang, she dressed me up and when my parents weren't looking, she would eat the vegetables on my plate at supper. When I did something wrong, my sister would stand between me and my mother protesting my mother's punishment. She would say, "Hit me. Hit me. It won't hurt me. She's just a little girl!" My sister persuaded my parents to allow my crib to be in her room right beside her bed. She told them that they would get more sleep. She would be able to comfort me if I fussed in the night. What really happened is she simply took me out of the crib when she went to bed and snuggled with me in her double bed. I adored my sister. At times, my mother would be annoyed when she put out her arms to pick me up because I would chose to embrace my sister instead. My sister took me everywhere with her. When she hung out the laundry to dry, I was in the basket of clothes. I even went on dates with her when she was in high school. When she was in nursing school, she took me to a Reds baseball game. She took me to Coney Island. She took me to several Broadway shows in Cincinnati. We have always been very close.

My mother would tend to household chores during the day. Like most moms during that time, she didn't have a job outside of the home. Occasionally she would don her white stockings, white uniform and her little white RN cap from Christ Hospital Nursing School and be a private nurse for a sick relative or friend. Off she would go to a hospital many times saying that she didn't know when she would return. She might be gone overnight. My father could only prepare pancakes, so that's what we would have for supper in mother's absence. When polio became widespread, she went to Columbus to attain enough vaccine for the community and organized other nurses to give the immunizations at the school to the general public. Nursing was a means of service rather than an occupation for her. The only time she worked as a nurse was at the county fair for a few days and at the local Girl Scout camp for two weeks in the summer. I went with her to each place and had such fun.

My father would work most of the time on machinery while the employees worked in the fields and orchards. There was always something in need of repair between three trucks, eight tractors and the apple equipment. He was a distributor of spray material for fruit trees. After supper he would sometimes make a delivery to another fruit grower. As soon as I was old enough, I would go along. I would be very attentive as we traveled home for if I saw a dairy bar, I would say, "Shake, Daddy, shake!" I was sure of getting a chocolate milkshake with him. He loved ice cream and milkshakes. In the evening before taking a bath, my father would hold me and help me take off my shoes and socks. He would tickle my toes. As I grew older, when I would perform or sing, tears of pride would collect in his eyes.

My mother and father were very social. They would meet friends in Morrow for a fish fry or just go to visit friends. Obviously, this was not during the busy season. Being around friends made them happy. Traveling and socializing with Flying Farmer friends made them even happier. Occasionally after supper we would go to a friend's house or my parents would invite someone over. Farmers had time to spare in the winter on week nights. Their other friends with regular jobs would get together on the weekends. They would sit around the kitchen table and talk, laugh and drink beer. They all smoked cigarettes until about 1960. That's when the American Medical Association announced that smoking could cause lung cancer. Many stopped smoking including my mother. My dad had more trouble kicking the habit. He would smoke off and on and in time smoked a pipe. Most of their friends had children older than me, so I would watch television and eventually fall asleep on the couch. Once again I was perfectly content. One set of friends didn't drink alcohol, so my mother would bake an apple pie, make coffee and have them over. My mother made the best apple pies. If they didn't socialize in the evening, my parents would bicker. When my sister-in-law met them, she thought for sure they would get a divorce. We kids were used to it. It was never upsetting to us. It was always about some trivial thing. My father might leave something on the kitchen table. My mother would pick it up and move it or throw it away. He would yell at her, and she would yell at him. He might leave his shoes in the living room. She would yell at him and he would yell back. Many nights I fell asleep upstairs to the sound of them yelling. It's just what they did.

On a hot summer day my father would come in for supper around six. He would go in the bathroom, take off his work shirt and wash. He used a bar of Lava soap which had tiny grains of sand in it making it good for scrubbing. He would scrub and scrub at his hands, face and arms. Then he would come to the table with his sleeveless undershirt on. My mother would have a fit because he didn't have a shirt on. She would yell at him, and he would yell at her until she went upstairs and brought down a clean shirt for him to wear at the table. On one occasion the sweet corn was plentiful, and we had lots of vegetables from the garden. My mother invited their close friends, the Bolangers, for dinner along with my brother, his wife and two children. We were all seated at the table chatting and enjoying the fresh food. My father had come in and scrubbed then sat at the table in his undershirt. My mother started yelling about his appearance at the table in front of guests. He ignored her and said something like, "Pass the sliced tomatoes." My mother left the table and went in the bathroom. She came out wearing no shirt, in her bra and sat at the table. My father didn't bat an eye. We looked at her in disbelief. Frank Bolanger raised his hands before his face and said, "I'm not going to look, Lois. I'm not going to look!" Virginia said, "What are you doing?!" My mother said in a flippant way, "If he's going to eat dinner in his underwear, so am I." And so it was. To this day we occasionally talk about how much my parents fought and laugh about them eating in their underwear!

The Cincinnati Enquirer/Michael E. Keating

Myron and Lois Baker with daughter Jean Weisbrod and grandson Richard.

I remember going to town with my mother once, and while we were in a store, someone approached my mom to say our car horn was blowing. Sure enough, totally on its own, the horn was blaring. A few days later the same thing happened to my father when he was in town. He simply detached the connecting wire on the horn, plugged it back in, and it was fine. He did work on it when he came home, and thought he had the problem solved. A few days later in the middle of the night, the car horn sounded while it was parked in the barn. In the darkness I could hear my parents talking before I heard my father go down the stairs and out the back door. The horn continued to blow and blow for a long time. It finally stopped, and I heard the hood on the car slam shut. Then I heard my father come in the back door and up the stairs. I could clearly hear my mother say, "What's going on? Why did it take so long?" Now one would think that if you slept in the nude, you would put on some pants and shoes before going out. Not my dad. His reply to my mother was, "I couldn't reach to pull the wire without leaning on the car. The car is very, very cold!" I buried my face in my pillow and giggled. And, the next day he took the car to a mechanic.

I'm not sure why the orchard received so much publicity. Many times the Cincinnati or Dayton newspaper would write an article about Maplewood Orchard naturally in the fall. Often a magazine would write an article about our apple business. My dad often went to the Cincinnati radio station, WLW, for an interview. The local news would show a clip about the apple harvest at Maplewood Orchard. I suppose the novelty of the apple business was unique. It was a seasonal thing or perhaps my father with his charisma was easy to interview. Once when

Jeane as the flower girl at her brother's wedding with Blaine Amburgy

Jeane with her niece, Kathy

my father was interviewed on a local television show, the interviewer commented that my father probably loved apple pie. My father's reply was that he "much preferred cherry". Later, my mother scolded him for being so honest. He should have told a white lie!

In all of the time while growing up, I never felt that I was privileged or better off. Yes, we were on television or in newspapers and magazines. I thought nothing of it. Yes, we had an airplane. Others had boats and campers. However, we didn't live in a luxurious home. We lived in an old farm house with one bath that had no shower. My father claimed that the cistern couldn't provide enough water for us to all take showers. To me, I was a kid simply living an average life. Only as an adult did I see my life as being far different from one who grew up in the suburbs or other farm kids.

My brother went off to college when I was three. I don't really remember him being at home.

When I was six, he was married, and I was the flower girl. By the time I was seven, Loron and his wife, Dixie, had a baby girl. I loved being called Aunt Jeane. They lived across the road for a couple of years in a small, rather primitive house that had been a rental. Later they moved to Morrow. In the first two years it was so convenient for me to go and play with the baby. I was so excited two years later when they had a baby boy. On holidays and when we visited, I had the treat of playing with little children. I was a built-in babysitter as they grew older, and I grew older. Their children, Kathy and Ty, became more like the siblings, something I truly never had. Often in the spring and summer, my parents would go away for a couple of days to attend a flying meeting. I would be left at my brother's house giving me another opportunity to play with my niece and nephew. Sometimes I stayed at the foreman's house or occasionally at my Great Uncle John's house in the suburbs of Columbus. I was always happy to go and stay with other people in their house. To me it was like a mini adventure.

By the time I was seven, my sister went off to college. By then I had my own friends at school, but I still missed her. The retail apple business was increasing considerably at this point. The whole family would work at the market on the weekends in the fall. I loved the fall with all the hustle and activity of harvesting. Sometimes after school I would go out to the barn and help on the apple grader or simply talk to the employees.

In junior high and high school I became involved in chorus and cheerleading. I possibly could have been on the track team, for I could run fast. In those days girls could be nominated for track queen, but they couldn't run track. Sports were more male oriented. I was the stereo-typical cheerleader that dated the quarterback in high school and found high school to be a tremendous joy. Just as my whole family was active in their life, I was very active in school. I sang in several small groups as well as in the chorus. One small group was called "Folksingers". We never used written music. We simply played the piano and two guitars and sang songs that we liked or that our music teacher suggested. We performed for various civic groups especially at Christmas. We also performed for criminals at the local prison which was rather eerie. We tried out for live shows at Kings Island at the end of my junior year. We made the cut and spent the following summer singing away. After an extremely active summer of working, preparation for and going to cheerleading camp, dating and being with friends, I was diagnosed with mono at the beginning of my senior year. I slept around the clock for six weeks before gradually returning to school. Not only did I miss school and most of the football season, but I missed the beginning of probably the last year I would be home for apple season. In the spring of my senior year, the music teacher decided to present a musical. With an ROTC program in the school, South Pacific was the perfect choice for a musical. The costumes for the military actors were right there. I played the leading female role of Nellie Forbush and did it with gusto!

When my sister and I were young, my mother encouraged us to be nurses as she was. My sister followed her suggestion and became a registered nurse and then later earned a college degree in nursing. Between my mother and my sister, I was often encouraged to be a nurse, too. I wasn't receptive to the idea. Finally my mother gave up on the idea of a nursing career and encouraged me to be a teacher. A teaching career I could handle – no blood, needles and sick people! After my experiences in singing and performing, many suggested that I seek a degree in music education. I auditioned and was accepted into the music school at a small college, Wittenberg University in Springfield, Ohio.

During this time period, festivals were popping up in every small community. Locally there was a wine festival in Morrow, a honey festival in Lebanon and a sauerkraut festival in Waynesville. Included in their events, every festival crowned a queen. The state commodities decided to join in by having a queen. At the time my father was involved in the Ohio State Horticulture Society. That group sponsored a state apple queen contest. I was chosen as the Ohio Apple Queen after graduating from high school.

I traveled across the state to various festivals and was given special recognition in the parade at the Johnny Appleseed Festival and the Ohio Apple Festival. There was also a contest among the commodity queens at the Ohio State Fair. It might seem a bit absurd to be the apple queen, but believe me, it was far more appealing than being the tomato queen or, heaven forbid, the pork queen!

The pageant was scheduled on the main stage right before a popular African American recording artist was to perform. Thousands of spectators for the concert were in the crowd making it difficult for my family to get anywhere near the stage. The crowd was anxious and rocking to hear the famous singer. The Ohio Boxing Queen, who was African American, was crowned as the Ohio State Fair Queen. A National Apple Queen contest was held in Pennsylvania as well in the fall which I attended. I soon realized that it was a contest of beauty over brains when Miss North Carolina answered one of her questions stating there were three varieties of apples – red, green and yellow. She was very attractive and was chosen as the national queen. I didn't stand a chance in either contest. I was the wrong race, and I wasn't a beauty.

With all of my experiences in performing and speaking, having perfect pitch and a few years of piano lessons, it wasn't enough to make me successful as a music major in college. I flunked the first quarter of college. I had no background in music theory or classical music as the other students had. Many of the other music students played several instruments. I changed my major to elementary education. That horrible first quarter I cried myself to sleep most nights. I came home at Thanksgiving and watched my college football team on television win

the division III national game. Now that was exciting. When I returned to campus, I asked my advisor if being on academic probation would prevent me from trying out for cheerleading. For the next three years I cheered for Wittenberg University. Yes, I fearlessly did flips in the air after standing on the shoulders of guy cheerleaders among other acrobatic stunts. I was invincible. Lots of traveling

in the eastern U.S. was involved as the football and basketball teams would advanced to state, district and national levels. In those three years the football team won another national title and the basketball team won two national titles. It was time consuming. I was motivated to study every free moment I had, and gradually I brought my grade point average above a 3.0 before graduation.

Miss Jean Baker

My father served on the local school board for many years. For several years he and my mother attended the national school board convention and became acquainted with many school administrators. One of those administrators was at St. Bernard Schools right outside the city limits of Cincinnati. That's where I got my first teaching job out of college. Within the boundaries of the district were the factories of the Proctor and Gamble Company. Because the tax revenue from the company was great, the schools were on the cutting edge, physically and academically. The student teacher ratio was sixteen to one, and the staff was the best. The elementary building won an architectural award with its open classrooms and large stainless steel slides that the students used as they went down from one floor to a lower floor. Within a year I was working with the music teacher to produce a student variety show annually. I had some of my best teaching years at St. Bernard Elementary. While I was teaching, I also worked at the orchard in the fall.

During this time period I met my husband, Chuck Weisbrod, and we were married. We moved to Madeira, a suburb of Cincinnati, Ohio, where my husband had grown up. He was a mechanical engineer, and his family owned their own engineering business. His mother worked for the business one day a week taking the responsibility of accounts payable. The company was doing well. After I had taught for five years, I resigned. His mother had decided to retire, and I took her position. We had two children, Susan and Richard, in the next few years. I was delighted with my part time job at the office and working at the orchard in the fall. I loved being a mom and having time to spend with my kids as they grew. Chuck became active in the community and served as mayor for two years.

As businesses in Cincinnati began to change or relocate, the family engineering company was suffering. General Electric no longer built jet engines in Cincinnati which had supported a portion of the local businesses. Health insurance costs increased drastically around the same time. Our family went for a few years with no health insurance because we simply couldn't afford it. I picked up a part time job at a nearby nursery school to help with our expenses. By the time our youngest child entered second grade, I realized that I needed to go back to a full time teaching job with benefits. I had been fortunate enough to be home with my young children for several years.

As I was interviewing at Loveland City Schools, the middle school principle noticed on my college transcript that I had taken several music classes. Obviously he didn't see the failing grades! The school was growing rapidly but not enough to hire another full time music teacher. I was hired to teach chorus, math and language arts the following year which was quite a challenge. For the next nineteen years I taught only language arts before retiring. I continued to work at the orchard in the fall on the weekends until my kids were involved in sporting events on the weekend. I didn't want to miss being a spectator while they played soccer or ran in cross country meets.

Twelve years after I had gone back to teaching (1999), my father died of heart failure. When he died, Maplewood Orchard died, too. The business was not nearly as encompassing as it had once been in the 1960's and 1970's. The retail market was going strong along with the wholesale cider business. "Pick Your Own Apples" and hayrides were popular. A big problem was it was nearly impossible to hire employees who would pick apples. Some of the orchards on the farm were left unattended and soon grew up in weeds and saplings. My father bought apples to resell from orchards in Indiana, Ohio and sometimes Michigan. My brother's family members had kept the retail business going as my father had aged.

After my father's death, my mother moved to a retirement community nearby and lived for another eleven years. The apple trees were bulldozed, and the acreage was leased for growing soy beans or corn. She sold forty acres in order to pay for her expenses. She never expected to live to be ninety-six!

When both of my parents had died, the farm was divided between my brother, my sister and me. My sister was well established in Phoenix, Arizona for she had moved there in the 1970's. She sold the third of the acreage which she inherited. On that property the apple barn still stands, but the house we grew up in was dilapidated and therefore razed by the new owners. My brother already lived in our grandfather's house, and he inherited acreage around his house. My kids were grown and off on their own far from home when I inherited a third of the acreage. My husband and I decided to build a house on our property and move. Just as we were about to move in our new house, I was diagnosed with breast cancer. It was difficult to grasp because I appeared to be so healthy. It was a hardship to move while enduring the effects of chemo therapy. My niece from Phoenix, Elizabeth, came to help us move. What a blessing. Other family members, especially Dixie, and friends from Madeira helped me with meals and transportation in the coming months. I survived surgery and a year after moving I could finally enjoy my new home. The setting of our house is so picturesque. It stands right beside one of the ponds that my father built several decades ago when he was an aspiring young man, anxious to plant more apple trees. The surrounding area is more developed than when I was a child, but it's still in the country. We love our new home. One might say I have returned to my roots.

This is the land that was once owned by the Stubbs, the Worleys, the Watkins and the Bakers. Each family came here from afar with not much more than a wagon and the clothes on their back. They bought and farmed the land and provided a service to others through their mills, hotels and blacksmith skills. Nothing was given to them. They earned it through their labor in a country that offered them life, liberty and the pursuit of happiness. They had such courage as they forged their way into an unknown land and into new business ventures. I am grateful for my ancestors who wrote down their family history. It is a true blessing to have and an honor to pass on their stories, bits of their lives.

This is not the end. As we live and have families, the story continues. We are all in the midst of our life, working and pursuing our happiness. Yes, indeed, we all have a story to tell. That's not all we have. We all have a place from where we came.

APPENDICES

STUBBS APPENDIX

The Stubbs Family Tree – England

William of Stubbing 1280 - ?

William of Stubbing 1312 – 1360 b Stubbing, Yorkshire

William Stubbe 1339 – 1393 b Rawmarsh, Yorkshire

John Stubbe 1367 – 1414 b Birstwuth, N. Yorkshire

William Stubbs 1392 - 1430 b Birstwith, N. Yorkshire

Thomas of Birstwith Stubbe 1421 – 1489
m Matilda ?
Thomas of Birstwith Stubbe 1442 – 1514

William Stubbe 1480 – 1550 b Norfolk

Thomas Stubbe 1507 - 1557 b Gloucestershire

Thomas Stubbe 1535 - 1604 b Staverton

William Stubbs 1576 – 1645 b Staverton, England
m Julia Trenton 1582 – 1639 *6 children*
William Stubbs 1606 – 1681 b Stavertonshire, England
"William Captain of the Horse Royal Army"
m Alice Hullnos 1618-1655 *7 children*
Daniel Stubbs 1646 – 1719 b Eldersfield, England
m Mary Neast 1649 - 1719 *8 children*
Thomas Stubbs 1692 – 1763 died Kennett, PA,
British Colonial America
m Mary Minor 1692 – 1745 *9 children*
1. **Joel Stubbs** 1715 – 1746
2. **Daniel Stubbs** 1722 – 1808
3. **William Penn Stubbs** 1723 - 1773
4. **Martin Stubbs** 1724 - ?
5. **Ann Stubbs** 1729 – 1774
6. **John Stubb**s 1732 – 1803
m **Ester Maddock** 1733 – 1786
7. **Sarah Stubbs** 1734 – 1776
8. **Joseph Stubbs** 1736 – 1770
9. **Thomas Stubbs Jr.** 1738 – 1769

The Stubbs Family Tree

Thomas Stubbs 1695 - 1763 Born in England
   m Mary Minor in Chester Co., PA
   John Stubbs 1732- 1803
      m Esther Maddock 1733-1786 *14 children*
       Isaac Stubbs I 1761 – 1838
      m Margaret Carter 1766 – 1805 6 children
        I. **John Stubbs** 1785 – 1853
          m Rhoda Whitcomb *10 children*
          1. **Huldah Stubbs** 1815 - ?
            m Silas White
          2. **Zimri Stubbs** 1816 – 1873
            m Mary Masterson
          3. **Margaret Stubbs** 1817 - 1877
            m Thomas Eaglesfield
          4. **Mary Stubbs** 1822 - 1852
            m ? Shurts
          5. **James Stubbs** 1823 - ?
          6. **Joshua Stubbs** 1825 - 1906
          7. **Elizabeth Stubbs** 1827 - 1863
            m Jacob Emeirson
          8. **Isaac Stubbs** 1829 - 1884
          9. **Anthony Stubbs** 1833 - ?
          10. **Emma Stubbs**
            m ? Hanch

        II. **Samuel Stubbs** 1790 – 1875
          m Rachel Whitacre 1799 – 1858 *9 children*
          1. **Harvey Stubbs** 1820 - 1891
          2. **Eliza Stubbs** 1823 - 1915
            m Edward Smith 1817 - 1874 *5 children*
            A. **Samuel Smith**
            B. **Elizabeth Smith**
            C. **Emma Smith**
              m George Diebold
            D. **William Smith**
            E. **Edward Smith**
              m Olive Mount
          3. **Isaac Stubbs** 1826 - ?
            m Emma Kelly *1 child*
            A. **Laura Stubbs**
          4. **Benjamin Stubbs** 1828 – 1849
          5. **Jonas Stubbs** 1828 - ?
          6. **Isaac W. Stubbs** 1832 - ?
          7. **M Sarah Hufford** 1841 – 1866
          8. **Jonas W. Stubbs** 1832 – 1903

m Elizabeth Pearson 1839 - 1922 *7 children*
- A. **Horace Stubbs** 1858 - 1899
  - m Mary Smith
- B. **Ernest Stubbs** 1860 - 1890
- C. **Charles Stubbs** 1862 - 1924
  - m Minnie Gerlach
- D. **Caroline Stubbs** 1865 - 1941
  - m Joseph Long
- E. **Clifford Stubbs** 1867 - 1943
  - m Gabriella Robb
- F. **Edward Stubbs** 1873 - 1961
  - m Caroline Benham
- G. **Stephen Stubbs** 1875 - ?
  - m Margaret Brown
8. **Margaret Stubbs** 1836 - ?
  m John Tyler Baker 1838 - ? *2 children*
  - A. **Florence Baker**
  - B. **Frank Baker**
9. **Rachel Stubbs** 1838 - 1903
  m Clarkson Kelly 1843 - 1917

III. **Isaac Stubbs II** 1793 – 1874
m Elizabeth Sherwood 1809 - 1872 *5 children*
1. **Margaret Stubbs** 1840 - 1921
2. **Darcus Stubbs** 1842 – 1843
3. **Albert Stubbs** b 1844 - 1914
  m Eunice Hufford
4. **Samuel Stubbs** 1847 – 1848
5. **Isaac Stubbs III** 1850 – 1882
  m Eunice Hollingsworth 1849 – 1892 *2 children*
  - A. **Sarah (Sallie) Stubbs** 1877 – 1957
    - m Alva J. Patrick *1 child*
  - B. **Elizabeth (Bessie) Stubbs** 1882 – 1921
    - m Harry L. Kneisly *1 child*

IV. **Zimri Stubbs** 1797 - 1883
m Mary Irons 1807 – 1878 *14 children*
1. **Rebecca Stubbs** 1828 – 1832
2. **Achsa Stubbs** 1830 – 1918
  m Stewart Brown
3. **Martha Stubbs** 1831 - 1931
4. **Amasa Stubbs** 1832 – 1902
  m Ann Nixon
5. **Abram Stubbs** 1934 – 1901
  m Monroe Wilkerson
6. **Jane Stubbs** 1836 - 1913
  m John Worley 1832 - 1859 *2 children*

A. **Althe Worley** 1860 - 1936
   m Clinton Watkins 1861 - 1934 *7 children*
   1. **Fairy Watkins** 1882 - 1958
       m Charles Stanley Baker *2 children*
       I. **Lorena Baker** 1903 - 1980
           m Bill Bellamy *3 children*
       II. **Myron Baker** 1914 - 1999
           m Lois Hartman 3 children
   2. **Arthur John Watkins** 1885 - 1968 m Hariet Ramsey
       m Mina Burd
   3. **Jane Watkins** 1886 - 1967
       m Hal Brant
   4. **Blanche Watkins** 1888 - 1978
       m Ford Sanford
   5. **Stanley Watkins** 1892 - 1968
       m Mary Connor
   6. **Adarene Watkins** 1892 - 1977
       m Leon Hunter
   7. **Catheryn Watkins** 1898 - 1954
       m George Dugan
B. **Zimri O. Worley** 1865 – 1954
   m Martha Kratzer
   m Della Vanriper 1873 – 1931 *2 children*
   m Amy Vanriper 1867 – 1937
   1. **John Worley** 1891 – 1968
   2. **S. Glenn Worley** 1897 - 1956
7. **Eden Stubbs** 1838 - 1838
8. **Mary Stubbs** 1839 - ?
   m Jasper Wilkerson
9. **Noah Stubbs** 1841 – 1926
   m Lavicae Glazier
10. **Abiah Stubbs** 1843 - ?
11. **Samuel Stubbs** 1844 – 1937
    m. Letitia Bush 1847 - 1925 *8 children*
    1. **Edward Stubbs** 1869 - ?
    2. **Horace Stubbs** 1871 - 1923
    3. **Laura Stubbs** 1872 - 1959
    4. **Oscar Stubbs** 1874 - ?
    5. **William Stubbs** 1877 - ?
    6. **Wilbur Stubbs** 1879 - 1959
    7. **Alberta "Allie" Stubbs** 1881 – 1911
    8. **Zimri Stubbs** 1881 - 1949
12. **Milton Stubbs** 1846 – 1847
13. **Quincy Stubbs** 1847 – 1937
    m Martha Washington Young *1 child*
    1. **Clara Stubbs**
14. **Harriet Stubbs** 1852 - 1930

m Alonzo Burns

V. **Achsah Stubbs** 1800 – 1840
   m Samuel Kelly *3 children*
   1. **Hannah Kelly**
   2. **Anna Kelly**
   3. **Isaac Kelly**

VI. **Hannah Stubbs** 1802 – 1840
   m Jacob Doan *2 children*
   1. **Mary Ann Doan**
     m Riley Nixon
   2. **Jemima Doan**
     m Ferguson

Myron Baker is my father.

Fairy Watkins Baker is my grandmother.

Althe Worley Watkins is my great grandmother.

Jane Stubbs Worley is my great-great grandmother.

Zimri Stubbs is my great-great-great grandfather.

Isaac Stubbs I is my great-great-great-great grandfather.

John Stubbs is my great-great-great-great-great grandfather.

Thomas Stubbs is my great-great-great-great-great grandfather.

Genealogy of the Stubbs family, not signed, but believed to be completed by John Watkins in the late 1940's or early 1950's as it references Blanche Sanford (his sister) as living in the Stubbs homestead. She sold the house in the 1950's.

ORIGIN OF THE STUBBS FAMILY IN OHIO.

Thomas Stubbs came from England to Chester, Pa. in 1718. Thomas Stubbs was born in England in 1695, and died 1763. In 1720 he married Mary Minor. They belonged to Kenneth Square Friends Church. This building of 1716 still stands near Philadelphia, Pa. John Stubbs, son of Thomas, moved to North Carolina, thence to Georgia, where he died in 1803. John Stubbs married Esther Maddock, daughter of Joseph Maddock and Rachel Dennis. John Stubbs' will is in court-house at Appling, Ga.

He had 14 children of which 13 came to Ohio and Indiana including Isaac Stubbs and his oldest brother Nathan Stubbs.

On November 17, 1784, Isaac Stubbs married Margaret Carter, daughter of Samuel Carter and Mary Barnes at Cane Creek, N. C.

On coming to Warren County, Ohio, Isaac Stubbs and wife settled near Waynesville, where he engaged in the milling business, in 1804.

As the years passed, a number of mills for the manufacture of flour, lumber, paper, woolen goods and whiskey were built along the Little Miami River. He and his sons were interested in several of them, of which were mills at Millgrove, Freeport (now Oregonia), Stubbs Mills, 2½ miles below the mouth of Todd's Fork, Deerfield (now South Lebanon) and Gainesboro (now Kings Mills).

In 1804 Isaac Stubbs built the mill at Millgrove. About 1812 to 1815 he built in Millgrove the house, now occupied by his great-grandson, Zimri O. Worley. Isaac Stubbs later moved to point 2½ miles below Fredericksburg, and purchased the Flour-Mill, Saw-Mill and Woolen-Mill, built by Jabish Phillips in 1801. He operated the mills for many years, they being known as Stubbs' Mills. Later the management was taken over by his son, Zimri Stubbs, who operated it for a number of years. Near this mill, Isaac Stubbs built, in 1822, a fine brick home, which at this time is still occupied by one of his descendants, Mrs. John F. Sanford, a great-great-grand-daughter.

Isaac Stubbs and his sons were for many years interested in the operation of the following :

Millgrove Mills, consisting of a flour mill, paper mill and the conducting of a general store. These mills were built in 1804. He disposed of them in 1819. The flour mill was operated from 1819 to 1835 by Thomas Kephart. Afterward it passed into various hands, the last of which being Charles Nixon, when it ceased operation.

Jabish Phillips Mills, consisting of a flour-mill, Saw-mill and Woolen-Mill, after being operated by Mr. Phillips short time, passed into the control of Samuel McCray, who continued it's operation until 1819, when Isaac Stubbs took over the management. He and his son, Zimri, operated these mills until 1860. From 1860 to 1867 they were under the management of William C. Nixon, after which they again returned to the management of Zimri Stubbs, and then into the hands of his sons, Samuel and Quincy Stubbs. Grinding was done in the the flour mill until 1897, when flood waters so badly damaged the machinery of both the flour and saw-mills , that futher operation was discontinued. The Woolen-mill ceased operation in 1860 and was dismantled.

Wood's Mill, built in 1799, by William Wood at Gainesboro,
                Ohio, (now Kings Mill), who operated it for
                a number of years, disposed of it to Hunt &
                Lowe, by whom it was operated for many years.
                It later became the property of Isaac Stubbs,
                who managed it for a time.   The Isaac Stubbs
                estate sold to A & J.W.King in 1877, who con-
                vetted the property into a plant for the man-
                ufacture of blasting and gun-powder, and es-
                tablished " Kings Great Western Powder Works."

Nebo Gauntt's Mill, built in 1804, in Freeport, (now Ore-
                gonia) Ohio. This mill was destroyed by fire
                in 1852. Before its destuction by fire it
                passed from Mr. Gauntt to the ownership of
                Judge Ignatius Brown and David Brown. A large
                frame building was erected in Freeport in 1844
                to be used for a paper mill; but was not used
                for that purpose.   After the Gauntt Mill was
                burned in 1852, Isaac Stubbs, a son of Isaac
                Stubbs,Sr. moved the machinery from the old
                Whitehall Mill, on the Warren County Canal,
                three miles west of Lebanon, to the frame build-
                in Freeport, and established a flour-mill un-
                der the name of Stubbs & Sherwood. This mill
                continued under their management until 1873,
                when it passed into the hands of Isaac Stubbs'
                sons, Albert and Isaac Stubbs. In 1880 Isaac
                purchased his brother's share and operated it
                for five years when Albert Stubbs again became
                the owner.   In 1903 he sold the mill to Spen-
                cer & Monroe. It was later destroyed by fire
                and was not rebuilt.

An item in " History of Warren County " is noted where Isaac
Stubbs, in 1810, successfully petitioned for a road to be con-
structed from his mill in Millgrove, via Salem (now Roachester)
, Todd's Fork, Second Creek, to Goodpastures, on First Creek, to
intersect with the road from McCray(s Mill to the Salt Works, via
First Creek and Rossburg.

        Another item of interest is that John Stubbs and Isaac Stubbs
were members of a committee to finish the upper part of the Friends
Meeting House in Waynesville, Ohio, in the year 1813.

        Nathan Stubbs, Oldest brother of Isaac Stubbs,1st. also
came from Georgia, and settled on Paint Creek, near West Elkton,
Preble County, Ohio. Many descendants have issued from Nathan
a complete record of which has not as yet been perfected.

X

The union of Isaac Stubbs and Margaret Carter, who were foundation of the Stubbs name in Warren County, and were pioneers in settlement and development of The county#; and were pillars in the Quaker Church and of society in the community wherein they lived, furnished the following issue:-

Samuel Stubbs	- who married -	Rachel Whitacre
Zimri Stubbs	- who Married -	Mary B. Iorns, in 1827
Hannah Stubbs	- who married -	Jacob Doan, in 1822
Isaac Stubbs	- who married -	Elizabeth Sherwood, in 1838
Achsa Stubbs	- who married -	Samuel Kelly, in 1828
John Stubbs	- who married -	

The original marriage contract, as consumated between Isaac Stubbs, Jr. and Elizabeth Sherwood, in the Friends Church, and signed by the congregation of that church, is now a keepsake in the hands of their great-grandson George Stubbs, of Lebanon, Ohio.

2nd. Gen.   The union of Samuel Stubbs and Rachel Whitacre furnished the following issue:

Eliza Stubbs	- who married -	Ned Smith
Harvey Stubbs	- who never married.	
Isaac Stubbs	- who married -	Emma Kelly
Margaret Stubbs	- who married -	Tyler Baker
Jonas W. Stubbs	- who married -	Elizabeth Pierson.
Rachel Stubbs	- who married -	Clarkson Kelly

The union of Zimri Stubbs and Mary B. Iorns furnished the following issue:

Rebecca Stubbs	- Died when 2 yrs. Old .
Achsa Stubbs	- who married - Steward Brown
Martha Stubbs	- Died when 2 months old.
Amasa Stubbs	- who married - Ann Nixon
Abiah Stubbs	- who married - Monroe Wilkerson
Jane Stubbs	- who married - John Worley
Eden Stubbs	- Died when 5 months old.
Mary Stubbs	- who married - Jasper Wilkerson
Noah Stubbs	- who married - Lovicae Glosier
Samuel Stubbs	- who married - Letitia Bush
Milton Stubbs	- Died when 1 year old.
Quincy Stubbs	- who married - Martha Young
Sidney Stubbs	- Died when 4 years old.
Harriet M. Stubbs	-who married - Alonzo Burns.

The union of Hannah Stubbs and Jacob Doan furnished the following issue:

| Mary Ann Doan | - who married - Riley Nixon. |
| Jemima Doan | - who married   Ferguson. |

The union of Isaac Stubbs and Elizabeth Sherwood furnished the following issue:

| Albert Stubbs | - who married - | Eunice Hufford |
| Isaac Stubbs | - who married - | Eunice Hollingsworth |

4

The union of Achsa Stubbs and Samuel Kelly furnished the following issue :-

    Hannah Kelly - who never married
    Anna Kelly   - who never married
    Isaac Kelly   - who never married

The union of John Stubbs and   furnished the following issue:

    Hulday Stubbs - who married -   White
    Margaret Stubbs-who married -   Eaglesfield
    Zimri Stubbs - who married -
    Mary Stubbs - who married -   Shurts
    James Stubbs - who never married
    Joshua Stubbs - who never married
    Elizabeth Stubbs- who married-   Fuqua
    Isaac Stubbs - who never married.
    Anthony Stubbs- who never married.
    Emma Stubbs   - who married -   Hanch.

Zimri Stubbs was born at Wrightsboro, Columbia County, Ga. November 23, 1797, died March 31, 1884. He was married May 27, 1827 to Mary B. Iorns, who was born near Ellisburg, Gloucester County, N. J. on August 29, 1807, and died July 26, 1878.

There are thirty-nine in the Stubbs family grave-yard on the old Stubbs Homestead at Stubbs Mills, near Morrow, Warren County, Ohio.

3rd.
Gen.

The union Eliza Stubbs and Neddie Smith furnished the following issue:

    Samuel Smith - who married -   in Clay Center, Kan.
    Elizabeth Smith- who never married.
    Emma Smith   - who married - George Diebold .
    William Smith - who never married.
    Edward Smith - who married Olive Mount.

The Union of Isaac Stubbs and Emma Kelly furnished the following issue:

    Laura Stubbs - who married - I. J. Jeffries.

The union of Margaret Stubbs and Tyler Baker furnished the following issue:

    Florence Baker - who married -   in Excelsior Springs.M
    Frank Baker   - who married   in Ness City, Kans.

The union of Jonas W. Stubbs and Elizabeth Pierson furnished the following issue:

    Horace Stubbs - who married - Mary E. Smith
    Ernest Stubbs - who never married.
    Charles Stubbs - who married - Minnie Gerlach
    Caroline Stubbs- who married - Joseph A. Long   Lucinda Stubbs
    Clifford J. Stubbs- who married- Gabriella Robb   died
    Edward F. Stubbs-who married - Caroline Benham   Unmarried.

Children of Zimri Stubbs (1797—1883) and Mary Irons (1807-1878)

*Harriet Stubbs (1853—) with husband,
Alonzo Burns. She is the sister of Mary
(pictured bottom of page.)*

*Samuel Stubbs, teacher at the
Washington School, corner of Trovillo
and Stubbs Mill, January 15, 1900. He
is the grandson of Zimri. His father was
Samuel (1844—1937).*

*Mary Stubbs Wilkerson (1839—) married
Jasper Wilkerson. She is the sister of Harriet.*

Copper stencil used to mark flour sacks from the Stubbs Mill.
This was found near the Little Miami River at Stubbs Mill Road.
(Stencil owned by a private collector)

Note the mention of "scantling". This is a specific cutting of wood that was used in ship building. (Ledger photo part of a private collection) This ledger is from the Stubbs saw mill 1818—1820.

Page from the Mill ledger, showing items received. (Photo courtesy of a private collector)

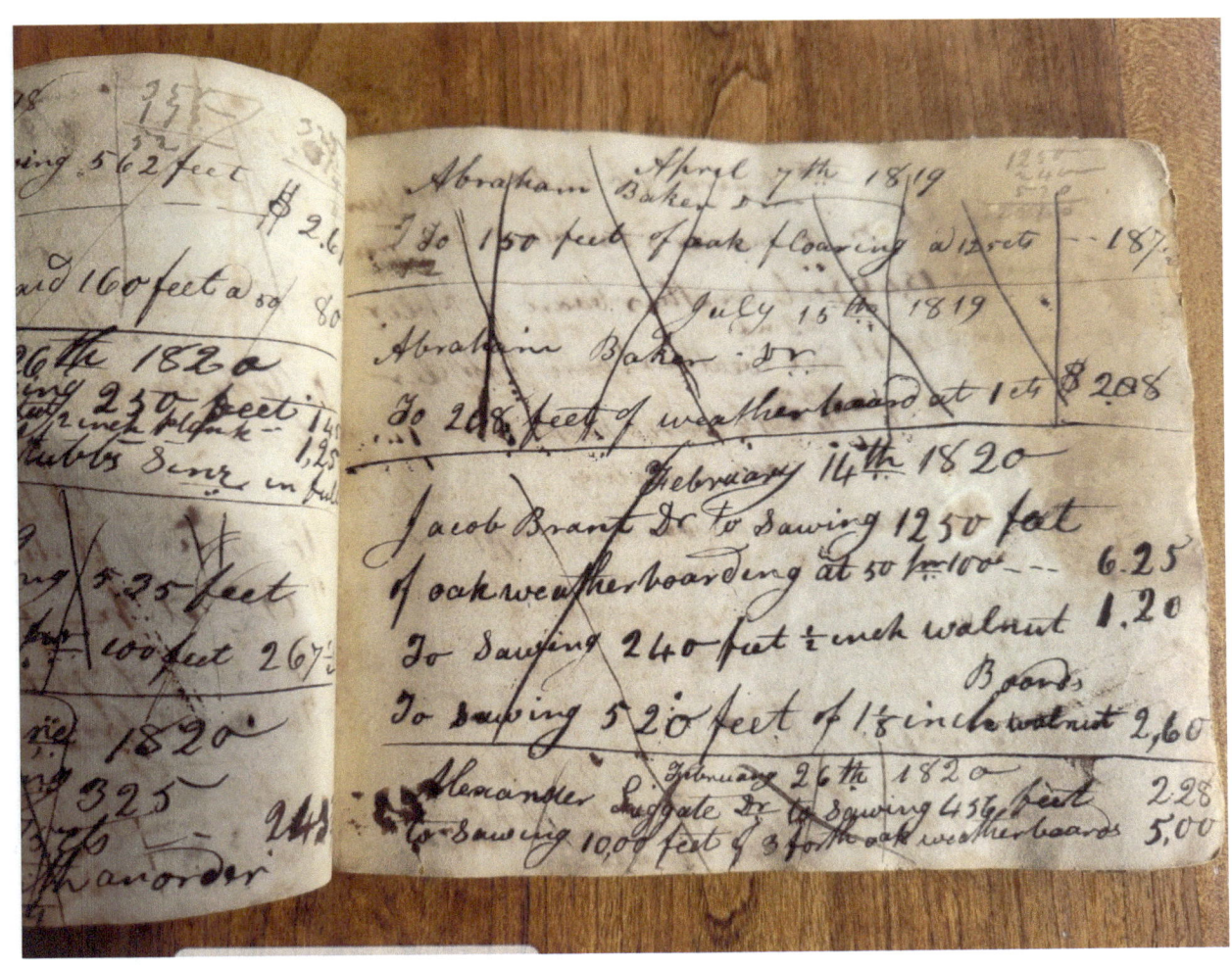

Mill Ledger 1819 (Photo courtesy of a private collector)

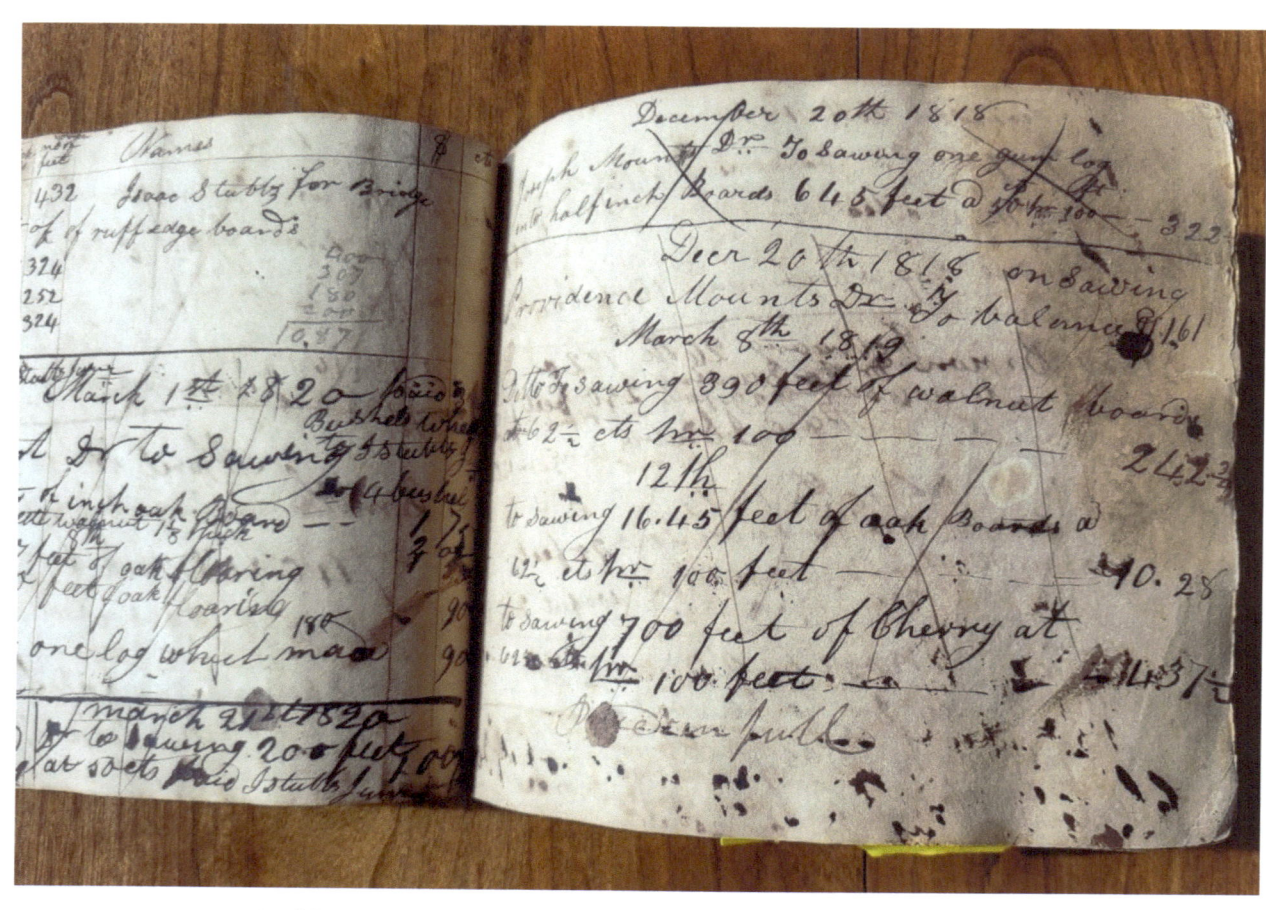

Stubbs Saw Mill—Ledger from December 20th 1818 and March 8, 1819 (Photo courtesy of a private collection)

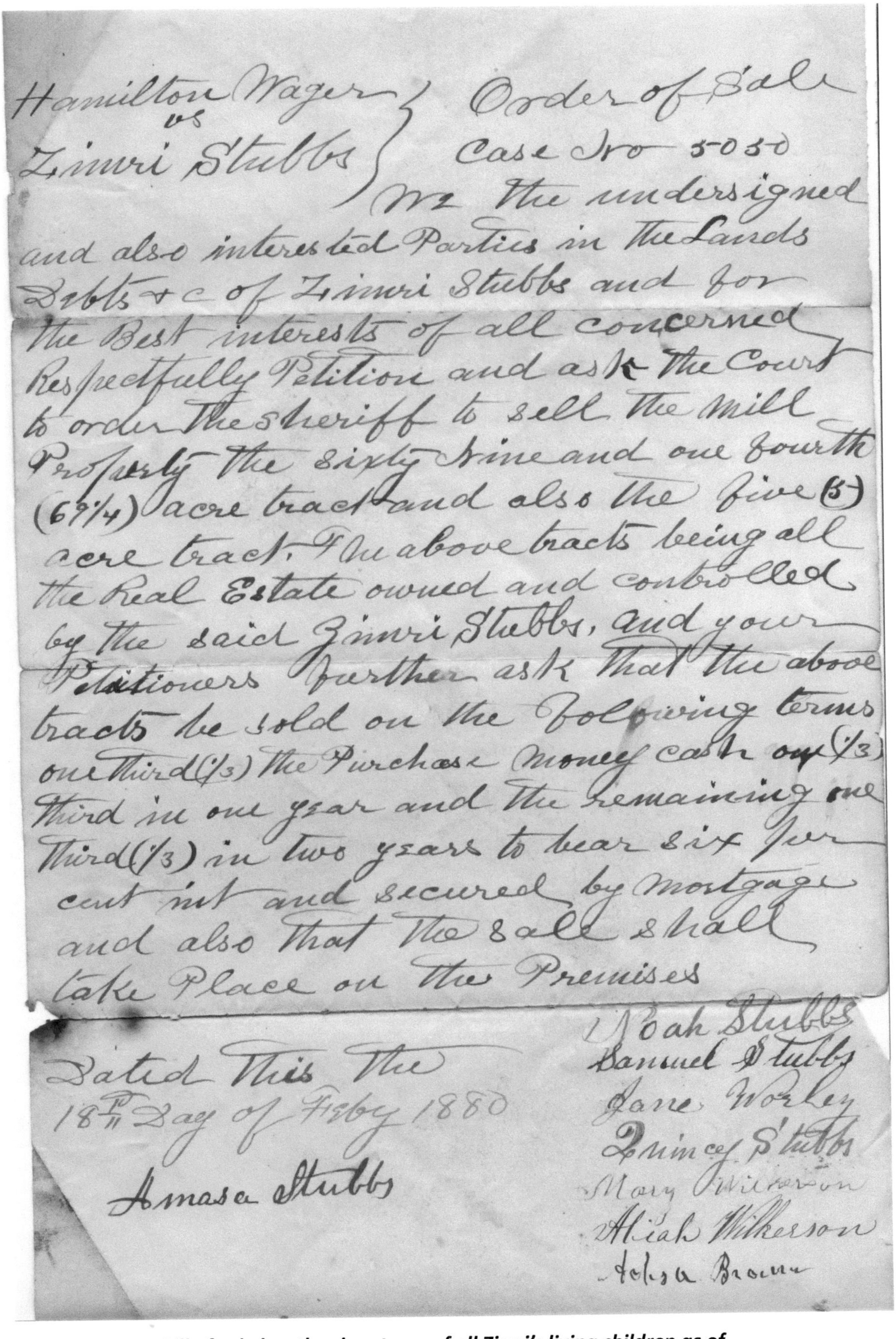

Hamilton Wager } Order of Sale
vs }
Zimri Stubbs } Case No 5050

We the undersigned and also interested Parties in the Lands Debts &c of Zimri Stubbs and for the Best interests of all concerned Respectfully Petition and ask the Court to order the sheriff to sell the Mill Property the sixty nine and one fourth (69¼) acre tract and also the five (5) acre tract. The above tracts being all the Real Estate owned and controlled by the said Zimri Stubbs, and your Petitioners further ask that the above tracts be sold on the following terms one Third (⅓) the Purchase Money cash one (⅓) Third in one year and the remaining one Third (⅓) in two years to bear six per cent int and secured by mortgage and also that the Sale Shall take Place on the Premises

Dated This The
18ᵗʰ Day of Feby 1880

Amasa Stubbs

Noah Stubbs
Samuel Stubbs
Jane Worley
Prince Stubbs
Mary Wilkerson
Aliah Wilkerson
Achsa Brown

Bill of sale has the signatures of all Zimri's living children as of 1880. Zimri was 83 at the time of this document. (Document part of a private collection)

Mill north of current day Corwin, Ohio (Warren County, Ohio)

1856 Atlas of Union Township, Ohio

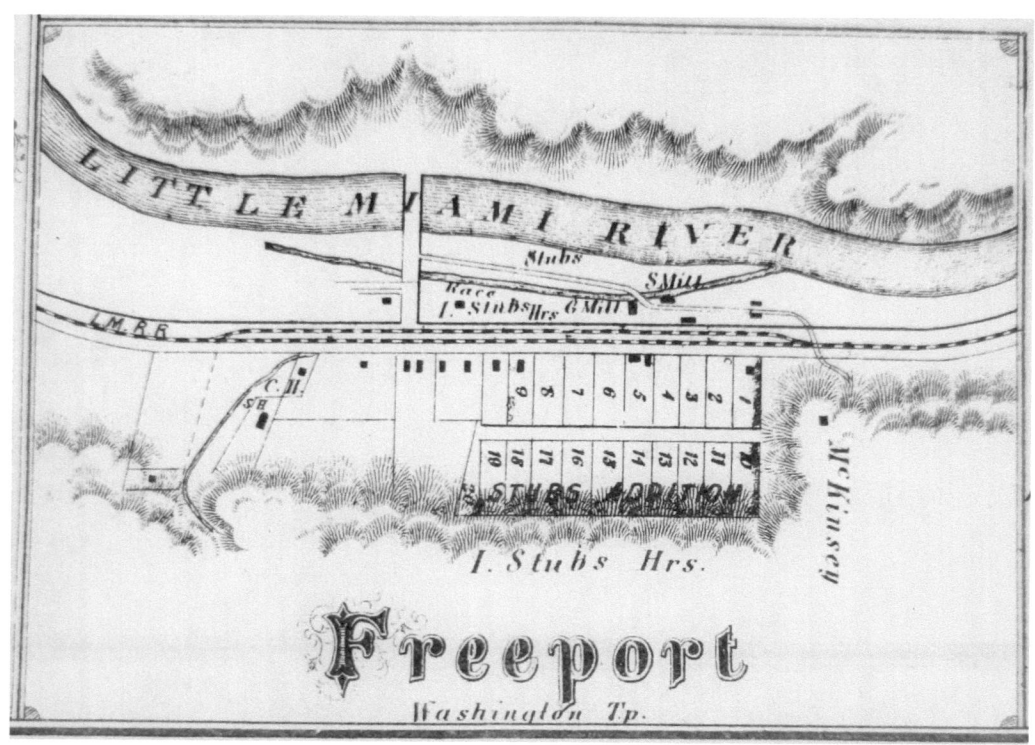

Freeport, now known as Oregonia, was established in 1802.
Note the Stubbs Mills.

Map of Oregonia. Note the development
along the School Lot.

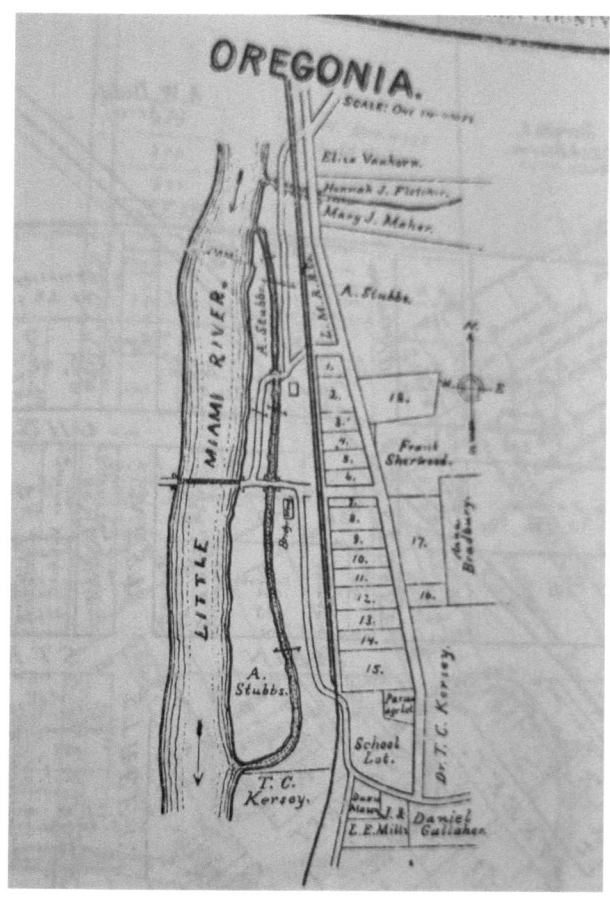

MORROW OF YESTERYEAR

By Marion Snyder

The once bustling little village of Stubbs Town is now only a memory. Once a couple of mills on the north bank and one on the opposite side of the river plus the homes of the Stubbs family and other relatives made up this little center of community life. Some of our older readers will recall the house pictured here which remained in the family for many years after the village ceased to be a manufacturing cen-

Waynesville for First Day worship. Isaac I saw no future at the Gainesborough site and concentrated on his mills at what we call Stubbs Town.

The 1882 Beers History of Warren County does not give any mention of Stubbs Town as an entity although Fredericksburg and Mill Grove received brief mention under Salem Township and that no plant was registered at the courthouse. During the Civil War years

"later it was owned and operated by Isaac Stubbs, Sr. who had emigrated from Georgia in 1804 and had first built a mill on the Little Miami at Mill Grove." The Stubbs family, including Zimiri (for whom his grandson, Zimiri Worley was named) owned several tracts of land in the area adjoining Stubbs Town and some of it is in the possesion of a direct descendent, Myron Baker.

Mr. Baker's mother was Fairy Watkins, daughter of Clinton DeWitt and Mrs. Watkins, and this family resided in the house pictured here for many years. The land across the road was Worley property and Jane Stubbs married John Worley there and as stated became grandmother to Z. O. or Zimiri Worley, longtime "squire" of Mill Grove Farm where an ancestor on the Worley side had operated a mill, no doubt after Isaac Stubbs moved southward to the now ghost town of Stubbs Town. Just about everyone says Stubb Town, dropping the "s" but if it had a legal name it would be Stubbs Town.

The red brick house stood on the north side of today's Stubbs Mill Road just before it crosses over the Mason-Morrow-Millgrove Road. Mr. Watkins had a number of children, all of whom have passed on but in addition to Myron Baker and his second and third generation, there are other direct descendents of Isaac Stubbs I and II around, mostly in the Lebanon area.

Bottom of article is continued on the next page.

to be a manufacturing center, giving way in more recent years to progress also known as gravel mining.

Isaac Stubbs I came to Ohio early in the nineteenth century, having been born in Georgia. His son, Isaac II, was born when the Stubbs were at Gainesborough, now known as Kings Mills, Isaac II being born in 1850. He devoted much of his adult life to operating a mill at Freeport, now known as Oregonia. He started there in partnership with his brother, Albert, but in a few years purchased his brother's interest.

The latter came to Lebanon and took over the management of the Lebanon House, now known as the Golden Lamb, owned by Isaac I for many years but leased to various managers who never seemed to make too good a go of it. The Stubbs were Quakers and had to drive a horse and buggy all the way to

During the Civil War years Zimri Stubbs operated the mills at Stubbs Town and his flour business suffered tremendously as a result of the war because he could no longer ship flour by water down the Ohio or Mississippi Rivers.

The Beers history mentions that the first or one of the first mills in Warren County was built as early as 1798 on the north bank of the Little Miami River midway between the mouths of Todds Fork and Turtlecreek which empties into the Little Miami just west of South Lebanon. This may or may not have been at what we know as Stubbs Town but the half way point is west of the Stubbs Mills Road bridge by a mile or so. It is said in the 1882 History that the mill started grinding grain in 1801 by Jabish Phillips.

The History continues that the mill's ownership passed to Samuel McCray and that

Morrow of yesteryear—bottom of article

WORLEY APPENDIX

The Worley Family Tree – England

William de Warley 1024 - ?

  William de Warley 1044 - 1095

    Robert de Warley 1086 - 1136

      Adam de Wirley 1124 - 1172

        Robert de Wirley 1170 - 1220

          William de Wirley 1210 - 1260

            Guy De Wirley 1248 - 1294

              John de Wirley 1277 - 1323

                Roger de Wirley 1324 - 1370

                  Eudo de Wirley 1352 - 1388

                    Cornelius de Wirley 1398 – 1434

                      Roger de Wirley 1423 – 1469 Staffordshire, England
                      m Joane 1423 - ?

                        Cornelius de Wirley 1455 – 1501
                        m Elizabeth Barton 1455 - 1494

                        James Worley 1492 – 1539
                        m Bridget Umn 1492 - 1519

                        Stephen Worley 1516 – 1564
                        m Anna Bateman 1516 – 1541

                        Henry Worley 1538 – 1583
                        m Ann Mayney

                        John Worley 1562 – 1603
                        m Alice of Kent Worley 1570 - 1601

                        John Worley, Sir 1594 – 1638
                        m Alicia Cushman 1590 - 1619

                        Henry Worley 1616 – 1662 London, England
                        m Anna Stone 1620 – 1696

                        Henry Worley 1642 – 1674 London, England
                        m Ann Young 1645 – 1725

The Worley Family Tree

Francis Worley 1668 – 1728
   m Mary Brassey 1673 – 1728 *6 children*
   1. **Caleb Worley** 1694 – 1751
   2. **Francis Worley Jr.** 1694 – 1768
   3. **Brassey Worley** 1696 – 1783
      m Lurena Christopher 1698 – 1750 *6 children*
      A. **Anthony Worley** 1730 – 1795
      B. **Achor Worley** 1738 – 1812
      C. **Brice Worley** 1740 – 1809
      D. **Ezekial Worley** 1740— 1809
      E. **Joseph Worley** 1748 – 1809
      F. **William Worley** 1750 - 1828
         m Nancy Walling 1754 – 1837 *9 children*
         a. **Silas Worley** 1784 – 1833
         b. **Mary Worley** 1786 – 1857
         c. **Walling Worley** 1787 – 1854
            m Eleanor Beale 1796 – 1861 *12 children*
            1. **James Worley** 1815 – 1903
            2. **Deila Worley** 1817 – 1870
            3. **Richard Worley** 1819 – 1898
            4. **Eliza Worley** 1821 - ?
            5. **Andrew Jackson Worley** 1828 – 1899
            6. **Nancy Worley** 1830 – 1881
            7. **Amanda Worley** 1830 – 1904
            8. **John Q. Worley** 1832 – 1915
               m Jane Stubbs 1836 – 1913 *2 children*
               A. **Zimri Worley** 1865 – 1954
                  m Videlia Van Riper 1873 – 1931
               B. **Althe Worley** 1860 - 1936
                  m Clinton Watkins 1861 – 1934 *7 children*
                  1. **Fairy Watkins** 1882 – 1958
                  2. **Arthur John Watkins** 1885 – 1968
                  3. **Jane Watkins** 1887 – 1967
                  4. **Blanche Watkins** 1888 – 1978
                  5. **Stanley Watkins** 1892 – 1968
                  6. **Adarene Watkins** 1894 – 1977
                  7. **Catheryn Watkins** 1898 - 1954
           9. **Lucinda Worley** 1834 – 1866
           10. **John Worley** 1834 – 1877
           11. **Walling Worley** 1836 – 1836
           12. **Sarah Worley** 1848 - 1921
         d. **Prudence Worley** 1789 – 1835
         e. **Piety Worley** 1792 – 1867
         f. **Brice Worley** 1794 - 1847
         g. **Ruth Worley** 1797 – 1854

     h. **Elizabeth Worley** 1800 – 1829

     i. **Frances Worley** 1802 - 1879

4. **Rebecca Worley** 1697 – 1749

5. **Susannah Worley** 1698 – 1751

6. **Achor Worley** 1705 - 1775

Myron Baker is my father.

Fairy Watkins Baker is my grandmother.

Althe Worley Watkins is my great grandmother.

John Q. Worley is my great-great grandfather.

Walling Worley is my great-great-great grandfather.

William Worley is my great-great-great-great grandfather.

Brassy Worley is my great-great-great-great-great grandfather.

Francis Worley is my great-great-great-great-great-great grandfather.

Henry Worley is my great-great-great-great-great-great-great grandfather.

RESIDENCE OF MR. AND MRS. Z. O. WORLEY, NEAR MORROW.

Z. O. WORLEY was born November 25, 1865, on the farm which he now owns, and on which he has resided up to the present time. He is the son of John Worley and Jane Stubbs Worley. The Worleys were among the early settlers, their forefathers coming to this country with William Penn. The Stubbses were among the pioneers, being owners of large tracts of land, and several of the water-mills along the Little Miami River and its branches. Among their holdings was Mill Grove Farm and Mill property. Isaac Stubbs, the great-grandfather of Z. O. Worley, built the house that now stands on Mill Grove Farm about the year 1811. There are two pear trees standing in the yard that were planted nearly one hundred years ago. The Worleys and Stubbses were connected with the Quakers of Colonial days. Z. O. Worley was married February 15, 1891, to Videllia Van Riper, a descendant of the Van Riper and Perrine families, well known in Warren County. Mill Grove Farm is devoted to the breeding of Cadmus Horses, Jersey Cattle, Poland China Swine and Plymouth Rock Chickens.

Millgrove Stock Farm, near Oregonia.

WATKINS APPENDIX

The Watkins Family Tree

John Watkins 1610 – 1632 b Breconshire, Wales d Surrey, England m Mary Lawe 1610 - 1632

    Thomas Watkins 1629 – 1689 b Boston, MA

      m Elizabeth Baker 1632 – 1689 *9 children*

      Joseph Watkins 1663 – 1711

        m Johanna Blackman 1667 – 1729 *10 children*

        I. **David Watkins** 1691 – 1755

        II. **Samuel Watkins** 1693 – 1725

        III. **Jonathan Watkins** 1695 – 1696

        IV. **Joseph Watkins** 1697 - 1697

        V. **Joseph Watkins** 1699 – 1736

        VI. **Johanah Watkins** 1700 - ?

        VII. **Elizabeth Watkins** 1702 – 1738

        VIII. **Benjamin Watkins** 1704 – 1732 b Stratford, CN

          m Sarah Marsh 1698 – 1726

        IX. **Ephraim Watkins** 1706 – 1751

          m Joanna Birdseye *9 children*

          1. **Samuel Watkins** Esq. of Watkill 1728 - 1794

          2. **Tabitha Watkins** 1730 - 1770

          3. **Joseph Watkins** 1726 – 1800 b Elizabethtown, Essex, NJ

            m Elizabeth Frances Spinning 1730 – 1787 *8 children*

            A. **Phoebe Sarah Watkins** 1755 - 1823

            B. **Joseph Watkins** 1759 - 1817

            C. **John Watkins** 1759 - ?

            D. **Jeremiah Watkins** 1760 - ?

            E. **Hezekiah Watkins** 1761 - 1834

            F. **Jonathan Watkins** 1765 - 1819

            G. **James Watkins** 1768 – 1849 b NJ d Athens, OH

              m Rachel Badgley Utter 1770 – 1843 *3 children*

              a. **Sarah Watkins** 1804 - 1828

              b. **Joseph Watkins** 1805 – 1882 b Hamilton, OH

                m Catherine Pierson 1820 – 1905 *8 children*

              c. **Benjamin Utter Watkins** 1811 - 1890

            H. **Sarah Watkins**

          4. **Abel Watkins** 1734 - 1754

          5. **Ephraim Watkins** 1739 - 1786

          6. **Bridget Watkins** 1740 -?

          7. **Eunice Watkins** 1740 - ?

          8. **Joanna Watkins** 1740 - ?

          9. **Hezekiah Watkins** 1748 - 1782

        X. **Hezekiah Watkins** 1708 – 1765

A detailed family tree of Joseph Watkins and his son James Watkins follows.

Author's note - There is some discrepancy about the father of Joseph Watkins (1726 – 1800). Some genealogy sources claim Benjamin Watkins and Sarah Marsh to be his parents. I found two sources claiming Tobias Watkins to be his father. I found two other sources claiming Ephraim Watkins and Joanna Birdseye to be his parents, which is what I used in this family tree.

Family Tree of Joseph Watkins 1726 - 1800

Joseph Watkins 1726 – 1800 b Elizabethtown, Essex, NJ
    m Elizabeth Frances Spinning 1730 – 1787 *8 children*
    A. **Phoebe Watkins** 1755 - 1823
    B. **Joseph Watkins** 1759 - 1817
    C. **John Watkins** 1759 - ?
    D. **Jeremiah Watkins** 1760 - ?
    E. **Hezekiah Watkins** 1761 - 1834
    F. **Jonathan Watkins** 1765 – 1819
    G. **James Watkins** 1768 – 1849 b in N.J. d Athens, OH
        m Rachel Badgley Utter 1770 – 1843 *3 children*
        a. **Sarah Watkins** 1804
        b. **Joseph Watkins** 1805 – 1882 b Hamilton
          m Susan Bruin d 1834
          2nd m Catherine Pierson 1820 – 1905 *8 children*
          A. **Nancy Watkins** 1841 - 1842
          B. **James Watkins** 1842 - 1864
          C. **Squire Watkins** 1844 - 1845
          D. **Samuel H. Watkins** 1847 – 1919
            m Mary Ellen Harn b 1848 *3 children*
            1. **Edith Watkins** 1886 – 1889
            2. **Wilbert Watkins** 1875 – 1948
              m Antoinette (Nettie) Stark
            3. **Henrietta Watkins** 1873 –
              m Clinton Watson
          E. **Eliza Watkins** b 1849 – 1904
            m William Parker *2 children*
            1. **Clarence Parker** 1883 –
            m Harriet Coats
             2. **Joseph Parker** 1888 – 1890
          F. **Benjamin Watkins** 1851 -
            m Ada Price 1849 -
          G. **Joseph Watkins** 1853 - 1924
            m Susan Ford 1854 – 1879 *1 child*
            1. **Smith Watkins**
              m Callie Stock *1 child*
              1. **Joseph Watkins**
            2nd m Mary E. Johnson 1858 - 1922 *7 children*

1. **Christopher Watkins** 1882 – 1945

    m Callie Goodin ? – 1976

    1. **George Watkins** MD 1922 – 2017

       m Rita Maurer

       1. **Chris Watkins**

       2. **Rita Watkins**

       3. **Joe Watkins**

2. **Benjamin Watkins** 1884 – 1986

3. **Joseph Watkins** 1884 - 1900

4. **William Watkins** 1887 – 1951

5. **E. Eulalia Watkins** 1893 - 1935

    m Dwight Watkins *no children*

    son of Otis & Ella Watkins, Clinton Co. OH

6. **Elizabeth Watkins** 1893 - ?

7. **Alfred G. Watkins** 1896 - 1964

    m Edith Trisler

    1. **William Watkins** 1925 - 1998

       m Hilda

H. **Sarah Watkins** 1772 – 1852

  m Capt. John Ferris *4 children*

  1. **Isaac Ferris**

  2. **Frances Ferris**

  3. **Anna Ferris**

  4. **Cornelius Ferris**

Author's note:

My text about the Watkins is based upon what Julia Watkins Frost wrote in her book. She wrote that Joseph Watkins, her great- grandfather, had six children. Records show that Joseph and Elizabeth (Spinning) had eight children. Julia did not mention John and Jeremiah. Since they have no recorded date of death, it can be assumed that they died in infancy. Julia also wrote the daughters being named Elizabeth and Sarah. There is a discrepancy. Records show that the oldest daughter's name was Phoebe Sarah Watkins and the younger daughter was Sarah Watkins. According to Julia the older boys served in the Revolutionary War. She did not say specifically which of Joseph's sons served.

Family Tree of James Watkins 1768 - 1849

James Watkins 1768 – 1849 b in N.J. d Athens, OH

  m Rachel Badgley Utter 1770 – 1843 *3 children*

I. **Sarah Watkins** 1804

II. **Joseph Watkins** 1805 – 1882 b Hamilton

    m Susan Bruin d 1834

    m Catherine Pierson 1820 – 1905 *8 children*

    A. **Nancy Watkins** 1841 - 1842

    B. **James Watkins** 1842 - 1864

    C. **Squire Watkins** 1844 - 1845

    D. **Samuel H. Watkins** 1847 - 1919

m Mary Ellen Harn b 1848 *3 children*
1. **Edith Watkins** 1886 – 1889
2. **Wilbert Watkins** 1875 – 1948
    m Antoinette (Nettie) Stark
3. **Henrietta Watkins** 1873 –
    m Clinton Watson

E. **Eliza Watkins** b 1849 – 1904
  m William Parker *2 children*
  1. **Clarence Parker** 1883 –
    m Harriet Coats
  2. **Joseph Parker** 1888 – 1890

F. **Benjamin Watkins** 1851 -
  m Ada Price 1849 -

G. **Joseph Watkins** 1853 - 1924
  m Susan Ford 1854 – 1879 *1 child*
  1. **Smith Watkins**
    m Callie Stock *1 child*
    1. **Joseph Watkins**
  2nd m Mary E. Johnson 1858 - 1922 *7 children*
  1. **Christopher Watkins** 1882 – 1945
    m Callie Goodin ? – 1976
  2. **Benjamin Watkins** 1884 – 1986
  3. **Joseph Watkins** 1884 - 1900
  4. **William Watkins** 1887 – 1951
  5. **E. Eulalia Watkins** 1893 - 1935
    m Dwight Watkins *no children*
    (son of Otis & Ella Watkins, Clinton Co. OH)
  6. **Elizabeth Watkins** 1893 - ?
  7. **Alfred G. Watkins** 1896 - 1964
    m Edith Trisler
    1. **William Watkins** 1925 - 1998
      m Hilda ?

H. **Harriet B. S. Watkins** 1858 – 1878

I. **Clinton DeWitt Watkins** 1861 – 1934
  m Althe Worley 1860 – 1936 *7 children*
  1. **Fairy Watkins** 1882 – 1958
    m Charles Baker 1883 – 1973 *2 children*
    a. **Lorena Baker** 1903 – 1980
      m Bill Bellamy
    b. **Myron Baker** 1914 – 1999
      m Lois Hartman 1914 – 2010
  2. **Arthur John Watkins** 1885 – 1968
    m Harriet Ramsey *3 children*
    a. **Paul Watkins** 1923 - 1993
    b. **Robert Watkins** 1926 - ?
    c. **Marion Watkins** 1928 - ?

3. **Jane Watkins** 1887 – 1967
   m Hal Brant *3 children*
   a. **Harold Brant** 1908 – 1984
   b. **Sarah Brant** 1909 – 1972
   c. **Hal Brant** 1909 – 1912
4. **Blanche Watkins** 1888 – 1978
   m John Sanford 1884 - ? *2 children*
   a. **Clair Sanford** 1916 – 1944
   b. **Donald Sanford** 1918 – 1992
5. **Stanley Watkins** 1892 – 1968
   m Mary Connor 1893 - ? *2 children*
   a. **Nyale Watkins** 1915 - 1996
   b. **Dale Watkins** 1918 – 1981
6. **Adarene Watkins** 1894 – 1977
   m Leon Hunter MD 1892 - ? *no children*
7. **Catheryn Watkins** 1898 – 1954
   m George Dugan *1 child*
   a. **Audrey Dugan**

III. **Benjamin Utter Watkins** 1811 – 1890 b Cincinnati, OH
m Sophronia Keeler 1804 - 1870 *4 children*
1. **William Benson Watkins** 1836 – 1898
   m Julia Morris *3 children*
   1. **Rosamond Watkins** 1862 – 1944
   2. **Paul Watkins** 1865 – 1931
      m Florence Henderson *3 children*
   3. **Agnes Watkins** 1867 – 1919
2. **Julia A. Watkins** 1838 – 1920
   m Alvah Frost *3 children*
   1. **(no name)**
   2. **Adelaide Frost**
   3. **William Frost**
3. **Joseph Ray Watkins** 1840 – 1911
   m Mary Ellen Heberling 1840 - 1904 *2 children*
   1. **Grace E. Watkins** 1877 – 1975
      m Elroy King *2 children*
      1. **E. L. Jr.**
      2. **Mary Eleanor**
   2. **George B. Watkins** 1879 - 1881
4. **Ida Louis Watkins** 1844 – 1931
   m Datus Myers *2 children*
   1. **Stella Myers**
   2. **Julia Myers**

Myron Baker is my father.

Fairy Watkins Baker is my grandmother.

Clinton DeWitt Watkins is my great grandfather.

Joseph Watkins is my great-great grandfather.

James Watkins is my great-great-great grandfather.

Joseph Watkins is my great-great-great-great grandfather.

Ephraim Watkins is my great-great-great-great-great grandfather.

Joseph Watkins is my great-great-great-great-great-great grandfather.

Thomas Watkins is my great-great-great-great-great-great-great grandfather.

John Watkins is my great-great-great-great-great-great-great-great- grandfather.

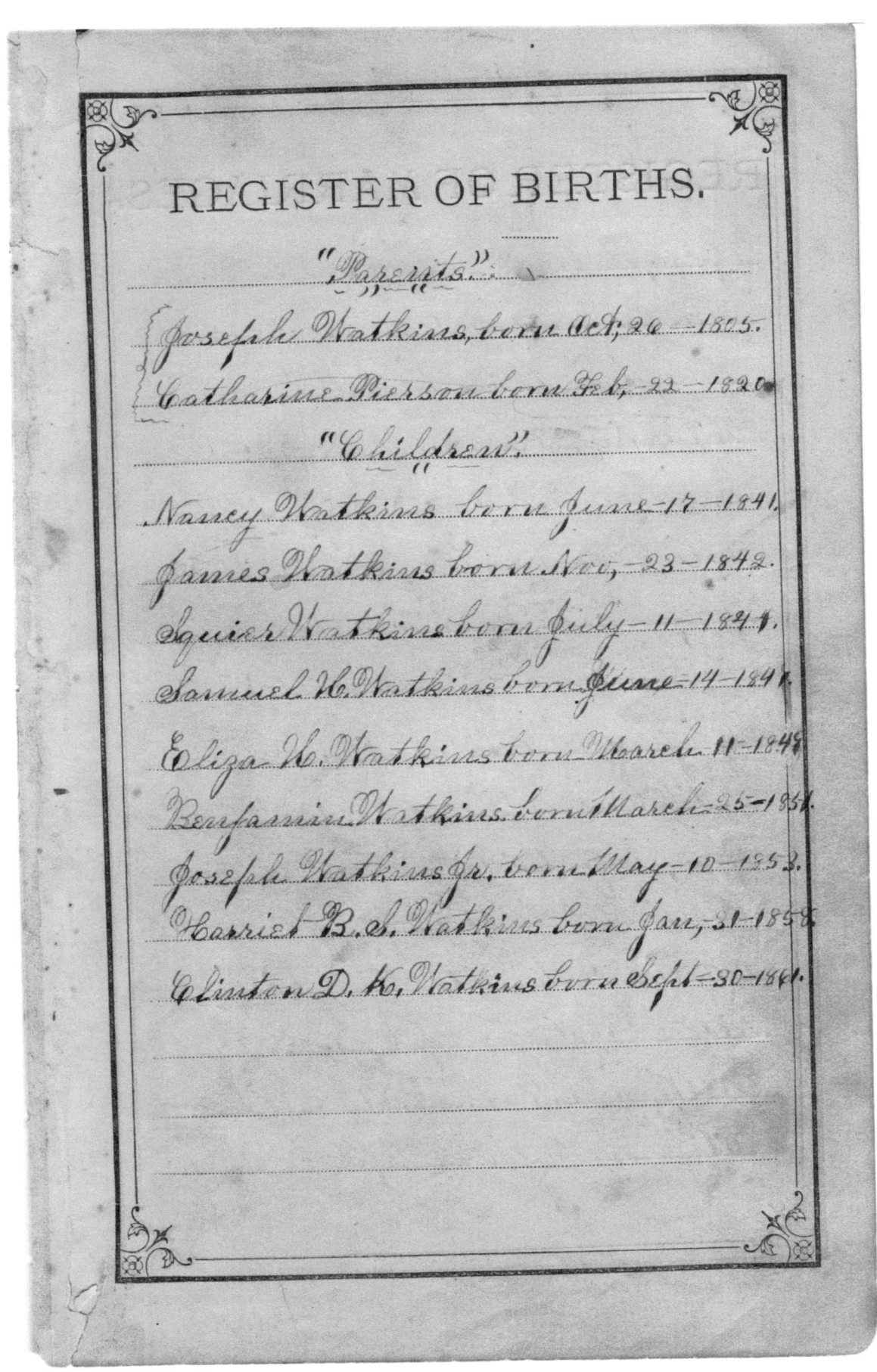

REGISTER OF BIRTHS.

"Parents"

Joseph Watkins, born Oct, 26 – 1805.

Catharine Pierson born Feb, 22 – 1820

"Children"

Nancy Watkins born June – 17 – 1841.

James Watkins born Nov, – 23 – 1842.

Squier Watkins born July – 11 – 1844.

Samuel H. Watkins born June – 14 – 1847.

Eliza H. Watkins born March 11 – 1849

Benjamin Watkins born March – 25 – 1851.

Joseph Watkins Jr. born May – 10 – 1853.

Harriet B. S. Watkins born Jan, 31 – 1856

Clinton D. K. Watkins born Sept – 30 – 1861.

Watkins Family Bible pages —possible from the middle?

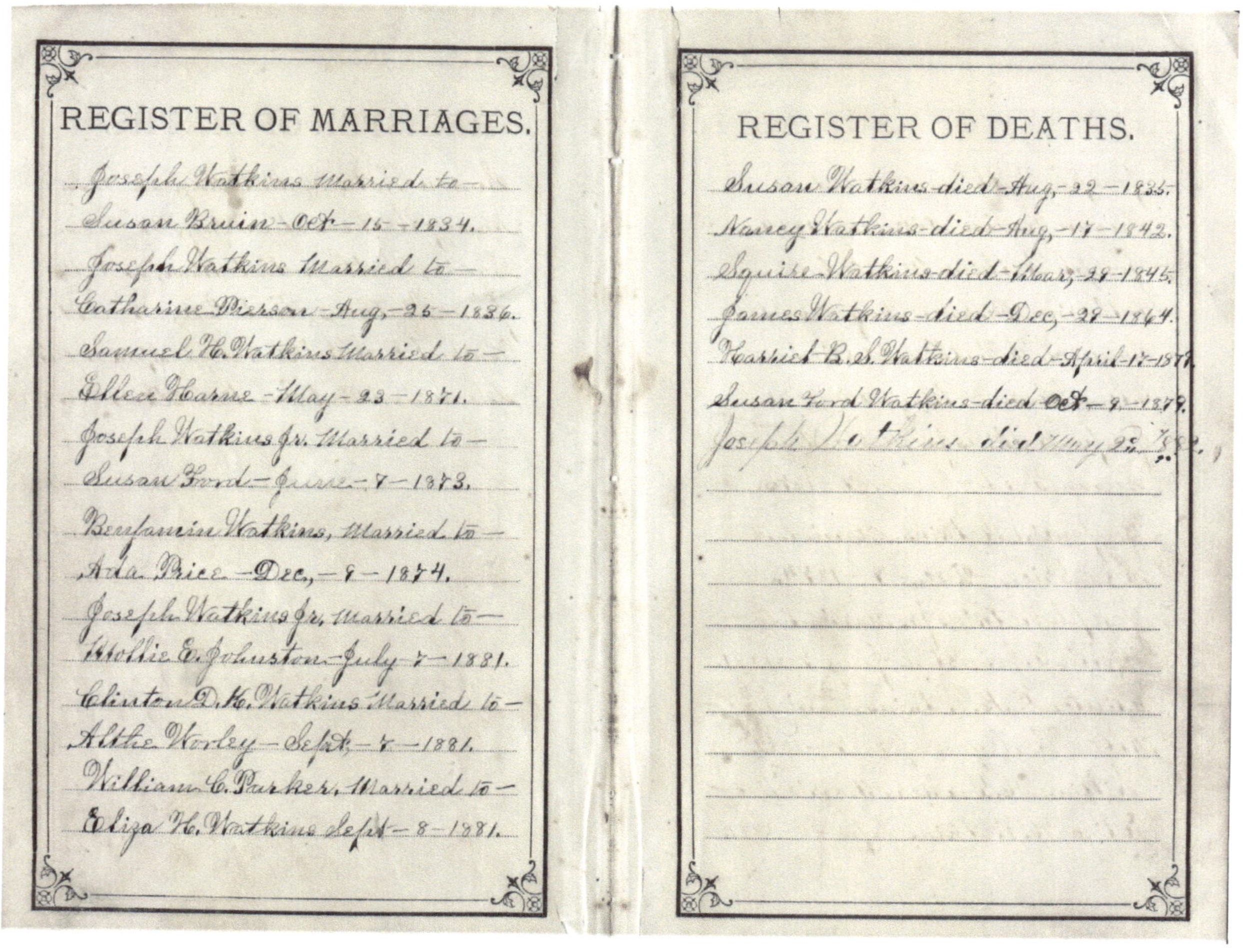

REGISTER OF MARRIAGES.

Joseph Watkins Married to Susan Bruin Oct. 15 1834.

Joseph Watkins Married to Catharine Pierson Aug. 25 1836.

Samuel H. Watkins Married to Ellece Hearne May 23 1871.

Joseph Watkins Jr. Married to Susan Ford June 8 1873.

Benjamin Watkins, Married to Ada Rice Dec. 8 1874.

Joseph Watkins Jr. Married to Mollie E. Johnston July 7 1881.

Clinton D. H. Watkins Married to Althe Worley Sept. 8 1881.

William C. Parker, Married to Eliza H. Watkins Sept. 8 1881.

REGISTER OF DEATHS.

Susan Watkins died Aug. 22 1835.

Nancy Watkins died Aug. 17 1842.

Squire Watkins died Mar. 28 1845.

James Watkins died Dec. 28 1864.

Harriet B. S. Watkins died April 17 1871.

Susan Ford Watkins died Oct. 8 1879.

Joseph Watkins died May 22 7___

Watkins Family Bible pages —possible from the middle section with marriage and death dates

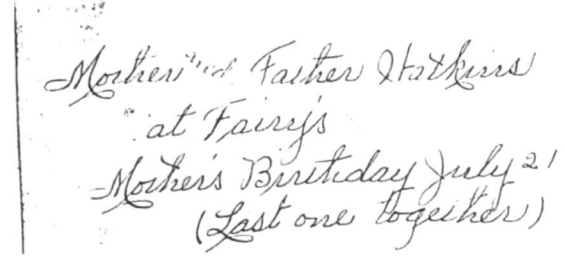

Mother and Father Watkins
at Fairy's
Mother's Birthday July 21
(Last one together)

Grandmother Worley
Mother Watkins &
Daughter Catherine

Foto from Cousin Jackie Watkins shows Grandmother Worley (R), a sister to Althea Worley Watkins. Althea was mother of Stanley J. Watkins, Maria Christina Conner's husband.
Do not know who "Mother Watkins" is nor daughter Catherine?

GRANDMOTHER WORLEY WAS A SISTER TO ALTHEA, WHO MARRIED CLINTON WATKINS (NYALE'S GRAND-PARENTS) SHE WAS STANLEY WATKINS' AUNT.

Althe Worley Watkins, Catherine Watkins "Aunt Kate" and Jane Stubbs Worley, mother of Althe and grandmother of Catherine.

C. D. Watkins and wife with their Grandchildren.

478

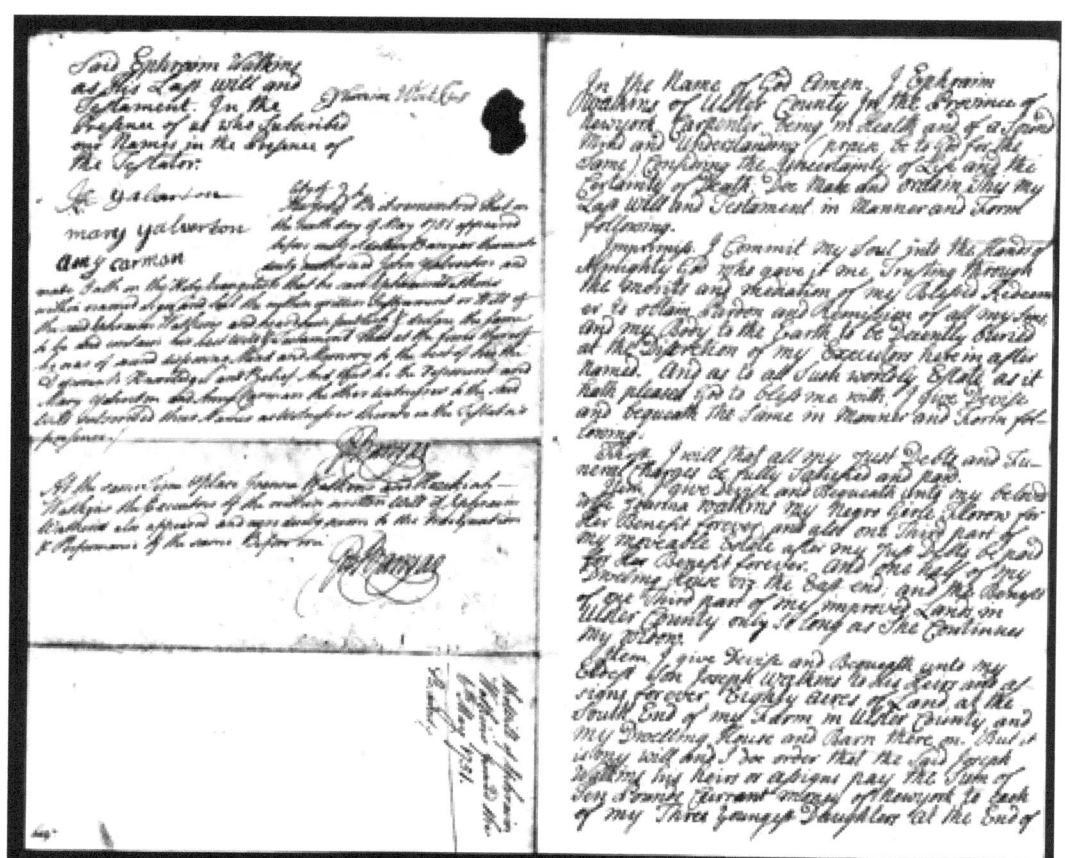

Cover and page 1 of Will of Ephraim Watkins, 1751

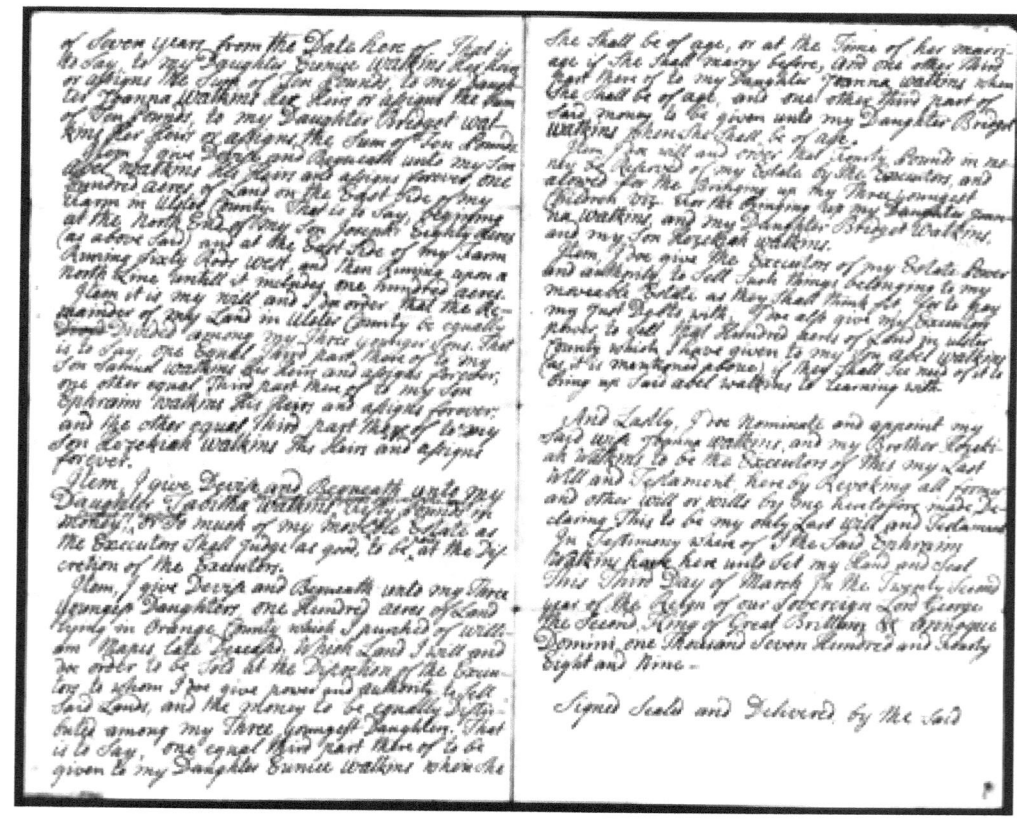

Pages 2 and 3 of the Last Will of Ephraim Watkins

Residence of Joseph Watkins where Samuel grew up

Joe Watkins (1853—1924) son of Joseph and Elizabeth Watkins, brother to Clinton.

James Watkins, (1842—1864) brother of Samuel, son of Joseph and Catherine.
This is a tin type and we know he served as a cook in the Civil War.

Marriage Certificate - Clinton and Althe

Jane Stubbs Worley is seated in the center of this picture, holding a baby.
To Jane's left is her son, "Z.O." Worley and Althe is standing behind him. (Those are Jane's 2 children).
Joseph and Mary Watkins (parents of Clinton Watkins) are seated to the right . Mary is holding the boy
with the big bow. Clinton Watkins is in the back on the right hand side,
Eulialia Watkins and Christopher Watkins (brother and sister) are standing behind Joseph and Mary
Watkins (their parents). (Cousins to Clinton).

BAKER APPENDIX

The Baker Family Tree

Jacob Baker 1778 – 1840
   m Adiamy Sipes 1788 – 1827 *9 children*
   I. **Catherine Baker** 1807 – 1887 b PA
      m Alexander Montgomery *9 children*
   II. **Henry Baker** 1809 – 1891 b PA
   III. **Mary Ann Baker** 1811 – 1878 b OH
      m Caleb Phillips *11 children*
   IV. **Joseph Baker** 1813 – 1905 b Sycamore, OH
   V. **Fredrick Baker** 1816 – 1904 b Warren, OH
      m Rieshel Harris
   VI. **Charles Baker** 1818 – 1880 b Hamilton, OH
      m Mary Ann Phillips 1825 - 1878 *6 children*
      1. **Joseph Baker** 1844 – 1872
         m Eliza Winteringer *7 children*
      2. **John Quincy Baker** 1852 – 1924
         m Mary Jane Toms Tintagel, Eng. 1862 – 1944 *3 children*
         A. **Charles Stanley Baker** 1883 – 1973
           m Fairy Watkins 1882 - 1958 *2 children*
           1. **Lorena Baker** 1904 - 1980
              m William Bellamy 1901- 1977
              I. **Norman Bellamy** 1928 - 2006
              II. **Charles Bellamy** 1927 – 2002
                 m Alice Ingram 1928 – 2007
                 1. **Duane Bellamy**
                 2. **Glen Bellamy**
              III. **Bobbie Bellamy**
                 m Joseph Edge *1 child*
                 1. **Stacy Rdge**
           2. **Myron Baker** 1914 - 1999
              m Lois Matilda Hartman 1914 - 2010
              I. **Loron Baker** 1939 –
                 m Dixie Amburgy 1939 -
                 1. **Kathy Baker** 1961 –
                 2. **John Ty Baker** 1963 -
              II. **Margery Baker** 1944 –
                 m Frank Simchak MD 1942 -
                 1. **Elizabeth Simchak** 1969 -
                 2. **Melanie Simchak** 1973 –
                 3. **Laura Simchak** 1978 -

      III. **Jean E. Baker** 1954 –
          m Charles Weisbrod 1953 -
          1. **Susan Weisbrod** 1984 -
          2. **Richard Weisbrod** 1988 -
    B. **Jacob Earl Baker** 1885 – 1950
      m Julia Irons *1 child*
    C. **Alma Eve Baker** 1889 – 1982
      m Henry Runyan Harris 1881 – 1972 *2 children*
      1. **Helen Louis Harris** 1914 – 1983
      2. **Ruth Marjorie Harris** 1921 – 1972
  3. **Charles Q. (Quimby) Baker** 1856 – 1922
  4. **Alva P. Baker** 1859 - 1876
  5. **Henry L. (Linc) Baker** 1862 – 1934
  6. **Mary Kate Baker** 1866 – 1945
    m Raymond E. Sparks
VII. **Susan Baker** 1820 – 1830 b OH
VIII. **John Baker** 1823 – ? b IN
IX. **Hannah Baker** 1826 – 1863 b IN

Myron Baker is my father.
Charles Stanley Baker is my grandfather.
John Quincy Baker is my great grandfather.
Charles Baker is my great-great grandfather.
Jacob Baker is my great-great-great grandfather.

A Platt of Zimri Stubbs's orchard South Side of orchard

March 1848

1	2	3	4	5	6	7	8	9	10	11	12	13	14	15			24
2	16	17	18	19	20	21	22	23	24	25	26	27	28	29			42
3	30	31	32	33	34	35	36	37	38	39	X	41	42	43	199		243
4	44	45	46	47	48	49	50	51	52	53	54	55	56	57	200		
5	58	59	60	61	62	63	64	65	66	67	68	69	70	71	201		
6	72	73	74	75	76	77	78	79	80	81	82	83	84	85	202		
7	86	87	88	89	90	91	92	93	94	95	96	97	98	99	203		
8	100	101	102	103	104	105	106	107	108	109	110	111	112	113			
9	114	115	116	117	118	119	120	121	122	123	124	125	126	127	205		
10	128	129	130	131	132	133	134	135	136	137	138	139	140	141	207		
11	142	143	144	145	146	147	148	149	150	151	152	153	154	155	208		
12	156	157	158	159	160	161	162	163	164	165	166	167	168	169	209		
13	170	171	172	173	174	175	176	177	178	179	180	181	182	183	210		
14	184	185	186	187	188	189	190	191	192	193	194	195	196	206	211		
15	212	213	214	215	216	217	218	219	220	221	222	223	224	225	226		

227 228 229 230 231 ... 240

North Side

Winesap 2=16=30=44=58=72=73=59=45=31=17=3

dormal 4=18=32=46=60=74

Smith cider =5=19=33=47=61=75=6=20
34=48=62=76=7=21=35=49=63=77 one dead
or buy

Green Pipen 8=22=36=50=64=78=9=23

Jennetting 37=51=65=79=10=24=38=52=66=80=194

Maidens blush 11=25=39=53=67=81=96

French Pipen 12=26=40=54=68=82 one dead

Newtown do 13=27=41=55=69=83

Roman Stem 14=28=42=56=70=84=71=85=197=198=199=200=201=202

White Pipen 15=29=43=57=197=198=199=200=201=202

Ridge do 86=100=114=128

Romanite 142=156=241=242 all dead

Wine apple 170=184

Gillow or Newark pipen 87=101=115=129

Apple or melon 165

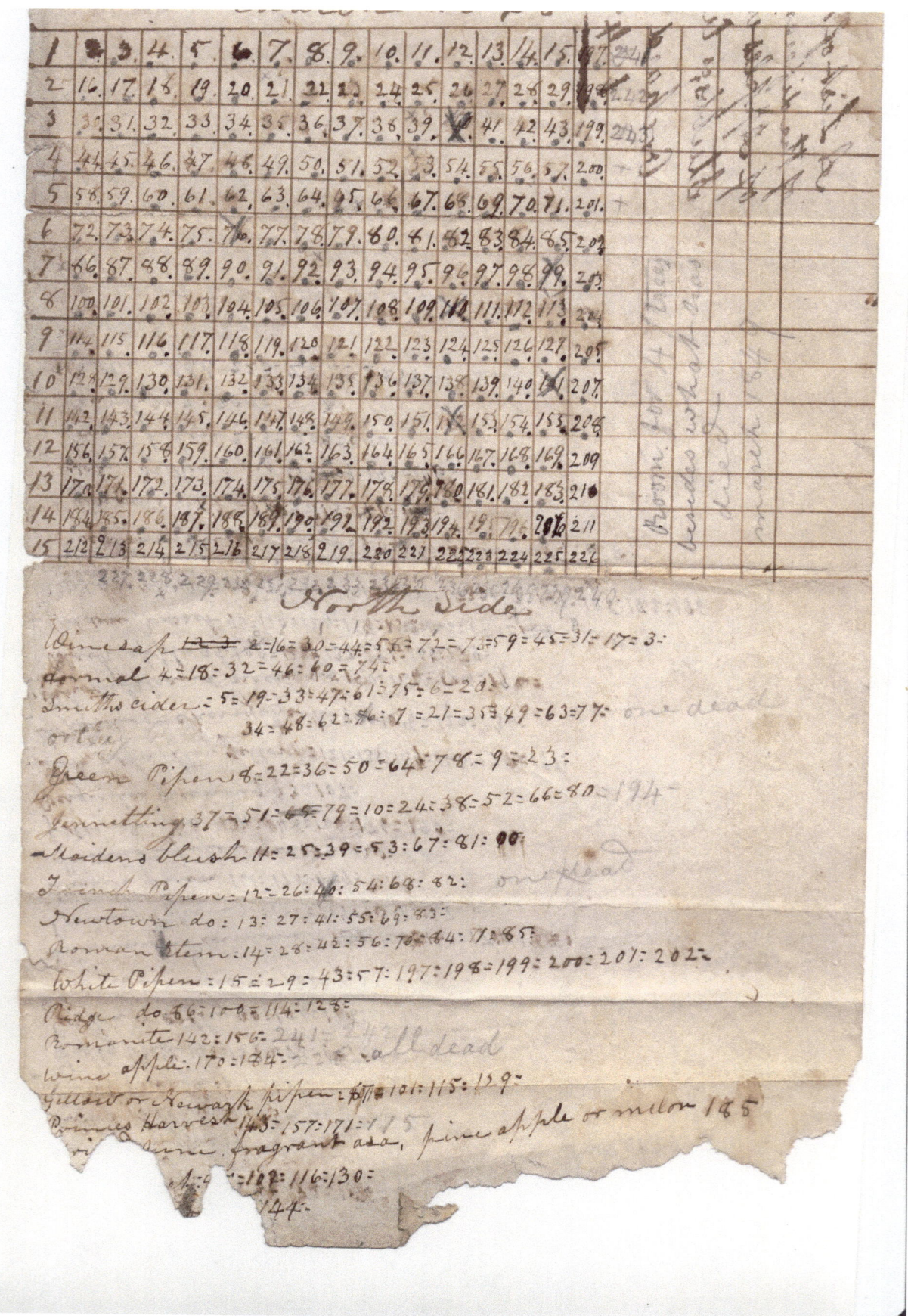

1	2	3	4	5	6	7	8	9	10	11	12	13	14	15	197	241	
2	16	17	18	19	20	21	22	23	24	25	26	27	28	29	198	242	
3	30	31	32	33	34	35	36	37	38	39	X	41	42	43	199	243	
4	44	45	46	47	48	49	50	51	52	53	54	55	56	57	200		
5	58	59	60	61	62	63	64	65	66	67	68	69	70	71	201		
6	72	73	74	75	76	77	78	79	80	81	82	83	84	85	202		
7	86	87	88	89	90	91	92	93	94	95	96	97	98	99	203		
8	100	101	102	103	104	105	106	107	108	109	110	111	112	113	204		
9	114	115	116	117	118	119	120	121	122	123	124	125	126	127	205		
10	128	129	130	131	132	133	134	135	136	137	138	139	140	141	207		
11	142	143	144	145	146	147	148	149	150	151	X	153	154	155	208		
12	156	157	158	159	160	161	162	163	164	165	166	167	168	169	209		
13	170	171	172	173	174	175	176	177	178	179	180	181	182	183	210		
14	184	185	186	187	188	189	190	191	192	193	194	195	196	206	211		
15	212	213	214	215	216	217	218	219	220	221	222	223	224	225	226		

227. 228. 229. ... 240.

North Side

Vinesap 1. 2. 3 = 2 = 16 = 30 = 44 = 58 = 72 = 73 = 59 = 45 = 31 = 17 = 3:

Hormal 4 = 18 = 32 = 46 = 60 = 74:

Smiths cider = 5 = 19 = 33 = 47 = 61 = 75 = 6 = 20:
or bug 34 = 48 = 62 = 76 = 7 = 21 = 35 = 49 = 63 = 77: one dead

Green Pipen = 8 = 22 = 36 = 50 = 64 = 78 = 9 = 23:

Jennetting 37 = 51 = 65 = 79 = 10 = 24 = 38 = 52 = 66 = 80 = 194

Maidens blush 11 = 25 = 39 = 53 = 67 = 81: 90

French Pipen = 12 = 26 = 40 = 54 = 68 = 82: one dead

Newtown do: 13: 27: 41: 55: 69: 83:

Roman Stem: 14 = 28 = 42 = 56 = 70 = 84: 71: 85:

White Pipen = 15 = 29 = 43 = 57: 197: 198 = 199 = 200: 201: 202:

Ridge do 86: 100: 114: 128:

Romanite 142: 156: 241: 242 all dead

Wine apple: 170: 184:

Yellow or Newark pipen: 87: 101: 115: 129:

Primes Harvest 143: 157: 171: 175 pine apple or melon 185
or June fragrant asa,

A 9 = 102: 116: 130:
144:

... 8 : 72 : 186 :

... ough : 89 : 145 :

Sweet Bellflower 103 = 218 = 229 +

Sweet Bough : 117 : 131 :

Early Red 145 : 159 : 173 : 187 :

Gustin or Ortley 90 : 104 : 118 :

Lady Washington = 132 : 130 = 210 :

Summer Pairmane = 146 : 160 : 174 : 188 : 229 = 214 = 215 = 216 =   or 23 : 231 = 217

Greasey Pippen 91 : 105 : 119 : 133 : 147

Summer queen 161 : 175 : 189 : 215 = 229

American pippen 92 : 106 : 120 : 8 6 :

fall ——— Do 134 : 148 : 162 : 176 : 190 =

Virginia greening 93 = 107 :

Seek no farther yellow = 121 : 135 : 149 : 163 : 177 = 191 :

Topside or Cherrycheek = 94 = 108 = 122 : 136 :

Rhode Island greening 150 : 164 : 174 : 192 :

Black apple 95 : 109 : 123 : 137 : 151 : 165 : 179 :

Golden Russet 96 = 110 : 124 : 138 : 152 : 166 : 180 : 197   Date

Bellflour 193 = 194 = 97 : 111 : 125 : 139 : 153 : 167 : 181 : 195 : 182 : 196

Newtown Spitzenburg = 98 : 112 : 126 : 140 : 154 : 168 :

Putnams Russet 99 : 113 : 127 : 141 :

Esopus Spitzenburg 155 : 169 : 183 : 206 :

Pound pippen 203 = 203 = 204 :

Penock 207 = 208 :

Butter apple 223 : 224 = 225 = 4 = 222 : 221 : 220 :

Kyle 18 = 29 :

Seuoual 233 = 234 = 235 = 235 = 236 = 237 = 243

Sulphurock 21 = 22

296

A List of the Medicine of Apples Studdies ...

Orchard 184...

xlix

Charlie Baker with family and friends at gathering

1893 — Charlie Baker, aged 10; Alma Baker, aged 4; and Jacob Baker, aged 8

Jacob Baker, aged 18.

50th Anniversary Pictures — Charlie and Fairy

Myron Baker, Lois Baker, Norman Bellamy and girlfriend, Bill Bellamy, Lorena Bellamy, unknown woman, Alice Bellamy, Charlie Bellamy, Sue Poston, Loron Baker, Margery Baker, Fairy Baker and Charles Baker.

Alma Baker, daughter of John Q. Baker and Mary Jane Toms. She lived on Summit Avenue in Lebanon after she moved from the Harris farm. She was married to Henry Harris.

Herry Harris and Alma Baker Harris

Photo of 1917 Baker Family reunion
From left: Charlie Baker, Grandma "Toms" Baker, Fairy, Kate's husband (?) with Kate in front,
unknown, "Link" Henry Lincoln Baker, and John Q. Baker.
Front row: Myron Baker, 2 girls,

In the orchard — Grandma "Molly" Toms, Fairy, a young girl, Adrene, and Charlie Baker

Left to right:
Ella Calloway, Fairy Watkins Baker,
Mary Jane Baker, Henry Harris, Alma
Baker Harris, Lorena Baker, Grandma
Baker, Charlie Baker, John Q. Baker
The group is standing in front of the
Stubbs barn which was located on the
Stubbs homestead. The house was
located (out of the picture) to the right.

From the back to front:
Aileen Smith with Mr. Rust, her husband.
Bill Bellamy, Mary Jane "Molly" Baker, Bess Rust, Aderene Watkins Hunt, Charlie Baker
Two unknown individuals, Grandma Baker, Lorena Bellamy, Jane Rust, Leon Hunt
Children in front: Charlie Bellamy, Norman Bellamy, Bobbie Bellamy

Butter churning. Mary Kate
Baker is the young woman on the right.
At the death of her
mother in 1878, Mary Kate was
placed under the guardianship of John
Shawhan, who lived
close by and was as attorney in Lebanon.

Fairy and Charlie—date unknown.

Charlie and Fairy's 50th wedding anniversary picture with their 2 children, Myron and Lorena Baker

John Q. Baker, around 1900s.

this union were born two children: one daughter, Lorena C., and one son, Myron C.

Born in the country, she loved nature, and a great part of her life she spent in the culture and development of fruits and flowers, assisting Mother Nature in her display of various forms of beauty. Such was her greatest hobby, and from it she derived much pleasure.

She loved God, and believed firmly in all His great principles and precepts; she lived as she interpreted His lessons—"By their deeds ye shall know them."

She leaves to mourn her passing: her husband; one daughter, Lorena Bellamy, of Valrico, Florida; one son, Myron C. Baker, of Morrow, Ohio; three sisters: Mrs. Jane Brant, of Morrow, Ohio; Mrs. Blanche Sanford, of Lebanon, Ohio; Mrs. Adarene Hunter, of Cincinnati; two brothers: John Watkins, of Columbus, Ohio, Stanley Watkins, of Lebanon, Ohio; six grandchildren; four great-grandchildren, and many neighbors and friends, who will miss her kind and cheery greetings of life as she passed them to those whom she met and loved.

Sunset and evening star,
And one clear call for me!
And may there be no moaning of the bar
When I put out to sea;
But such a tide as moving seems asleep,
Too full for sound or foam,
When that which drew from out the boundless deep
Turns again home.

Twilight and evening bell,
And after that the dark!
And may there be no sadness of farewell,
When I embark;
For tho' from out our bourne of Time or Place
The flood may bear me far,
I hope to see my Pilot face to face
When I have crossed the bar.

EXPRESSION OF THANKS

We wish to express our heartfelt thanks and gratitude to all our friends, neighbors and relatives for their kind rememberance with cards, beautiful flowers, deeds of helpfulness and consoling words at the time of the passing of our dear wife and mother, Mrs. Fairy E. Baker. We also wish to thank Rev. Wones for his consoling words and the Vale Funeral Home for their efficient services.

MR. CHAS. S. BAKER,
LORENA C. BELLAMY,
MYRON C. BAKER

OBITUARY
4-10-1958
FAIRY ELMA BAKER

Fairy Elma Watkins, eldest daughter of Clinton D. Watkins and Althe Worley, was born near Morrow, Ohio, on July 3, 1882; and passed away in Bradenton, Florida, on March 27, 1958, aged 75 years, 8 months, 24 days.

Her entire life was spent in and near the community in which she was born. Her education was received in the local schools.

She was married on September

ROBERT

Fairy Baker, nee Watkins, obituary 4-10-1958

Farm tour— Myron driving the tractor and Loron standing in front of him. Frank Alderson is on Loron's left.

Carmel Apple Recipe in Myron's handwriting.

4 generations of Bakers:
Loron in Myron's arms, Charlie and Grandma Toms

Myron in his airplane, Columbus
Dispatch, July 20, 1946

It Takes Apple Grower To Get To Core Of Thing

BY BILL THOMAS
Of The Enquirer Staff

LEBANON, Ohio — Myron Baker was born practically in the midst of an apple orchard with a model airplane in his hand and he's been plucking fruit and flying planes ever since.

In 1959, he was named Ohio's "Flying Farmer of the Year" and continues to be one of the state's most active flying farmers. He's also one of the state's most active apple pluckers.

Myron Baker operates an orchard of apple trees halfway between Lebanon and Morrow on Stubbs Mill Road in Warren County and finds the occupation both challenging and fascinating. He rides herd on 4000 apple trees and sometimes crates up to 30,000 bushels of juicy delicious fruit annually.

"That's in a good year," he said. "Last year now, was one of our worst and we only picked 2500 bushels of apples. That early May freeze just killed us."

There are other headaches in the apple orchard business, too, and Myron Baker, who grew up there and spent all of his 50 years learning how to produce a better apple at less cost, knows all about them.

He's had headaches at various times of various consequences. There's the scab, the apple worm, and all kinds of insects and diseases that can make either the apple or the apple tree very, very sick. And of course, that makes Myron Baker sick, too.

"IT'S A constant battle against something," he said, spraying his fruit trees during a light rain. "But when you think you've got the battle half won, then comes along something else to upset your plans. I said it was chalenging . . . hell . . . it's sometimes just plain discouraging."

But Myron Baker has weathered most of the storms of the apple orchard. And he's weathered most storms among flying farmers, too. Being director of Region Three of the International Flying Farmers, which includes Michigan, Indiana, Ohio, Kentucky, West Virginia and Ontario, Canada, for the past four years has taught him much.

He has seen the organization grow, however, and become an influential group in the nation.

Mr. Baker says there are about 75 flying farmers who are members of the International Flying Farmers Association in Kentucky and a like number in Ohio and Indiana.

The airplane is very much a part of farm operations for these men. They use their planes to dust crops, to run errands, to fly in supplies or to feed livestock marooned by high water or blizzards.

Some folks around Warren County who know Myron Baker suspect he uses his to pick apples from high in the trees, but he says "No."

He does find it handy in sales work, however, and many times when he could not fill an order from his own supplies of apples, he has flown north to other apple territory to buy hundreds of bushels of fruit to fulfill the order.

Myron Baker has been flying since he was 16 years old and has owned his own plane since 1940. He's had four planes now, the latest a Tri-Pacer, which he keeps in his own metal hangar.

"Flying is a hobby and a business, pleasure and work combined," said Mr. Baker.

—Enquirer (Thomas) Pho

Myron Baker Plots Flight Course

. . . a toy airplane in one hand, an apple in the other

"I would no more think of being without my plane than I would a tractor on my farm. I'll never be without one again."

The flying farmers have set up their own set of objectives which include, among other things:

● The promotion of the practical use of the airplane in the agricultural industry.

● Sponsor education a research in agricultural a ation.

● To encourage close - landing strips for tow and cities.

● And to express ide and opinions of farm fa ilies at the national level

Myron Baker is a push of all these goals and has seen progress made. hopes to see more.

lx

6-2-60

Ohio Flying Farmers Elect Queen

The Ohio Flying Farmers at the annual meeting held recently at Pomerene Hall, Ohio State University, elected Mrs. Myron Baker of Lebanon-Maplewood Orchards, near Lebanon, as Ohio Flying Farmer Queen for 1960. The Queen and her husband own and operate the orchards.

Queen Baker's duties are to act as hostess at all activities of Flying Farmers and to head women's activities and encourage them to do more flying. Main project this year set up by the national queen is the "Land-it" program. This is a safety measure, so the wife may take over the controls from her seat and safely land the plane in case of illness or incapacitation of her flyer husband. This program is expected to encourage more women to learn to fly and earn a private pilot's license.

The Ohio Queen is responsible for publishing a monthly news letter of the activities of the Ohio group. She also submits a condensed article for publication in the National Flying Farmer monthly magazine.

Queen Baker's husband is a charter member of the Ohio Flying Farmers. It was organized 14 years ago. The Bakers last year made a trip to the Bahamas with the National FF group. Baker this week is at Dawson Creek, British Columbia, with the National FF. President Vernon Pond of Scott, Ohio.

There are a number of active and associate members in the area with John Lane, an OFF director and Baker happy to furnish information to interested persons. Flying Farmer members in this area are Mr. and Mrs. Roy Hayes, Springboro; Mr. and Mrs. Leslie Shaffer, Mr. and Mrs. Jerry Cooke, Mr. and Mrs. William Davidson, Lebanon; members who have facilities to land at their back door are Mr. and Mrs. Corwin S. Fred, Leslie Kearns, Mr. and Mrs. Baker; Mr. and Mrs. John Lane who operate the Lebanon Airport on Greentree Road; Charles Smith who operates the Warren County Airport on Rt. 48 just south of Lebanon and Mr. and Mrs. George Beltzhoover, who have a golf course beside their airstrip.

In August Queen Baker will go to the National Convention to vie for the national crown. Forty-one states and five provinces of Canada have organized Flying Farmer groups and will participate. More than 1,500 members and their families will fly to this convention in Oklahoma City, Okla. Oklahoma.

The many air strips in Warren County indicate progress. Flying Farmers of the area will a look to the future, Mrs. Baker explained. Farmers who own planes find they are valuable to their business as well as enjoyment for the family — and it is surprising how many wives like to pilot these planes, the queen concluded.

OHIO FLYING FARMER QUEEN—Mrs. Myron Baker of Morrow Route 2, was signally honored recently when she was elected Ohio Flying Farmer Queen for 1960. She will compete for national honors in August at Oklahoma City. (Rueppel Photo)

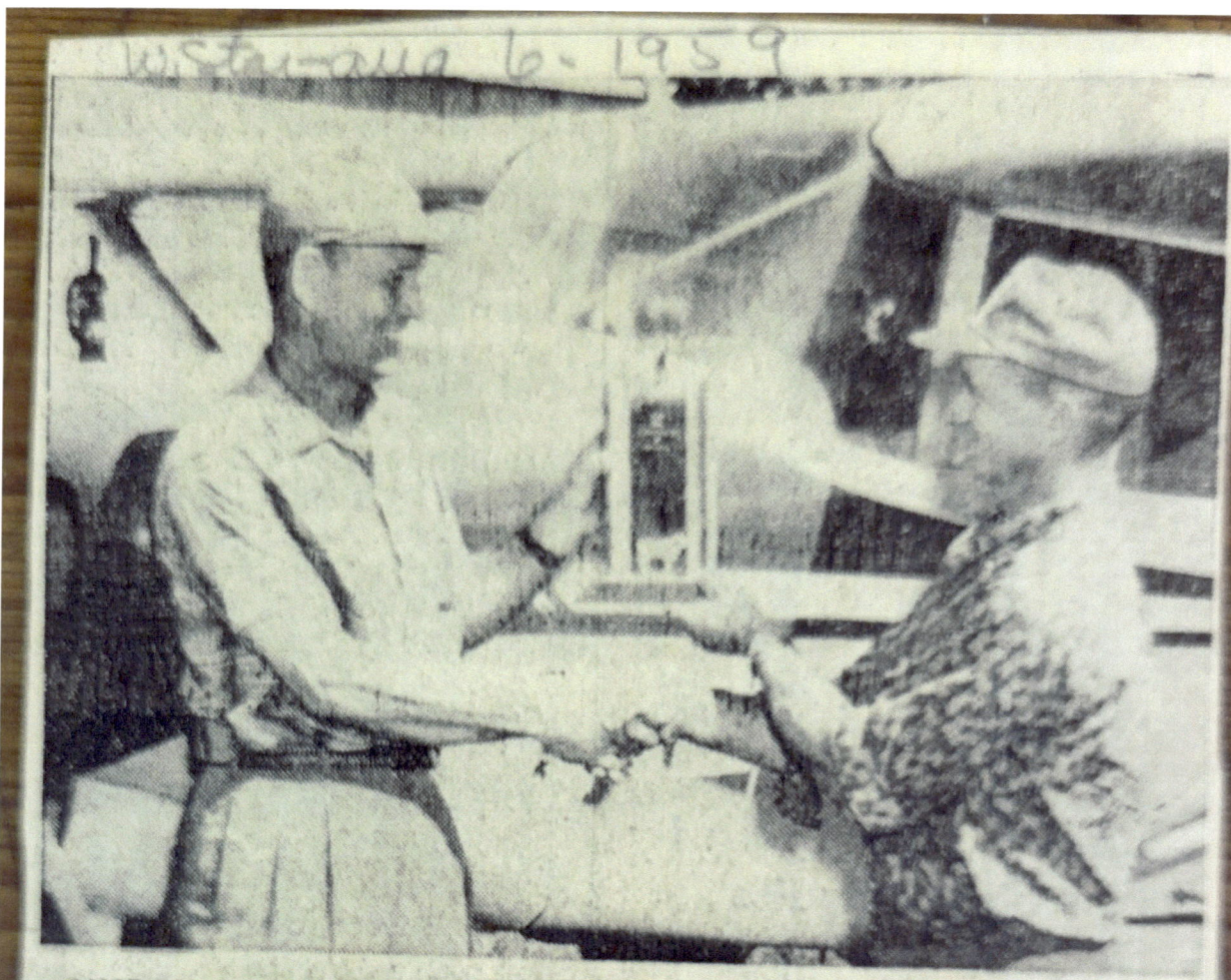

W.Star-aug 6-1959

MYRON BAKER IS NAMED FLYING FARMER OF THE YEAR in Ohio and is being presented the trophy of the honor by Dale Studebaker, president of the Ohio Flying Farmers. The ceremony took place at Dale Scott airport, Columbus. Baker will vie for the National Flying Farmer honors at the convention at Ft. Collins, Colorado on August 9-14. Baker was honored for work in the legislative field in promoting private flying.

The Cincinnati Post and Times-Star

All Week MAGAZINE

Saturday, October 18, 1969

One Small Step... To Treats In Tree

Michael Mikula, year-old son of Mr. and Mrs. Al Mikula, Oxford, O., takes one small, faltering step toward the goodies high above his head. Photos by Joseph P. Herring.

Karen Games, nine-year-old daughter o
Mrs. Richard Games, Finneytown, mu
watches as Kent Willis, six-year-old son
Mrs. Bruce Willis, Springdale, looks on

By Jo Thomas

On sunny fall days the apple trees at Maplewood Orchard, Morrow, O., are full of children.

They come by the dozens with their families to pick Jonathan, Winesap, Yellow Delicious—20 varieties of apples in all. They usually eat as many as they pick while Mom and Dad fill bushel baskets with apples for lunch boxes, pies and apple-sauce.

Afterwards, in the barn, there's all the cider you can drink for a dime. And if you can still eat, there are candy apples made on the spot for 15 cents. The caramel is still warm and sticks to teeth.

Myron Baker opens one orchard on his 300-acre farm to families from September until Nov. 1. He gives them a numbered guide to the 600 trees so they can find the apples they want.

Maplewood's 300 acres have about 4000 trees, and the apple crop is 35,000 bushels if the weather has been good.

The apples are crated for shipment or stored for everything from Halloween apple-bobbing to Christmas stockings.

Baker has built a candy apple machine—a Rube Goldberg device—that turns out 700 to 800 boxes of candy apples a day—28 to a box. Candy apples must be tart and firm enough to hold a stick, he explains.

Baker also makes 1000 to 1500 gallons of cider a day, blending at least three varieties of apples into each. Cider, he explains, is not the same as apple juice, which is pasturized.

Baker lets families pick apples for $3 a bushel. If they buy the apples he's picked instead, they pay $4.50. Most families pick —and munch—their own.

Baker's Country Store: Located on Stubbs Mill Road several miles north of Little Miami River cross-ing.

Western Star—fall of 1985

Maplewood Orchard—located on Stubbs Mill Road, Morrow, Ohio

Apples aplenty this year

By Nadine Louthan
Post Staff Reporter

If the fr___ ___ crop left your fr___ basket empty, you may f___ for the winter from a bum___ crop of apples.

T___ __ol, wet weather in June ___ __ugh frustrating for peo___ ___ was just what the apples __ded. Their growth was excellent, said Richard C. Funt, horticulturist at Ohio State University.

The often unpredictable weather this year produced an unusually cold spell last January that froze the buds then forming on peach trees in the Greater Cincinnati area. Most of the peach crop was lost.

BUT APPLE trees endured the cold better and now are on their way to producing the second largest harvest since 1960, Funt said. He estimates a harvest this year of 165 million pounds in Ohio, about 65 million pounds more than average, but about 5 million pounds less than 1980's record crop.

Mr. and Mrs. Myron Baker of Maplewood Farms at Morrow have been picking apples for their customers since July 4. Their apples are mostly cooking varieties for pies, applesauce and jelly. Their main crop of apples will begin to ripen in about two weeks, Mrs. Baker said, and their pick-your-own operation begins Sept. 10.

"Every tree in our orchard has apples on it," she said. "The trees are loaded. We're going to have plenty of apples this year."

Apples of almost every kind are being picked now at Hollmeyer Farm, 3241 Fiddler's Green Road, Green Township.

"WE HAVE A bumper crop of apples," Ray Hollmeyer said. "We're picking both cooking and eating apples—Early Blaze, Paulared, Prima and by the weekend we will have an early Delicious apple ready to harvest."

Hollmeyer said he doesn't offer pick-your-own service, but his family will sell "from one apple to a truck load" at the fruit and vegetable stand at the farm.

Vaughn Hempfling of Parlor Grove Farms at Hebron, Ky., said his orchard has a pretty good crop but it is not one he would call a bumper crop this year. The farm is open now from 8 a.m. to 8 p.m daily.

NATIONWIDE, the apple crop is forecast to be 8.56 billion pounds, or 11 percent more than last year. The country's total harvest will be about 3 percent below the record 1980 yield, Funt said.

The apple boom is bypassing some of the warmer states this year, however. Four states are predicting losses. Apple yield in North and South Carolina, Georgia and California is expected to be 450 million pounds less that in 1981. But Michigan, New York, Pennsylvania and West Virginia will produce about 1.1 billion pounds more than in 1981. Michigan's super crop this fall is estimated to be 950 million pounds, 44 percent or 50 million pounds more than the state harvested in 1981.

Myron and Lois Baker and their daughter, Jeane Weisbrod, are happy to see the bumper crop of apples this year on their farm near Morrow, Ohio.

Article from Cincinnati Post—August 18, 1982

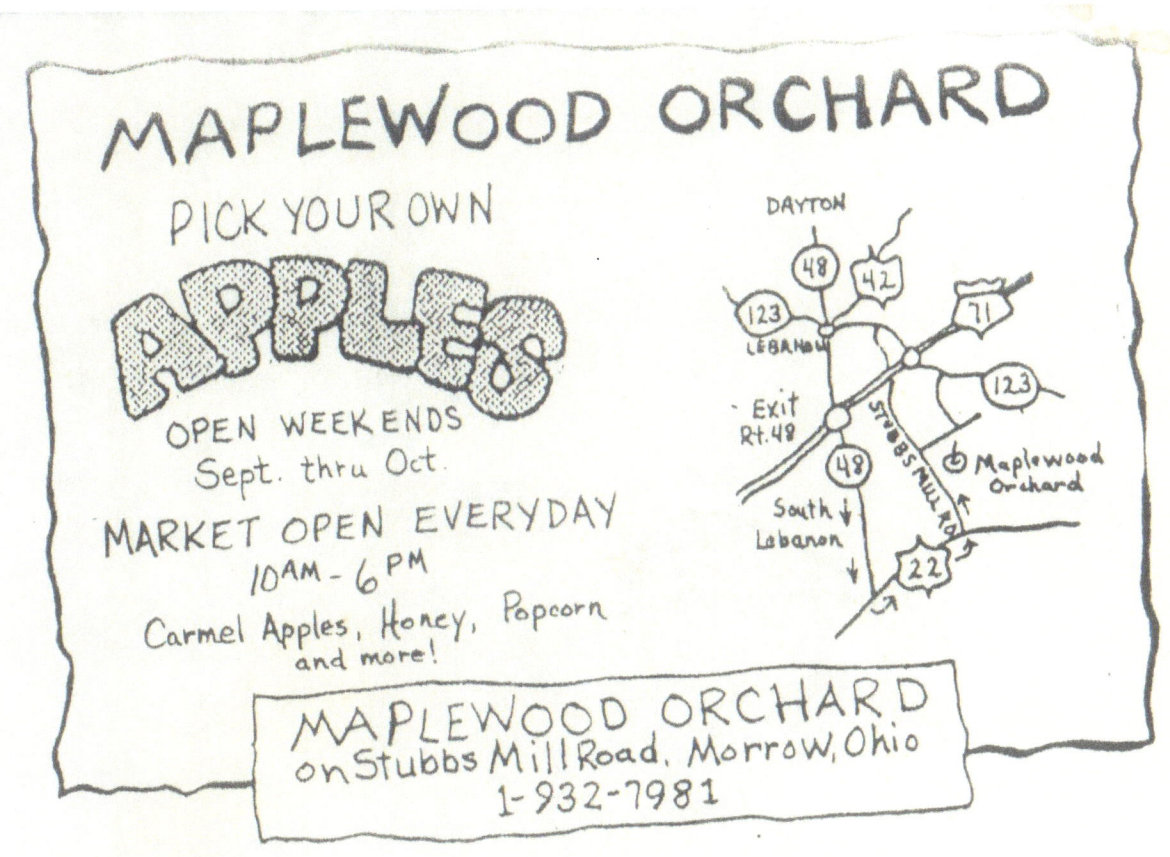

Advertising, drawn by Jeane Baker Weisbrod for local newspapers

State Apple Queen No Longer
Teased About 'Delicious' Wardrobe

By JIM ROHRER
Lebanon Bureau Chief

MORROW, Ohio — It used to be [th]at [cl]assmates teased red-haired [Jea]ne Baker about her "apple" [cl]o[thes].

"I've always had all kinds. Ap[pl]e dresses, shoes, apple jewelry, [ev]erything," J e a n e remembered. [An]d her mother, Mrs. Myron Bak[er] [still] recalls the expense of the [va]st apple wardrobe.

They probably wouldn't tease so [mu]ch now, though, because 18[ye]ar-old Jeane, a June graduate of [Litt]le Miami High School, now [rei]gns as Ohio's 1973 apple queen.

She g a i n e d that distinction [Ju]ne 21 at the Ohio State Horticul[tur]al Society summer meeting at [Em]mons Peace Valley Orchard [ne]ar Youngstown in Columbiana [Co]unty, edging out six other con[tes]tants who held such titles as [Ja]ckson County apple queen and [Jo]hnny Appleseed Festival queen.

After all that talk about apples [an]d festival queens, Jeane figures [it] was probably her knowledge of [pes]ticides, of all things, which won [he]r the title.

"The one crucial question was [to] answer what our response would [be] to someone who talked to us [abo]ut pesticides in a negative [wa]y," she remembered.

[S]he quickly warms to that sub[jec]t. "Pesticides are absolutely nec[ess]ary to grow apples," she stated. [Th]ey are only harmful when used [in] the wrong way. It's not orchard[ist]s but people who don't read the [lab]els or aren't familiar with the [pro]duct who cause damage," she [ad]ded.

[I]t just happens to come natu[ral]ly to Jeane, since ever since she [ca]n remember she was surrounded [by] apples and worked in an apple [orc]hard.

[H]ER PARENTS own and operate [Ap]plewood Orchards on Stubbs [Mil]ls Road near Morrow in Warren [Cou]nty. The 75-acre layout is noted [for] its large cider press, which sup[pli]es cider to roadside stands [thr]oughout the tri-state, and for [its] "pick your own" days which [are] held in the fall, when custom[ers] come in and fill up their own [bus]hel baskets. There is also a car[am]el apple "factory" which takes [20] people to operate in the fall.

"My playpen was an apple [cra]te," Jeane is fond of saying.

"Before I was even old enough to count right, I could make change for a bushel of apples."

One of her early childhood memories, in fact, dates from when she was about four years old, left in charge of the place while her parents were out. Customers trying to cheat the diminutive seller came in for a shock when asked for the "right amount of money" from a little tyke who had to stretch to reach the cash register.

THESE DAYS, she most enjoys working during the pick your own days, when customers are given printed sheets to show locations of different varieties, then clamber up ladders to fill their plastic bushel bags.

Two important stops for Jeane this year will be the Ohio State Fair in Columbus, where she will compete in the "Queen of Queens Contest," and the national Apple Queen Contest in Gettysburg, Pa., in October.

"Some of the o t h e r apple queens weren't raised on apple or-chards," she said. This knowledge will help as she promotes apples throughout the state, she feels. She already knows this has been a bad year for many apple growers.

"We're at a perfect location here. We're up on top of a hill and we have good air drainage. All the cold air goes in the valley. But some growers have just about been wiped out by frost," she said.

Jeane's plans now call for a ma-jor in vocal music at Wittenburg University in the fall. A vocalist all through school, she spent last sum-mer as a singer for "Tinfolk," for-merly the Little Miami Folk Sing-ers, at Kings Island. There she spent six-day weeks performing at the park's rivertown section.

In 1967, as a 12-year-old, Jeane wowed them at the International Flying Farmers Teen Talent Con-test, singing "Second Hand Rose," and "In The Shadow of the Old Apple Tree There's a Beach," win-ning first place and $100.

If the main idea is for the apple queen to push apples, the young miss with the apple clothes and apple-red hair, the daughter of ap-ple growers, fills the bill nicely.

She worries that national apple consumption is down. But con-sumption may go up by the time Ohio's 1973 apple queen has ended her reign.

—Enquirer (Jim Rohrer) Photo

Jeane Baker Checks Green Fruit
. . . yes, that's an apple design on her dress

Instructions for "PICK YOUR OWN APPLES"

FIRST AND FOREMOST, because of the danger of fire, please **NO SMOKING** in the orchard at any time.

2. Apples should be handled like eggs, carefully. A bruised apple is a second grade apple, we want you to take home only perfect fruit.

3. Be careful you don't fall, people have been known to fall out of trees. Take no chances at any time.

4. Stay within the area assigned to you. Those who do not abide with this request will be told to leave. It will save embarrassment for us as well as for those who do not care to co-operate.

5. If you have children with you, and we hope you have, do not allow them to throw apples, someone may get hurt.

6. We have tried to restrict our "pickers" to real folks, we hope all of you will live up to our expectations. Rough talk or any other type of rudeness will not be tolerated.

7. We hope all of you will have a profitable and enjoyable experience and we hope it will work out so that we can do it again sometime. It is the first time a "pick your own" has been tried on apples in the middle west, to our knowledge, and we hope we have thought of everything which will make it work. If you have any suggestions, we would appreciate them.

8. If you cannot put a lid on your basket, you have picked more than a bushel. This will be checked at the gate when you leave.

9. AGAIN, **PLEASE DO NOT SMOKE.** A FIRE WOULD KILL THE TREES AND PUT US OUT OF BUSINESS. THANKS FOR YOUR CO-OPERATION.

10. Ladders and picking baskets are scattered in the orchard. When finished using them, please place so the next picker can find them.

BAKER'S MAPLEWOOD ORCHARDS

STUBBS MILL ROAD
MORROW, OHIO 45152

MYRON C. BAKER
OWNER

Mm-Mm Good...
Apple Harvest In Full Swing

By TARA ENGEL

Jean Weisbrod remembers being urged awake on a cold night in 1966.

"My mother led me to an upstairs window, saying 'you just have to see this,'" she recalls.

As the youngster rubbed the sleep from her eyes, she gazed across a familiar landscape turned surreal by a patchwork of small fires and a black curtain of smoke clinging to the treetops.

The orchard was under siege by mother nature. Jean's parents, Lois and Myron Baker, were fighting back.

"Unfortunately, it didn't work. The frost came anyway and took our apple crop with it," she says. "We've learned over the years that all the technology in the world can be pretty useless against the forces of nature."

This year, however, the forces of nature were kind, and the Baker's trees – known collectively as Maplewood Orchard – are boasting a solid crop of large, crisp apples.

"You really don't want trees that are filled with apples, because the apples tend to be smaller. It's better to have fewer apples, but have them good-sized," Weisbrod explains.

She says that spring frosts, like the one in 1966, are a yearly concern for her family.

"The weather is so critical to every crop. The family is on pins and needles during the spring, never knowing if a late cold snap will destroy the crop," Weisbrod said.

And what if one does?

"You can't let the business stop, that's for sure. You have to get your supplies elsewhere. In 1966, we bought all our apples from North Carolina," she noted.

Big Cider Producer

For Maplewood Orchard, getting those apples in – one way or the other – is critical because the operation produces apple cider for other business throughout the region.

"We can press up to 1,000 gallons a day. We then sell to businesses that don't have a cider press, and they put their own label on the cider ," she explained, adding that Maplewood provides all the cider for Waynesville's upcoming Saurkraut festival.

Maplewood matriarch Lois Baker talks about the origins and evolutions of her beloved orchard, noting that the first plot of land destined to become Maplewood was not bought, but traded for a turkey. Myron Baker's parents wanted to settle on 33 acres of land, around the turn of the century, but did not have enough money to purchase it. The owner of the tract explained that his family was in need of a Thanksgiving turkey and perhaps a trade could be worked out.

"And the family has been here ever since," Lois Baker said.

In the beginning, Maplewood earned its moniker by focusing on maple syrup production.

"But during World War II Myron's father could get enough help with the sap collection and syrup making, so he turned to selling apples," Baker explained.

The former nurse is quick to sing praises of apples, calling them "nature's most perfect food."

"There are 7,000 different kinds of apples, and Maplewood started out selling about 65 varieties," Baker said. "Today, we've whittled that down considerably, focusing on the most popular and hardy types, such as Jonathan, Red and Yellow Delicious and Winesap varieties."

She adds that apples vary based on their growing season and level of sweetness.

Kids And Apples

"I am never happier than

Pictured at top, Lois Baker dons an apple picking bag and demonstrates to spellbound youngsters the art of getting the freshest, juiciest apple. Below, two of the generations responsible for Maplewood's success, from left, Jean Weisbrod, Myron Baker and Lois Baker.

when I see a child eat and apple," Baker said. "Apples have vitamins and calcium. They have bulk, which so much of our diet lacks and they are good for heart trouble because they have the ability to pick up and remove cholesterol."

Baker says that apple harvest runs from July, when the earliest varieties are ready, to November. The early apples, she says do not keep well but make excellent apple sauce.

"September and October are the prime months for apple harvesting," she says.

They are also the months

when Lois Baker is constantly in motion. Schools begin bringing field trips to the orchard in September and Baker is always on hand to guide and educate the youngsters about nutrition and the life cycle of an apple. She admits that the daily visits for school children can be tiring, but she loves to visit with them and pass along her apple-mania.

Although July through October are harvest months, the work doesn't end when winter frosts coat the orchard. That is when the entire process of pruning, preparing, watching and waiting begins anew.

"It can be nerve wracking, but it's just such rewarding work. I can't imagine us doing anything else," she says.

Maplewood orchard offers the chance to pick your own apples every weekend after Labor Day until November. Pickers can visit the orchard from Friday noon until Sunday dusk. Maplewood will provide containers and apple-picker poles to assist in the process. For more information, call 932-7981.

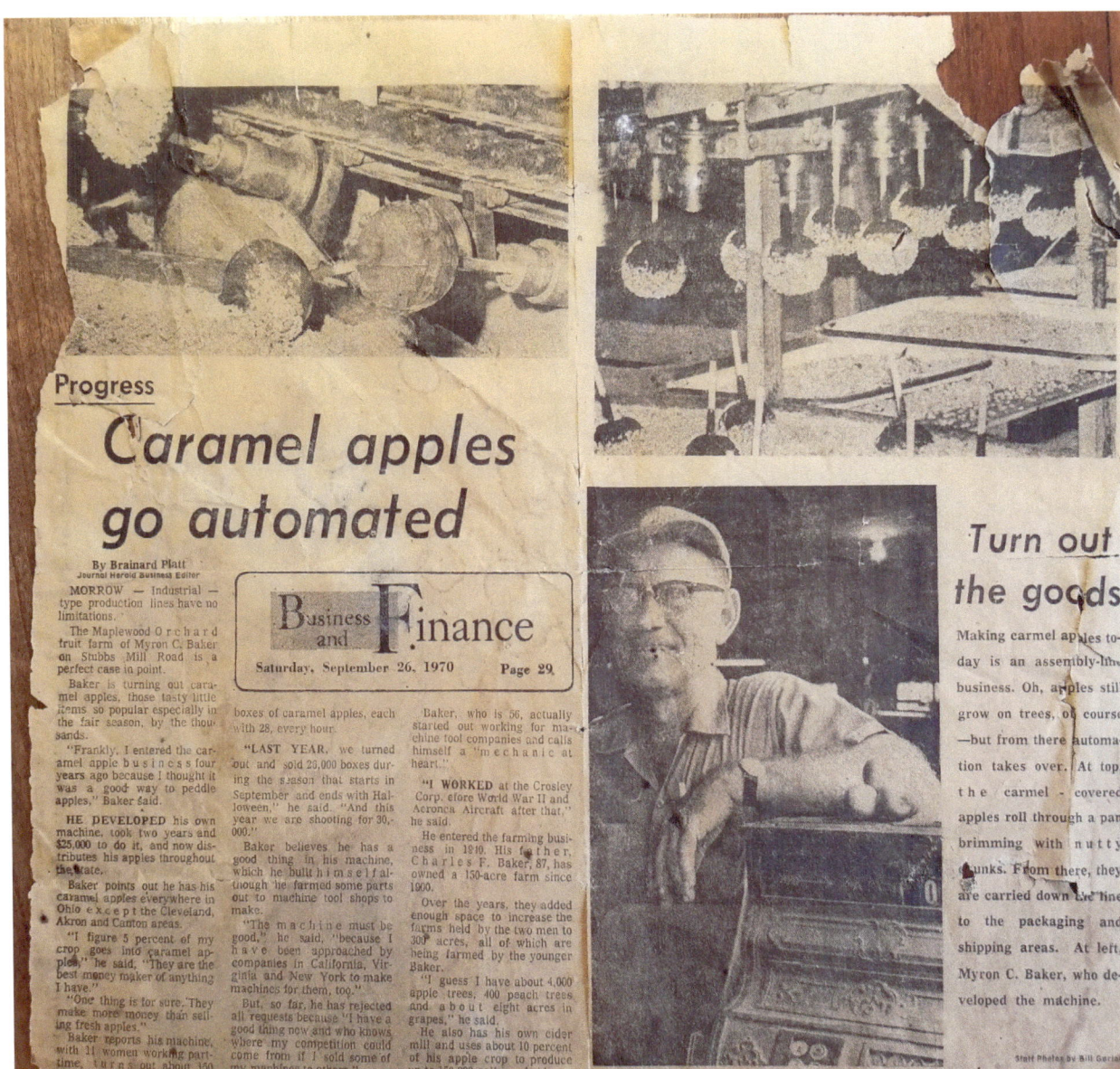

Progress

Caramel apples go automated

By Brainard Platt
Journal Herald Business Editor

Business and Finance

Saturday, September 26, 1970   Page 29

MORROW — Industrial — type production lines have no limitations.

The Maplewood O r c h a r d fruit farm of Myron C. Baker on Stubbs Mill Road is a perfect case in point.

Baker is turning out caramel apples, those tasty little items so popular especially in the fair season, by the thousands.

"Frankly, I entered the caramel apple b u s i n e s s four years ago because I thought it was a good way to peddle apples," Baker said.

HE DEVELOPED his own machine, took two years and $25,000 to do it, and now distributes his apples throughout the state.

Baker points out he has his caramel apples everywhere in Ohio e x c e p t the Cleveland, Akron and Canton areas.

"I figure 5 percent of my crop goes into caramel apples," he said. "They are the best money maker of anything I have."

"One thing is for sure. They make more money than selling fresh apples."

Baker reports his machine, with 11 women working part-time, turns out about 150 boxes of caramel apples, each with 28, every hour.

"LAST YEAR, we turned out and sold 26,000 boxes during the season that starts in September and ends with Halloween," he said. "And this year we are shooting for 30,000."

Baker believes he has a good thing in his machine, which he built h i m s e l f although he farmed some parts out to machine tool shops to make.

"The m a c h i n e must be good," he said, "because I h a v e been approached by companies in California, Virginia and New York to make machines for them, too."

But, so far, he has rejected all requests because "I have a good thing now and who knows where my competition could come from if I sold some of my machines to others."

Baker, who is 56, actually started out working for machine tool companies and calls himself a "mechanic at heart."

"I WORKED at the Crosley Corp. efore World War II and Aeronca Aircraft after that," he said.

He entered the farming business in 1910. His father, C h a r l e s F. Baker, 87, has owned a 150-acre farm since 1960.

Over the years, they added enough space to increase the farms held by the two men to 300 acres, all of which are being farmed by the younger Baker.

"I guess I have about 4,000 apple trees, 400 peach trees and a b o u t eight acres in grapes," he said.

He also has his own cider mill and uses about 10 percent of his apple crop to produce up to 150,000 gallons of cider.

Turn out the goods

Making carmel apples today is an assembly-line business. Oh, apples still grow on trees, of course —but from there automation takes over. At top, t h e carmel - covered apples roll through a pan brimming with nutty chunks. From there, they are carried down the line to the packaging and shipping areas. At left, Myron C. Baker, who developed the machine.

Staff Photos by Bill Garlow

'Most solid evidence yet'

MERRY-GO-ROUND RIDE BEGUN — Mrs. Ruby Alderson works beside Mrs. Lyons. This team fits raw material on a revolving wheel for a merry-go-round ride to a device that thrusts a wooden handle into the core.

APPLES ARE 'HANDLED' HERE — Maplewood's candy apples in the raw are shown above during the first stages of preparation. Mrs. Erma Lyons is shown here as she places apples between the spokes of a wheel apparatus that moves the fruit to an air compressor for stick insertion. On the left an air valve drives a stick handle into an apple. The completed process is shown in the foreground as apples move to the elevator which carries them to a conveyor for a caramel dip.

FRUIT GETS 'NUTTY' TREATMENT — Caramel coated apples receive a nutty rolling as they are conveyed from a candy bath to a bed of crushed peanuts. Peanuts are ground at Maplewood Orchard to insure freshness. Apples reach this stage after placement in conveyor trucks by a worker situated above the pictured equipment.

Orchard Sales Tuned To 'Caramel-ody'

By DENNIS DALTON

Autumn pungency has been confectionized for the orchard.

A tasty 18,000 cases of candy apples have already been distributed by production teams employed to handle an "appleanche" of crispy sales promotion.

Maplewood owners, Mr. and Mrs. Myron Baker have changed the complexion of fruit sales by giving their apples a caramelized polishing via a candy bath.

Baker began caramel apple operations Sept. 1 after purchasing equipment from the Martin Potato Chip Company at Cincinnati.

Two 10 person production staffs have candied 2,320 bushels of apples since the starting date. Seven bushels will manufacture 50 cases of candy coated fruit. Each case termed a tray will hold 28 apples.

Apples begin their journey to "candy-dom" on a revolving wheel-like device. They are first affixed to spoke-like holders which rotate them until an air compressor that jabs them with a stick handle.

The scoured fruit passes to an elevator which lifts them to a worker who inverts them in truck holders of a conveyor. From there the apples ride through a caramel bath in trough below.

Next the apples roll over bed of crushed peanuts and are dropped from their trucks a short distance beyond on a nut covered turntable for packaging.

Five tons of peanuts have been exhausted since production began the first week in September. Nuts are purchased in 300 pound barrels.

Caramel ingredients to date have included twenty-two barrels of condensed sweet milk; 12 barrels of corn syrup; 55 cases of six, six and one half pound cans of sweetened milk and four tons of sugar.

Baker said that his candy appling equipment was capable of producing 100 cases, 2,800 apples, per hour.

However, operations have yielded only 600 cases of approximately 1,200 trays per shift daily. Maplewood's biggest production day tallied 1,219 trays.

Apple size has been regulated at circumferences of 2¼ to 2½ inches. Jonathans have become the preferred fruit since their flesh is solid and their tartness combines easily with a caramel coating.

Grimes Golden and Golden Delicious were found suitable substitutes when numerous rains caused the Jonathan to outgrow candy size.

The candy apple business has successfully adapted itself to maplewood since Jonathan trees compose 75 per cent of the orchard's population. This year the Bakers used 80 per cent of their Jonathan crop. The remaining percentage has to be purchased elsewhere due to climatic conditions.

Lebanon candy apple sales are being handled by the G.C. Murphy Company and the Marsh Distributing Company of Cincinnati.

Other state distribution firms include the Schlater Distributing Company, North Star; Seyfert Potato Chip Company, Zanesville and the Coon Potato Chip Company, Lancaster and Zanesville.

The Bakers and their production crews plan to extend apple operations throughout October although the candy coated fruit "is a September item."

Warm weather for some unknown reason squelches the demand. Baker attributes this to the financial status and appetite capacity of the business's biggest customer, the youngster.

"The children love them so much that when the apples first hit the market the children use every extra penny to buy them," he commented. After gorging to a delightful fill youngsters apparently "burn out" their caramel apple appetites, according to him.

"Health wise we don't believe in this business," declared Mrs. Baker, a registered nurse. "Apples are a healthful food." "They don't need a sugar coating."

Numerous amounts of Maplewood's tasty products have been purchased by area high school Booster clubs. Large quantities have also been consumed at football game concession stands.

Baker said that he planned to fill two football game orders after Halloween. Then production will be halted until next year.

Late August has been calendared for next year's candy apple season. During the interim, Baker plans to design a machine that will eliminate hand placement of apples in their pleated paper cup containers. The hand apple-cup insertion has been this season's biggest bottleneck.

The approaching close hasn't silenced the air compressor's piercing punch or the dramatic bubbling of the caramel vat. Neither has it influenced the continuous activity of a staff relatived to conclude operations.

"I'm shooting for 25,000 trays," Baker exclaimed.

CANDY 'APPLING' IS CONTINUAL PROCESS — An elevator drops apples beside Ronald Traylor from the stick machine. Traylor is shown above as he inserts sticks in conveyor trucks. The conveyor pulls a train of apples to a caramel filled trough beneath him. Final caramelizing procedures are shown below Traylor as apples come to rest on a turntable of crushed peanuts after being caramel coated and bearded with nuts. Packers move them from the turntable to paper chip lined boxes.

— Dennis Dalton Photos

Bailey Bound Over To Grand Jury Friday

Oscar Bailey, 37, Lebanon, who attempted to flee from Sheriff's Deputies Sept. 30 after appearing before County Court Judge Paul Herdman, appeared in Lebanon Municipal Court Friday on charges of escaping confinement while in legal custody of an officer.

Bailey, who was shot in the leg and recaptured, entered a plea of innocent and requested the case be bound over. His Warren County Municipal Court Judge Albert Herrick bound Bailey over on $1,000 bond. Bailey was presently turned to the Warren County Jail where he has been since his return from Middletown hospital after the shooting incident.

Error Is Noted

Last week The Western Star reported in error that the Ladies Auxiliary of the Veterans of Foreign Wars Post 6009 was planning a dinner to raise money for the Warren County unit of the American Cancer Society.

APPLES ARE 'HANDLED' HERE — Maplewood's candy apples in the raw are shown above during the first stages of preparation. Mrs. Erma Lyons is shown here as she places apples between the spokes of a wheel apparatus that moves the fruit to an air compressor for stick insertion. On the left an air valve drives a stick handle into an apple. The completed process is shown in the foreground as apples move to the elevator which carries them to a conveyor for a caramel dip.

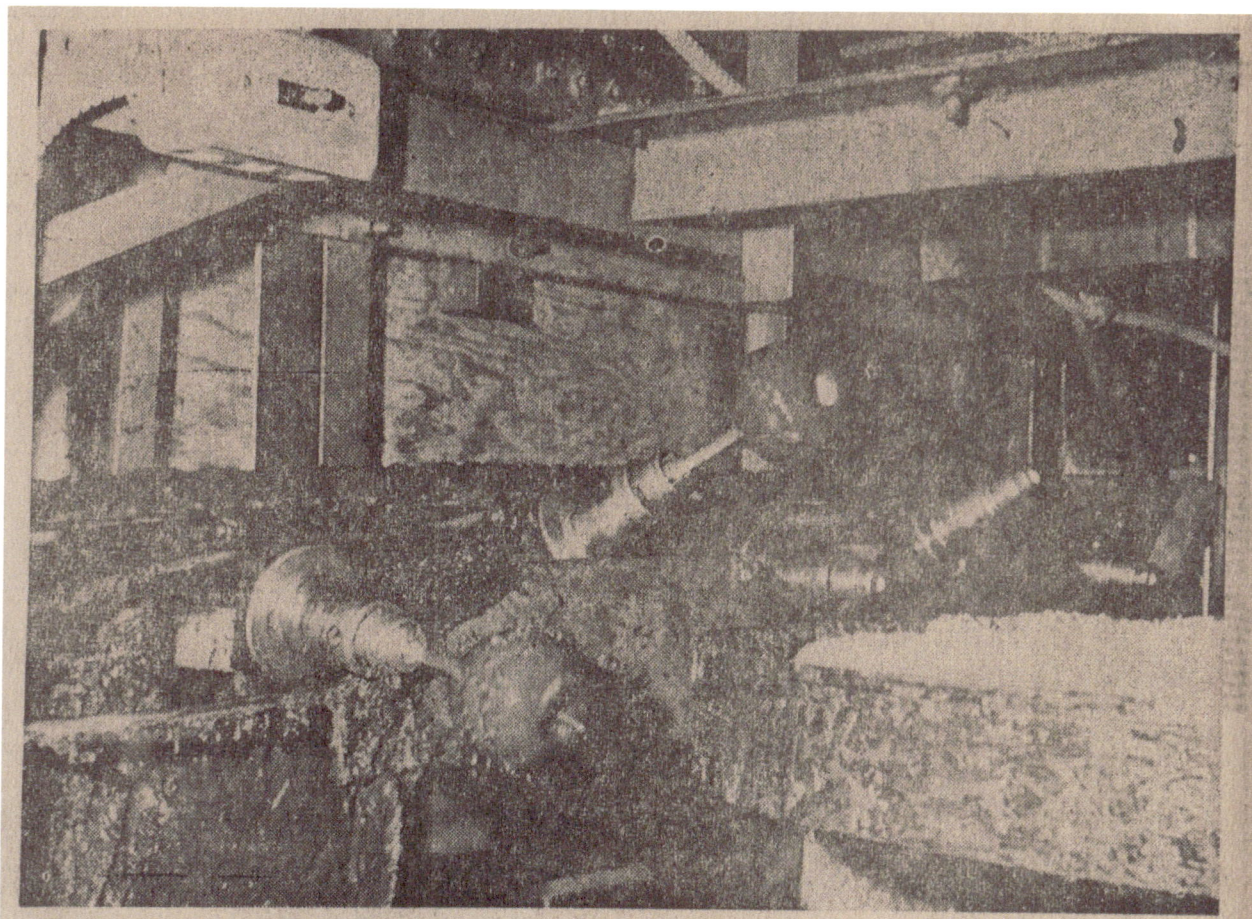

FRUIT GETS 'NUTTY' TREATMENT — Caramel coated apples receive a nutty rolling as they are conveyed from a candy bath to a bed of crushed peanuts. Peanuts are ground at Maplewood Orchard to insure freshness. Apples reach this stage after placement in conveyor trucks by a worker situated above the pictured equipment.

Lifestyle

MORE LIFESTYLE
Search for sexual cures
is an ancient one. Page 64

Orchard owners relish the 'simple' life

Old cider press is part of Tillie's buzz

Apple growing is a Baker family tradition

APPLE CAKE

APPLE CAKE FROSTING

Ices are a Turkish delight on a warm day

Common Cents

Frying Pan Follies

TURKS ICES

Bumper apple crop to stem from El Nino

Mild, wet winter works magic

BY DAVID ECK
Enquirer Contributor

LEBANON — El Nino is the apple of Ron Irons' eye.

The massive weather system that has wreaked havoc across the globe has been a blessing for Ohio apple farmers like Mr. Irons. El Nino brought a mild, but moist winter to most of the state, enabling apple trees to remain healthy and productive.

And thanks to a trouble-free spring, experts predict a bumper crop this fall.

"It looks like pretty much a full crop," said Mr. Irons, a third-generation fruit farmer on Stubb Mill Road near Lebanon. "It looks pretty good all over the state."

So good, in fact, that a past president of the Ohio Fruit Growers Society thinks 1998 could yield one of the state's largest apple harvests.

"We have an extremely full crop," said Dano Simmons, past president of the Ohio Fruit Growers Society. He has a 200-acre apple orchard near Youngstown. "We're putting on our first thinning sprays because there is such a large crop at our orchard."

Dave Gress, general man-

The Enquirer/Dick Swaim
Small apple blossoms on one of the Bakers' trees.

ager of the state's Fruit Growers Marketing Association, said this year's yield could be 2.8 million to 3 million bushels, about 700,000 more bushels than in 1997. "I wouldn't term it a bumper crop. I don't think we're going to be beyond that 3 million."

The state's potential total apple crop is about 3 million bushels a year, Mr. Gress said. The co-op in Newcomerstown, about an hour south of Akron/Canton, wholesales about 40 percent of the apples grown in Ohio. Though there will be more apples this year, Mr. Gress said he doesn't expect a noticeable increase in the price consumers pay for the fruit.

"Everything we deal with, as far as the growing end, just costs us more money," he said. "I don't think you're going to see a lot of difference in retail cost changes."

Back in Warren County, Myron Baker, 82, works the apple orchards his dad settled in 1903 in Morrow.

Sitting in an old wooden barn crammed with 50 years of machinery and tools, Mr.

The Cincinnati Enquirer/Dick Swaim
Maplewood Orchard owner Myron Baker, right, and his son, Loron Baker, check out some of the apple buds on his trees. "I'd say it's (this year's crop) going to be a little higher than average." Myron Baker said.

Baker said he expects his 20-acre grove of apple trees to have a good season.

"I'd say it's going to be a little higher than average," he said.

In addition to offering pick-your-own, Mr. Baker sells apples to Cincinnati bakeries such as Servatii, Busken and Bonnie Lynn. He makes and sells apple cider and in the fall maintains a country store.

"We get big crowds here on Sundays," said Myron's wife, Lois.

In Clermont County just east of Milford, Dan and Donna Rouster of Rouster's Apple House are watching their 18 acres of apple trees bloom.

"The apple crop's great," Mr. Rouster said. "I would say overall, we're in pretty good shape. The apples are set on the trees."

Farmers, who grow nervous during cold spring nights that could freeze their crop, said those worries are behind them for this year.

The growers' optimism is in sharp contrast to last year, when an April cold snap all but wiped out Ohio's apple crop. "Last year, we just didn't have any," said Mr. Baker, who bought apples to fill orders.

Loren Baker of Maplewood Orchards, Morrow, operates the hydraulic cider press, above. Maplewood employee Ray Sallee, at right, hauls another load of apples to the grinder, the last step before the apple pulp is pressed for cider.

Myron and Lois 50th wedding anniversary. 1987

*April 9, 1994 Myron Baker, Ty Baker
(standing) and Loron
Baker. (Three generations)*

Baker Family Wedding Photos

Charlie Bellamy wedding—1950 with Margery as flower girl

Loron Baker wedding—1960 with Jeane as flower girl

Margery Baker wedding picture with Jeane as a bridesmaid — 1968

Jeane Baker wedding—1979

Glen Bellamy wedding —1984

Kathy Baker—1988

Ty Baker wedding —1995

Melanie Simchak wedding —1997

Elizabeth Simchak wedding —2007

Laura Simchak wedding — 2008

Susan Weisbrod wedding — 2019

Richard Weisbrod 2019

Many of the flower girls gathered in Arizona in 2018 at the 50th wedding anniversary of Frank and Margery Simchak.
From left to right: Susan Weisbrod Lopez, Brooke Walker, Laura Simchak Moore, Jeane Baker Weisbrod, Mealnie Simchak Hull, Elizabeth Simchak Buchanan, Michelle Blackburn, Kathy Baker Blackburn

When an engagement is announced in the Baker family, one of the first questions is: "Who has the flower basket?" It has been carried in family weddings for over 60 years in Ohio, Arizona and Nebraska. The tradition began, not purposefully, but merely because my mother kept it when I carried it at my brother's wedding (Loron Baker) in 1960. It evolved into a tradition from there. Plans are set for it to be carried in Chicago in July 2023 for the wedding of Michelle Blackburn. She is the granddaughter of Loron and Dixie Baker. This will be the first wedding of the 3rd generation in the Baker family where the flower basket will be used.

ACKNOWLEDGEMENTS

All of the information is true to the best of my knowledge. I gathered information from books written by Julia Watkins Frost and Samuel Watkins which I mentioned in the text. The rest of the information came from various places. I gathered lots of dates from genealogy references. I also visited the genealogy room at the Warren County Court House and the Lebanon Museum. Some of my information came from newspaper articles, obituaries and old letters written by family members.

I was welcomed like a small town celebrity when I went to Winona, Minnesota to gather information on J.R. Watkins. The archivist at the Watkins Museum told me personal information about the family. Unknowingly I booked a room at a bed and break- fast, the Alexander Mansion, because the reviews stated that the owner knew about the town's history. I ended up sleeping in Maud King Alexander's bedroom, the step-daughter of J.R. That was a pleasant surprise!

The librarian at the Lebanon Public Library told me stories about the Stubbs that I would have never found in text. I heard repeatedly many of the family stories when I was growing up. The bulk of my information came by word of mouth from people in the family. My older brother and sister were a great source of information since they knew more and could remember things that I had no knowledge of. My greatest source of information by far was my nephew, Ty Baker. I am so grateful for his help. He has a wealth of information about the history of this area and our family. He has visited every grave site of our relatives, and he speaks of all of them with great enthusiasm. He is also the keeper of many items from our ancestors. He is truly the historian in the family. I am just the writer.

Deb Paris was the one who worked with me for countless hours as we put my text together with photos. Her knowledge of resources and her aid in research was amazing. Without her this book would have never come to be as it is.

I must acknowledge my husband for his patience throughout this project and his assistance in research and editing. He was my sounding board as I gathered information for two years.

ABOUT THE AUTHOR

Jeane Weisbrod lives with her husband on the corner of Stubbs Mill Road and Shawhan Road. She is very fortunate to live on
the property that was originally owned by the Stubbs, where she also grew up. It is within two miles of where the Stubbs had a mill on the Little Miami River more than two hundred years ago. She is a retired English-Language Arts teacher. She holds a
B.A. in education and a M. Ed. She enjoys the outdoors, gardening, bicycling, reading and visiting their two adult children who live out of town.